D1237162

SHIPHANDLING WITH TUGS

By George H. Reid

Primer of Towing, 1975

Boatmen's Guide to Light Salvage, 1979

Simulator Training Manual, 1983

Shiphandling with Tugs, 1986

SHIPHANDLING
WITH TUGS

BY

GEORGE H. REID

CORNELL MARITIME PRESS

Centreville, Maryland

Library of Congress Cataloging-in-Publication Data

Reid, George H.
    Shiphandling with tugs.

    Bibliography: p.
    Includes index.
    1. Ship handling.   2. Tugboats.   I. Title.
VK361.R45 1986   623.88′232   86-47712
ISBN 0-87033-354-2

Manufactured in the United States of America

First edition, 1986; second printing, 1994

This volume is affectionately dedicated
to that informal gathering of *salts*
known as the "Brotherhood of the Coast."
They know who they are.

CONTENTS

Preface   ix

Acknowledgments   xi

1. An Introduction to Shipwork   3

2. Piloting   6

3. The Tugs   11

4. Propulsion and Steering   24

5. Structural Considerations   42

6. Gear and Rigging for Shipwork   54

7. Communication between Ship and Tug   69

8. Handling the "Light" Tug   72

9. Basic Tug Handling for Shipwork   90

10. The *Hows* and *Whys* of Shipwork   102

11. Working Tugs Alongside   121

12. Working Tugs on a Towline   138

13. Using Torque to Advantage   146

14. Using Tugs in Current   149

15. Handling Dead Ships   164

16. Salvage and Emergency Situations   170

17. Using Tugs in Exposed Waters 184

18. Tugs and Anchors 189

19. Tugs and Tailboats 196

20. Handling the ITB 203

21. Conclusion 211

Answers to the Study Questions 213

Appendices

  I. Shiphandling at Ras Tanura Sea Island, 234
  II. Full-Scale Trials to Examine Tugboat
      Performance during Berthing of Tankers, 246
  III. Safety in Towing, 250

References 259

Index 261

About the Author 267

PREFACE

The writing of this book, like its predecessors, *Primer of Towing* and *Boatmen's Guide to Light Salvage,* was encouraged by what was perceived as evidence of "demonstrated need."

I recall the particular occasion that "inspired" this volume. It stemmed from a discussion relating to the most effective methods of using tugs to assist ships docking and undocking in a tidal river with a reversing current. This could oblige vessels to berth and unberth in varying conditions of fair and foul currents. I tendered my own opinions on this matter, based upon my own experience as well as my observations of practices commonly used in other ports throughout the world in similar situations. However, I was unable to cite any *authoritative sources* to support a number of my contentions.

This led me to review quite a bit of material on the subject of shiphandling and tugs that I had hoped would shed some light on this subject (and perhaps confirm my own expressed opinions). I was a little disappointed in this respect for the following reasons:

1. Some of the material was dated. Ships were generally much smaller at the time of writing, and the use of tugs was, for this reason, often optional.
2. Many excellent books on the subject of shiphandling devote a chapter or two to the use of tugs—but only in applications that the *authors happened to be familiar with.*
3. Technical papers on this subject presented at symposiums, both here and abroad, are informative—for those who attend them. But, unfortunately most of these papers do not deal very much with the *mechanics* of shiphandling with tugs from the mariner's standpoint—and those that do are hard to come by.

This volume has been written to remedy these deficiencies. It is intended for the pilot, ship's officer, or tug master. For this reason the emphasis is on the *practical,* rather than the theoretical, aspects of using tugs. It is my modest hope, however, that this material will not only prove useful to the professional mariner, but will be informative for those who follow other callings related to the handling of ships and tugs, afloat or ashore. Questions and answers have been supplied for many of the chapters. It is hoped that they will be helpful to beginners in tug work.

ACKNOWLEDGMENTS

The antecedents of this volume go back a "long way." And to a certain extent the material contained in this text is drawn from the freely shared experience of colleagues in the marine field and those from other related disciplines.

It would be impossible to list all of those that have been so generous with their insights—nevertheless, it is appropriate to acknowledge their contributions.

A small list of those who have been so kind would include: Captains Ernesto LaFontaine, Lowell Brentner, the late Tom Cuyler, Dick Griffin, Carmelo Martinez, and Raul Iglesias; also, Messrs. Bill Hurst, Guy Baldwin, Pat Boatright, and Kennedy Brown.

In addition I am grateful for material contributed by Captain Herb Taylor of Ship Analytics, Inc.; Voith-Schneider of America; Schottel of America; the Harbormaster Division of Murray & Tregurtha Co.; Philip F. Spaulding of Nickum & Spaulding Associates, Inc.; and Hydronautics, Incorporated.

My gratitude is extended to Captain John V. Noel and Van Nostrand Reinhold Co., the revising author and publisher (respectively) of *Knight's Modern Seamanship*.

I particularly want to thank Camilla H. Reid, my daughter, for the work she has done on the illustrations.

All these and others have made this volume possible.

SHIPHANDLING WITH TUGS

CHAPTER ONE

AN INTRODUCTION TO SHIPWORK

The purpose of this volume is to provide a comprehensive guide to the safe and effective employment of tugs doing shipwork. The text is primarily directed to the attention of pilots, docking masters, tug captains, and ships' officers who would have a professional interest in the subject. I hope also that the material will be of interest to those who may not be immediately involved in the mechanics of shiphandling (naval architects, marine engineers, etc.), but who have an affiliate interest in the process. The attention of the pleasure boatman or landsman with an inquiring mind is also welcomed.

Shiphandling is, of course, one of the maritime skills that is essential if marine trade is to continue. The recognition of this fact is indicated by the number of books on this subject—usually written by competent authorities. However, most of these texts are remiss in one respect: they fail to deal at any length with the use of tugs in shiphandling. The subject is usually taken for granted or touched on briefly. The *hows* are sometimes explained, but the *whys* are usually ignored. This is an unfortunate oversight since any witness to (or participant in) marine activity is aware of the importance of the tug's role in this highly specialized field of endeavor. Certainly the ability to use the tugs wisely and well must be regarded as one of the shiphandler's arts.

Shipwork is not a new business. The docking and undocking of vessels and the assisting of ships to navigate narrow channels and crowded harbors have been staple employments of tugs since sailing ship days. In fact, it is hardly likely that the "great age of sail" would ever have come to pass if the steam tug had not come into existence beforehand. Until the advent of tugs, sailing ships of any size were warped, towed by pulling boats, or kedged about whenever space was limited. This would have been impossible with ships the size of the great windjammers that plied the trade routes of the world during the latter part of the nineteenth century and the early years of the twentieth century. The big square-riggers (like their frequent companions, the albatross) were most at ease on the high seas. When crossing the bar or navigating in confined waters, they fared best secured to the end of some tug's tow hawser. A well-known painting entitled *The Fighting Téméraire* by J. M. W. Turner depicts such a scene. A famous ship of the line of Lord Nelson's days is shown in tow of the steam tug *Monarch*. The painting is dated 1838. Ships have changed since then, but the circumstances remain the same. Present-day ships, excluding some sail training ships and a few engaged in the sailing passenger trade, are propelled by machinery. Even these remaining sailing vessels have auxiliary engines for propulsion. Nevertheless, the congestion of our waterways and the size of the ships that call at our ports assure the continuing need for tugs to assist these vessels if they are to arrive, berth, and depart safely without delays.

The large oceangoing carriers of today—and there are many that exceed 100,000 DWT, the VLCCs (very large crude carriers)—and the ULCCs (ultra large crude carriers)—are just as much creatures of the high seas as the clipper ships of the past. They are designed for efficient operation *at sea*, and except for certain trades (cruise ships, etc.) their maneuverability and backing power are strictly secondary considerations. For this reason the tug's role is as vital to maritime commerce today as it was in the days when the wind ships lay offshore waiting for a tow across the bar. Shipwork with tugs differs now in several respects from the way it was done during the days of sail. In most instances the tug is no longer the prime mover since the ship will normally provide its own propulsion; and the tug's function is to *assist* the vessel rather than propel it. The ship, of course, is under command of its own master who will direct or will delegate someone to direct (usually the pilot or docking master) the tug's activities. The tug captain's role has changed also. Tug captains are still responsible for the handling of their tugs, but must do so in accordance with the pilot's or shiphandler's instructions, rather than acting on their own volition as was the case in sailing ship days. This imposes the responsibility for conning the ship and directing the tugs squarely on the shiphandler's shoulders. In order to respond to this responsibility effectively the shiphandler should be as proficient at employing the tugs as he (or she) is at maneuvering the vessel.

The essence of shipwork with tugs seems simple enough. After all, a tug can only push, pull, or lie there passively. Its function is to *assist* the vessel to steer, to turn the vessel, to move it laterally, or to hold it in position while heaving up or letting go its mooring lines. In addition the tug may be required to check a vessel's way (ahead, astern, or sideways), break a vessel's sheer, slow the vessel's swing, or even physically propel the vessel. In short, the tug permits a shiphandler to safely undertake maneuvers with a vessel that would otherwise be difficult, dangerous, or impossible.

You can easily imagine the difficulty that would be encountered in handling a large ship in ballast, in confined waters, with a strong beam wind blowing against the enormous area of exposed freeboard; docking a big ship with a strong fair current at a "shakey" berth; or maneuvering a deep-loaded bulk carrier with poor steering and limited backing power, in close quarters, without tugs. The appearance of simplicity, obviously, can be deceiving. It requires a great deal of understanding on the part of the shiphandler who directs the tug's maneuvers, plus a high level of skill on the part of the tug's captain to carry out the pilot's orders.

The methods used to accomplish these varying maneuvers may differ widely, often depending upon local custom. In shipwork, as in other endeavors, there may be several different ways to achieve the same result. Despite the methods used, however, the effectiveness of the tugs engaged in this employment will be determined by the knowledge and skill of those who operate and direct them.

CHAPTER TWO

PILOTING

One dictionary defines pilot as "a person licensed to direct or steer a ship into or out of a harbor or through difficult waters." In this book I use the term in a broader context, and it is applied to docking masters, mooring masters, and qualified ships' officers who may direct a vessel's maneuvers and, in essence, fulfill the same function as a pilot. The definition above doesn't shed much light on the special skills required of this person, nor how he or she acquired them. Perhaps the Spanish term for pilot, *práctico*, is more informative. As you can imagine, it means someone with considerable experience or "practice" at this art.

Most pilots or shiphandlers acquire their qualifying experience by serving an apprenticeship with a pilot's organization, working as a deck officer or master aboard commercial or military vessels, or working in the towing industry, where they may have operated tugs doing shipwork.

There are some training programs for shiphandlers which involve the use of simulators. The best known of these is the CAORF (computer assisted operational research facility) at the United States Merchant Marine Academy at Kings Point, New York. There is also the Maritime Institute of Technology and Graduate Studies facility at Linthicum Heights, Maryland, operated by the International Organization of Masters, Mates, and Pilots, and one operated by Marine Safety International at La Guardia, New York. Another installation, the Shiphandling Training Center at Grenoble, France, employs scaled-down versions of ships having characteristics similar to full-sized vessels.

There are several different aspects of piloting. Shiphandlers may be engaged to moor a vessel at a single-point mooring (SPM), or to anchor it where it can be connected up to an offshore pipeline. Others may berth a vessel alongside another ship to lighter off. The target vessel may be either anchored or steaming. For economic reasons the employers (usually oil companies) prefer to call these pilots "mooring masters." "Bar pilots" may only handle ships when they are crossing the bar, inbound or outbound, while river pilots may handle the entire transit of a river.

In some areas pilots board and disembark ships at the sea buoy and direct every phase of the operation, including docking and undocking the vessel. In other ports a docking master will relieve the pilot while the vessel is being docked or undocked. This is often the case when tugs are used. The docking masters are usually senior tug captains familiar with the use of tugs in shipwork. Except for the Suez and Panama canals (and certain ports in Germany) where pilots are *in command* of the ships, a pilot nominally serves in an "advisory" capacity. In reality, however, the pilot usually is the one who directs the maneuvers of a ship in pilotage waters.

A pilot's task is not an easy one. Pilots are frequently called upon to board unfamiliar ships (often in the middle of the night) and, despite high winds and restricted visibility, are expected to deliver a charge safely to its destination. The process is often further complicated by the fact that the pilot may have only a few minutes to "feel the vessel out," and some ships have idiosyncrasies that even the vessel's master is unaware of. It is an awesome responsiblity, and a miscalculation can be disastrous. The penalty for failure can be severe. In more robust times (until the seventeenth century) a pilot charged with the loss of a vessel was often beheaded on the spot. While an accident is no longer a capital offense, it can cost the pilot his license, and the courts can award damages against him for millions of dollars. Neither prospect is pleasant to contemplate—the consequences of a serious mistake can be ruinous.

It is apparent that the ability to handle ships of different types and sizes, in varying conditions of trim, and under varying conditions of wind and current, is fundamental to this employment. It is equally obvious that local and up-to-date knowledge of the pilotage area is essential. Last, but not least, if tugs are used, the shiphandler should have a good understanding of the dynamics involved so that the tugs can be employed safely and effectively. It is with respect to this last factor, the use of tugs, that many shiphandlers' failings are evident. Tugs are often underutilized or misused.

On occasion a ship will maneuver to stay in position alongside a dock while heaving up its lines with a tug standing by idly instead of breasting the ship to the dock until the vessel is secured. Often a pilot will be frantically maneuvering to keep a vessel from landing too heavily when coming alongside a dock. With a little anticipation and simple orders to the tug, the problem could have been avoided. The order to "back full at 90°'" given to a single-screw tug assisting a vessel making three knots headway is a standard joke among tug captains. (It's impossible for any tug to back at 90° to a ship traveling this fast, especially a single-screw tug.)

Some of these oversights can be attributed to a once-prevalent attitude among pilots that is, thankfully, less fashionable now. In the past it was common for pilots to pride themselves on their ability to handle ships without assistance from tugs. It must be admitted that many were excellent shiphandlers—without tugs. But unfortunately many of them were, at best, mediocre when tugs were used. The fallacy of this thinking is apparent. Shiphandling with tugs is like any other skill and "if you don't use it, you lose it," or perhaps never acquire it at all. The moral here is obvious, if you do not learn how to use tugs when they *may not* be absolutely necessary, then you are not likely to know how to use them properly in those desperate moments when they are essential.

Any undertaking involving the use of tools requires some familiarity with the tool itself. While it is hardly necessary for individuals who drive automobiles to be mechanics or automotive engineers, they must certainly be aware of cause and effect in the operation of their vehicles. By the same token, any pilot commonly required to use tugs to assist in shiphandling should have at least the same degree of familiarity with their functional limitations. In the past Panama Canal pilots were required to spend some time on tugs as part of their training. I have no doubt that this proved useful to them. I feel that anyone who is a candidate for a pilot's job and has not had some experience on tugs should at least ride them enough to get the feel of their capabilities and limitations.

Since they usually work with the same tugs and tug captains on a daily basis, pilots should make it a point to know something about the characteristics of the tugs as well as the people who operate them. There are good reasons for this. Most towing companies have a few underpowered *lumps* which they send out on jobs when their better tugs are laid up or busy, and they often use "horsepower stretchers" when referring to them. They will unabashedly call a tug capable of delivering only 750 horsepower a "1,200 horsepower tug." This is no problem if the pilot is aware of the situation, but if not, he or she may be sadly embarrassed by the lack of additional power.

Personnel, too, can affect a tug's performance. One pilot I knew consistently requested a smaller tug instead of a larger, more powerful unit available for the same price, saying he preferred some "horsepower in the wheelhouse." He obviously had a good working relationship with the captain on the smaller tug. I once operated an old tug with a direct-reversing engine. One pilot always asked which engineer was on duty at the time. He understood, as I did, that one of the engineers was much faster answering bells than the other one, and this made a difference in the tug's capability.

The pilot must also be alert to other factors that can affect the tug's performance. On one occasion I was assisting a passenger liner to dock on a very windy day. Passengers lined the rail, where my tug's line was fast, waving and smiling, unaware of their danger should the line part. The crew had, of course, cleared out. The ship took a swing toward the dock, and the pilot signaled for full astern. I backed the tug as hard as I dared, but the ship still landed heavily on the dock. The pilot and I had some heated words afterwards, until I explained my reluctance to risk parting a line. I had tried, without success, to call his attention to the peril of the passengers, but he had been so preoccupied with handling the ship he was unaware of their danger.

Lastly, do not ignore the tug. One pilot I know was halfway home after docking a ship before he remembered that he had failed to dismiss the tug. (After all, it's pretty stupid to leave a 2,000-horsepower tug at $350 per hour pushing for an hour and a half after the ship is docked.) Another pilot expressed the opinion that a tug's safety was not really the pilot's concern. He stated, "Tugs can look after themselves." They usually can, but that is not what they are there to do and if the tug's captain gets "spooked" a few times, the pilot in question won't get much cooperation.

Pilots should understand the dynamics of using a tug. They should know whether to place it forward, aft, midships, or fast alongside. They should also know if it is necessary to use a quarter line, towline, or no line at all. Their judgment in this respect will, to a large degree, determine their success in using tugs.

It is evident now that ships are hardly likely to decrease in size.

Large deep-draft vessels will continue to call at our ports and will sometimes berth at facilities built a generation or more ago and designed for much smaller ships than those of today. It is equally evident that these large ships with their limited maneuverability will require the assistance of tugs directed by shiphandlers familiar with their proper employment. Given these circumstances, perhaps the definition of the word pilot will be amended to read, "one also familiar with the art of shiphandling with tugs."

CHAPTER THREE

THE TUGS

A tug captain was once asked to describe a harbor tug. He obliged by saying:

> It is a vessel between 80' and 120' in length and of 750 to 4,000 horsepower. It may be single screw or twin screw. It may have a Kort nozzle, and may even have flanking rudders. However, there is one sure way you can tell if it is a harbor tug: The mast will be bent and the visor around the wheelhouse will be dented.

The description that the captain gave was accurate enough, even though it was very general. Most harbor tugs would fall into this range of characteristics and his reference to the bent mast and dented visor is also accurate. These battle scars are the inevitable consequence of working in close quarters situations.

Most tugs are intended for general towing service, but the appearance of some may indicate a specialized service for which they were originally intended or for which they were once employed. Railroad tugs have high pilothouses to give visibility over the loaded car floats. Canal boats have low wheelhouses and short stacks to enable them to pass freely under low bridges. Tugs designed for shipwork have narrow wheelhouses and masts that can be lowered easily to avoid damage when working under the flare of the ship's bow or overhang at its stern. However, the need for tugs to do shipwork has increased in recent years, and it is not unusual to see tugs built for different services working side by side while docking ships.

As the tug captain quoted above implied, the tugs assisting a ship are likely to be a diverse lot and will in all probability have different handling qualities and capabilities. These are important for the shiphandler or pilot to know. Principal among them are the following factors:

1. The size and shape of the tug's superstructure (i.e., height and width), which could prohibit the tug from working near the extreme ends of a vessel because of the flare at the bow or overhang at the stern;
2. The tug's power, both ahead and astern;
3. The tug's maneuverability and handling characteristics.

The first two factors cited are beyond the shiphandler's control, but he should be aware of any limitations on the use of the tug that they might impose. The last factor is likely to be the pilot's principal concern. His understanding of the tug's handling qualities and capabilities in this respect is essential if he is to use them to the best advantage. For those who are not familiar with the handling qualities of various types of tugs employed in shipwork, their capabilities and limitations are discussed below.

Single-screw tugs probably outnumber all other types of tugs combined that are used in shiphandling, and many of them have been around for quite a few years. There are good reasons for this. Tugs are durable because they are sturdily built to withstand the frequent heavy contacts that are inevitable in this kind of work. Also, many of them have spent most of their lives in fresh water which is much kinder to a vessel than salt water. Also, the demands of harbor work are usually not severe, and older equipment unsuitable for more demanding employment can be used in shipwork.

The limitations of the single-screw tug are fairly obvious. It cannot maneuver as readily as a twin-screw vessel, which can turn about in its own length by working one engine ahead and the other astern. Many of the maneuvers of the new generation of tugs (either those fitted with flanking rudders, a steerable Kort nozzle, or steerable propellers) are simply beyond its capabilities.

If a single-screw tug is required to turn in a short radius, it must "back and fill" by alternately coming ahead with the helm turned hard over and then going astern on its engine. It will also turn far more readily in one direction than it will in the other because of the torque effect of the tug's propeller when it backs. This will be turning to starboard in the case of a standard right-hand rotation propeller because while backing down the stern will walk to port. Most single-screw tugs do not steer well when going astern, and can be difficult to control if they are required to back a long distance.

In working alongside a ship, a tug may have to press heavily against the vessel in order to get into position when required to push or back at right angles to the ship's side. This can be a disadvantage, especially if the ship is of light draft. Since some of the older tugs are quite narrow, they are slow to turn. Their lack of beam can also make them susceptible to capsizing when working on a towline or when using a quarter line alongside, especially if the ship has too much way on.

If they are required to back for an extended period of time, it is likely that a single-screw tug will require quarter lines or stern lines (terms used interchangeably here) to maintain position. This is brought about because the effect of the torque of the tug's propeller will cause the tug to swing out of position even if the wind, current, or the vessel's movement ahead or astern does not. (Note that the stern line keeps the tug from swinging out of position.)

Unless the average single-screw tug has been repowered, few of the older boats have more than 1,600 horsepower, and many of them have much less. These smaller tugs may not have adequate power to handle the large vessels that now call at our ports, although 1,600 horsepower is usually enough power to handle vessels in the 30,000 to 40,000 DWT range.

In spite of these shortcomings, once single-screw boats are properly made up alongside the ship they can be just as effective as other tugs, especially if they are primarily required to push. More lines, however, may be needed to hold them in position, especially if the chocks on the ship are poorly placed. Finally, the single-screw tugs are generally preferred to twin screw and other more modern types of tugs (i.e., propeller steered) for assisting submarines since their underwater configuration is unlikely to damage the outer hull of the submarine. (Figs. 3-1, 3-2.)

Twin-screw tugs are gradually replacing the single-screw vessel. Most of the new vessels used in shiphandling are of this configuration. Many are quite powerful, in the 3,000-4,000 horsepower range, and are capable of handling the largest ships entering our harbors. Some tugs that are used overseas to handle VLCCs and ULCCs may have as much as 6,000 horsepower installed. (Fig. 3-3.) Aside from the fact that it is convenient to install two engines to achieve a higher aggregate horse-

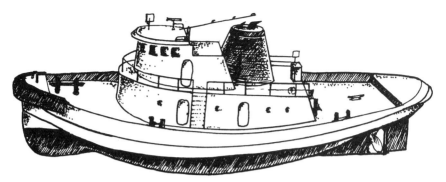

Fig. 3-1. An older type single-screw tug with a molded hull.

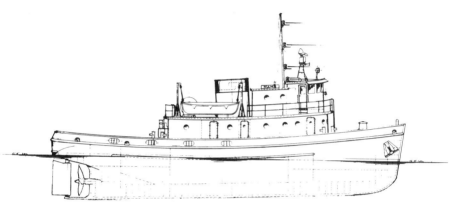

Fig. 3-2. A conventional single-screw tug. Courtesy: Nickum & Spaulding.

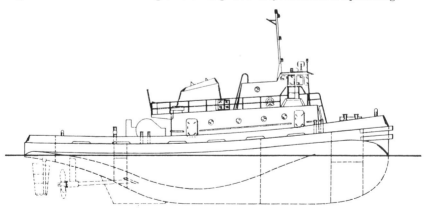

Fig. 3-3. Outboard profile of a 100-foot, twin-screw harbor tug with 3,200 horsepower. Note spade rudders. Courtesy: Atlantic Marine Inc.

power and provide backup in the case of the failure of one engine, the real advantage of twin-screw tugs is their exceptional maneuverability. When working a ship they can shift position readily, work handily in confined spaces, and can stay in shape (i.e., maintain an angle of approximately 90°) without pressing heavily against the vessel. However, on a horsepower-for-horsepower basis, discounting their mobility, they may be at a disadvantage compared to a single-screw tug since single-screw propulsion is normally about 20 percent more efficient than a twin-screw installation of the same aggregate horsepower.

If a ship is dead in the water and a twin-screw tug is required to back, the torque effect of the counter-rotating propellers will nullify each other, and the tug will back straight. However, if the ship is moving ahead or astern, or if there is much wind or current, the tug will only be able to maintain position at right angles to the ship by "twin screwing," i.e., by backing on one engine while maneuvering ahead on the other with the helm turned in the appropriate direction. Its backing power will naturally be less than half of its full astern capability on both engines. In the event that more backing power is required, the twin-screw tug will be obliged to use a stern line the same as a single-screw tug.

The shiphandler should also bear in mind that most tugs, single or twin screw, deliver much less power when backing than when coming ahead on their engines. (Refer to Table 3 in Chapter 4.)

A *new generation* of harbor tugs has appeared with capabilities that the conventional tugs of either single- or twin-screw configuration do not possess. I am referring to the tugs (more commonly seen in this country) that are fitted with flanking rudders, or steerable Kort nozzles, and to the propeller-steered tugs that have proven successful in Europe.

The characteristics that distinguish this new generation of tugs from the conventional tugs are their ability to steer when maneuvering astern, and to maintain position when backing without having to rely upon a stern line or quarter line to stay in "shape." The propeller-steered tugs also have the additional advantage of undiminished backing power.

Flanking rudders are installed ahead of the tug's propeller. There are usually two of them for each propeller and they function *independently* of the regular rudders. They are used to direct the water flow when the tug's engines are backed, permitting the tug to maneuver

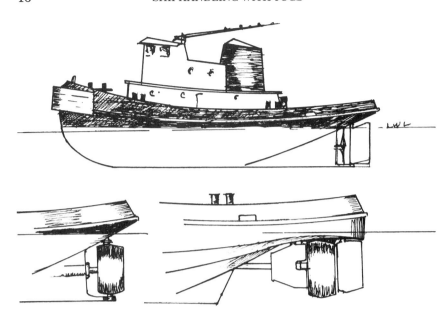

Fig. 3-4. *Above,* typical single-screw harbor tug. *Lower left,* a steerable Kort nozzle. *Lower right,* a fixed Kort nozzle installation with flanking rudders.

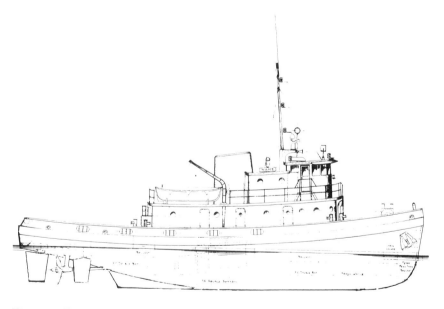

Fig. 3-5. Twin-screw tug with spade and flanking rudders. Courtesy: Nickum & Spaulding.

when going astern. Both single- and twin-screw tugs may be fitted with flanking rudders (Figs. 3-4, 3-5).

Naturally the handling characteristics of single- and twin-screw vessels with flanking rudders will differ considerably. The twin-screw tugs are quite maneuverable and can be walked sideways by working one engine ahead and the other astern, with the backing engine's rudders turned outboard. The term applied to this action is referred to as *flanking*, and the rudders derive their name from the capability.

Although single-screw tugs with flanking rudders cannot be flanked like a twin-screw tug, they nevertheless can turn in a very small area since the flanking rudders can be maneuvered to continue the swing when the engines are backed. However, single-screw tugs (like the twin-screw tugs) can maintain their position when backing their engines during shipwork without having to use a stern line. This is, of course, provided the ship is not moving at excessive speed.

Flanking rudders are usually installed in conjunction with Kort nozzles (a circular airfoil-shaped sleeve that shrouds the propeller). The Kort nozzle is generally conceded to increase the propeller thrust ahead by up to 40 percent. The backing power, however, is substantially less than its pushing power. Nozzles and flanking rudders of both twin- and single-screw configuration have proved most successful.

The *steerable Kort nozzle* (or Kort rudder) consists of a movable Kort nozzle that is controlled by the steering gear and directs the thrust of the propeller in the appropriate direction. It fulfills the function of a rudder when moving ahead or astern (see Fig. 3-4). It is not quite as handy as the flanking rudder since the helm must be turned the opposite way, when maneuvering from ahead to astern, in order to maintain the direction of the tug's swing. The steering gear itself must be more powerful than conventional steering gear because of the weight of the nozzle, and it sometimes responds slower than a conventional rudder for this reason. The Kort rudders are mostly used in single-screw configurations (Fig. 3-4).

PS *(propeller-steered)* tugs have enjoyed a favorable reputation in Europe for many years. This is because of their excellent maneuverability, their capability to stay in position when backing, and the fact that their backing power is equal to their pushing power.

These tugs differ considerably from conventional tugs since they are steered directly by their propellers rather than using rudders to direct the propeller wash. Several different types of propulsion systems are used to power these tugs. The most common ones in Europe are the Voith-Schneider, which utilizes a cycloidal propeller (a number of air-foil-shaped vanes that rotate about a vertical axis); and the Schottel drive, which employs a conventional propeller (usually fitted with a nozzle) driven by a right-angle drive from a vertical shaft—much like an outboard motor. The propeller can be turned through an arc of 360° to provide steering and reversing.

There are several other systems that are similar to the Schottel drive—the Z drive and the Harbormaster units both manufactured by Murray & Tregurtha in this country are good examples of these.

PS tugs, whether they are single- or twin-screw types, usually conform to one of two basic configurations—*pusher* tugs whose propellers are located aft, and *tractor* tugs that have their propellers located forward of midships.

PS pusher tugs respond similarly to conventional tugs since their propellers are located in the same approximate position. This type of tug can, of course, maintain position when backing, and can even push effectively when lying flat alongside a ship since the propeller can direct its force to the side. Its backing power is undiminished since the propeller is simply turned so that the thrust is directed forward.

The tractor tugs derive their distinctive name from their principal method of employment. They are designed for pulling and are much less likely to capsize than conventional tugs when doing shipwork on a towline. This is due to the forward location of the propeller. They are pretty versatile however, and work equally well ahead or astern. In fact, they usually work stern first when required to push against a ship. Incidentally, capsizing is probably the principal hazard to tugs doing shipwork, and this usually occurs when towline work is being done. This subject will be discussed in detail in Chapters 9 and 12.

The underwater configuration of propeller-steered tugs is often quite different from that of conventional tugs since some type of lateral plane is necessary to provide directional stability. A skeg or fin keel usually fulfills this function. The location of this appendage depends upon the position of the propeller. (Figs. 3-6 to 3-8.)

There is apparently no difference between the Voith-Schneider, Schottel drive, Harbormaster, and other systems with regard to their functional ability and maneuverability. But the Schottel drive and similar systems have an advantage over the Voith-Schneider system on

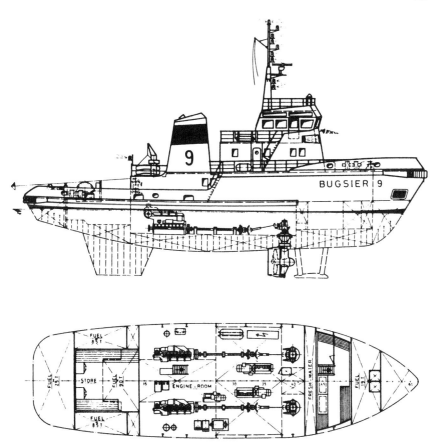

Fig. 3-6. Tractor-type tug propelled by two Schottel rudder-propellers for ship-work and general towing. Courtesy: Schottel of America.

the basis of bollard pull, especially if they are fitted with a nozzle, as is customary. Table 2 (Chapter 4) gives approximate values for different systems.

A tug evaluation table, Table 1 below, compares in a general way the relative merits of different types of tugs. You are, of course, aware that the better the equipment, the more it costs to construct, maintain, and operate it.

For towing companies and other marine operators the principal consideration is economic, and the expenditure for equipment is only justified if there is adequate return on their investment.

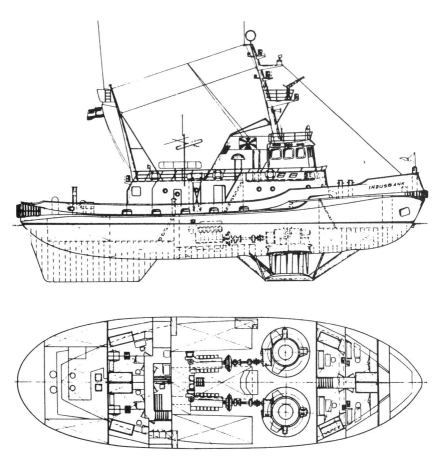

Fig. 3-7. A 3,400-horsepower Voith water tractor built for harbor service in Europe. Courtesy: Voith-Schneider.

Table 1.

Evaluation of Three Tug Types

Type of Tug	*Advantages*	*Disadvantages*
Single Screw Conventional	low costs, i.e., construction and maintenance; effective when maneuvering ahead or pushing	maneuverability only fair; backing power about one-half of power ahead; poor steerage astern; requires stern line when backing during shipwork

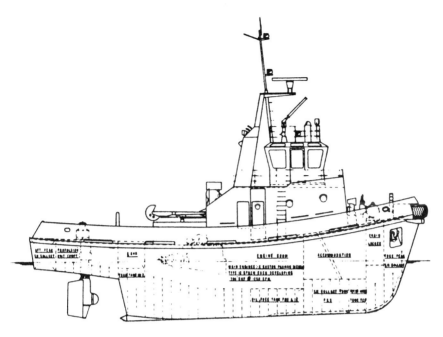

Fig. 3-8. A 1,400-horsepower tug intended for shipwork fitted with two aft-mounted Schottel steerable rudder propellers. Courtesy: Schottel of America.

Table 1. (continued)

Type of Tug	Advantages	Disadvantages
With flanking rudders and Kort nozzle	excellent power ahead; good maneuverability, ahead and astern; can work without a stern line	backing power one-half of power ahead; costs more to operate
With Kort rudder	same as above, except in maneuvering, it is slightly inferior	same as above
Twin Screw Conventional	excellent maneuverability; steers well astern	costs more to operate; may require stern line for shipwork in backing

Table 1. (continued)

Type of Tug	Advantages	Disadvantages
With flanking rudders and Kort nozzle	excellent power ahead; excellent maneuverability ahead and astern; works ships without stern line	costs still more to operate
Propeller-Steered Pusher type	power good to excellent depending on whether or not Kort nozzle is installed; maneuverability excellent ahead and astern; backing power undiminished; no stern line required when working ships	most costly to operate; tends to roll a lot when propeller thrust is directed to the side
Tractor type	same as above, except it is superior for towline work	same as above, except it is more suited to towline work and will usually push against a ship stern first

You should also remember that even a second-rate tug in the hands of a first-class operator, and directed by a top-notch shiphandler, can outperform much better equipment in the hands of those who are less competent. The real bottom line, of course, is the fact that even if the tugs are versatile and capable, unless the shiphandler and the operator know how to use them to best advantage, these exceptional capabilities may complicate the process of shiphandling instead of simplifying it.

STUDY QUESTIONS

1. What advantage does a single-screw tug have over a twin-screw tug?
2. What is the principal disadvantage of a single-screw tug?
3. What advantage does a twin-screw tug have?

4. What are the disadvantages of the twin-screw tug?
5. What are the *new generation* tugs?
6. What are the principal advantages of the new generation tugs over the conventional tugs?
7. List the new generation tugs in the approximate order of their effectiveness.
8. Are there different types of PS tugs?
9. How do they differ functionally?

CHAPTER FOUR

PROPULSION AND STEERING

The two elements that are vital to the movement of any vessel are its motive force (the propelling machinery, in the case of a tug), and the apparatus which controls its direction of movement—the steering gear. Both of these elements merit special attention and will be dealt with separately.

METHODS OF PROPULSION

A tug is a floating power plant and its function is to apply this power by pushing or pulling. The hull is the platform that supports the machinery as well as the other elements of equipment essential or incidental to the navigation and operation of the tug, and which permit the operator to control and deliver the power that the engine develops.

In its simplest form, the tug's main engine is directly connected to a shaft which has a propeller attached to the other end. The engine produces the necessary power to turn the shaft and propeller. The propeller then converts this rotative force into thrust. When tugs were propelled by steam engines, this arrangment worked quite satisfactorily. The reciprocating steam engines used on tugs were slow turning, which permitted the use of efficient, large diameter propellers. Furthermore, the engines were easily controlled and responded quickly when maneuvering ahead or astern. The engine speed could be adjusted to one that would best suit the situation, from barely turning to full speed.

The diesel engine has now almost completely replaced the steam engine as a source of power aboard tugs. It is more compact and efficient, and this has made it possible to increase both the range and power of tugs. However, certain disadvantages occur when the diesel engine is connected directly to the propeller shaft. The engine must be completely stopped and then restarted when it is necessary to reverse the rotation of the propeller shaft. Its speed range is fairly limited. Slow speed is generally about half of full speed, and the speed at which the engine turns may not permit the use of a propeller of the most efficient size. Nevertheless, this system has proven practical and economical in some applications. There are many direct-connected, direct-reversing engines in use aboard large motor ships. But these are less than ideal aboard tugs where a high degree of maneuverability is desirable and often necessary. For this reason several alternate methods for maneuvering the engine have been developed.

MANEUVERING SYSTEMS

The *DR (direct-reversing)* system is the simplest and least expensive system for maneuvering a diesel engine. It is also the oldest system. There is still a surprisingly large number of harbor tugs powered by direct-reversing engines, and these tugs will, no doubt, continue in service as long as engine parts are available. Nevertheless, the DR system must be considered obsolete and most tugs fitted with this type of engine will eventually be either replaced or repowered with more modern machinery.

DR engines of the size that would be installed aboard a tug are air starting. Compressed air from a bank of tanks is admitted directly into a cylinder where a piston is under compression. This, of course, starts the engine turning, and the firing cycle of the cylinders is begun. The direction of rotation is determined by the starting air valve and the position of the cam shaft which can be shifted by the operator.

This system is simple enough and, in less demanding applications, is satisfactory. But there are drawbacks other than those already noted. The number of maneuvers is limited and is determined by the volume of the starting air tanks and the capacity of the compressor to recharge them. The DR system can also fail. The engine may not start at a crucial time, or the cam shaft may fail to shift. The propeller shaft brake may not keep it from turning and if the vessel is moving ahead or astern too fast, the engine could then start up in the wrong direction. The results of these types of failures can be most embarrassing.

Many of the DR tugs have been fitted with wheelhouse controls. While this doesn't eliminate the fundamental problems, these controls do make it easier for the captain to maneuver. He does not have to adjust to the engineer's response time (which can vary amazingly), or suffer the shock of seeing the engineer casually leaning over the forward rail with a mug of coffee in his hand, while he, the captain, is ringing frantically for full astern!

DE (diesel-electric) drive was initially developed for marine use in submarines, and the system was later employed in tugs. It has proven to be an excellent method of harnessing and controlling engine output. DE drive can deliver any amount of shaft speed from dead slow to full speed ahead or astern, and responds without delay to changes in speed and direction of rotation. This propulsion unit consists of three basic elements: the main engine or engines (there are sometimes two or more); the generators which are engine driven; and the DC (direct current) electrical motors that in turn drive the propeller shaft and derive their power from the generators.

This type of installation has certain virtues in addition to its maneuverability. Principal among them is the fact that the diesel engine turns at a constant speed—which minimizes maintenance. The DE installation is not quite as efficient a system as one employing controllable-pitch propellers, but the engine fuel consumption reflects the load on the engines. In the case of multiple-engine installations, only the engines and generators required for propulsion at the time need to be run.

The drawback, of course, is the cost. Large generators (particularly the DC type) are expensive, and the DC motors are also costly. And, of course, any marine electrical system is vulnerable to dampness and salt in the atmosphere.

The SCR (silicon-controlled rectifier) system of DE drive has proven effective in recent applications aboard small vessels, including tugs. In the SCR system the main engine generators are AC (alternating current) which is suitable for ship supply and other applications. The current is delivered through rectifiers which convert it to DC for driving the propulsion motors.

The AC generators are cheaper than the DC types of the older units, and since the AC current is compatible with the vessel's electrical system, it can save the cost of some of the auxiliary generators.

CPP (controllable pitch propellers) have been around for some time now and until the advent of reliable transmissions for large diesel engines, they were the only alternative to DR or DE systems for maneuvering. They have been a favored and effective system even on very large and powerful engines, and have seen service on many different types of vessels. Both Ka-Me Wa and Bird-Johnson are well-known names in the manufacture of the CPP systems, some of which are built under license in this country. The pitch-control mechanism consists of a solid shaft inside the hollow drive shaft, which engages cams on the base of the propeller blades to alter the pitch. The control shaft can be operated mechanically by hand in some small installations, but on large ships the pitch control is usually operated by electrical or hydraulic servomotors.

The characteristics of the CPP system are interesting. The pitch can be adjusted to give very slow speeds, and the transition from ahead to astern is made very smoothly (unlike DR engines). The torque effect is the opposite of a conventional propeller of the same rotation, since the pitch of the propeller is reversed rather than its rotation.

There are advantages to this system. Unlike conventional propellers with fixed pitch that are most efficient at one particular engine speed and load condition, the controllable-pitch propeller can provide pitch that is appropriate for a wide range of conditions of load and speed ("light" tug versus tug with a tow). For this reason fuel savings are considerable. CPP and DR systems are more in use in large horsepower-engine installations than any other maneuvering system. The advantage that the CPP system has over the DR system is in the fact that the number of maneuvers is not restricted by the amount of starting air since the pitch of the propeller blades is changed rather than the direction of rotation of the propeller shaft.

On the deficit side, the CPP systems are complicated, expensive, and more vulnerable to damage if their propellers strike something. Since it is constantly turning, in neutral position, the propeller disrupts the water flow past the rudders, and a ship (even with good headway) may not "dead stick" very well. In the towing industry CPP systems have a reputation as "hawser suckers" since it is fairly easy to foul a towline in a propeller that is constantly in motion. Controllable-pitch propellers fitted with nozzles are a bit safer in this respect (Fig. 4-1).

Reverse and Reduction Gears. Transmissions of various types, usually combined with reduction gears, have been in service for years, and are the most common method of controlling engine output in use aboard tugs in this country. Mechanical and hydraulic clutches are in use on engines of relatively modest horsepower. The mechanical clutches are suitable for engines up to about 300 horsepower, and hydraulic clutches

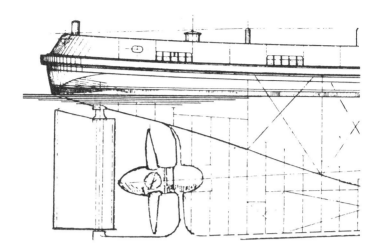

Fig. 4-1. Stern gear of a single-screw tug with controllable-pitch propeller.
Courtesy: Nickum & Spaulding.

are suitable for engines up to 1,200 to 1,500 horsepower. Some of these
have two-speed gear boxes that permit a higher shaft speed running
light, and a lower range that is used when the tug is towing or handling
a ship. This permits the tug to economize on its fuel consumption
whenever its engines are not under a heavy load.

Pneumatic clutches can be used in engine installations of considerably higher horsepower (up to about 4,000 at present). These utilize
heavy-duty "tires" that are inflated to engage the engines, either ahead
or astern. Some pneumatic clutches have a "slip mode" that permits
very slow shaft speeds for a *limited time*. This is convenient in powerful
tugs when a very light push is desirable.

The most notable difference between hydraulic and pneumatic
clutches is the time delay in shifting from neutral to ahead or astern.
The delay in hydraulic clutches can be adjusted but is usually 4 to 6
seconds. Pneumatic clutches, understandably, require more time to
respond, since the tires must be completely inflated before the throttle
can be advanced.

Magnetic couplings (clutches) have been around for a long time and
are most often used to connect two engines to one propeller shaft. In this
case the engines are coupled to input shafts of a reduction gear that has
one output shaft connected to the propeller shaft. This is a convenient
way to compound the horsepower of two engines. It also permits the

vessel to operate on one engine should the other break down. When the vessel is maneuvering, it is a common practice to run one engine ahead and the other astern (they are DR), and the engines are engaged as needed by energizing the appropriate magnetic coupling electrically.

This system is suitable for high horsepower ratings and has been used on large oceangoing tugs as well as on ships. However, its application for use on harbor tugs is probably limited as the tugs would normally require the full power of both engines to maneuver with when working a ship.

Fuel: Consumption and Conservation. An efficient diesel engine consumes about .348 pounds per horsepower hour. This amounts to about 1.2 U. S. gallons per horsepower day. Since engines are normally operated at about 80 percent of their rated horsepower, it is often convenient to estimate the consumption this way, if the fuel consumed by the generators is also included.

At today's prices this can amount to a sizeable sum of money. For this reason some operators are installing engines that are capable of burning cheaper grades of fuel, like heavy diesel (No. 6 oil) or blends (mixtures of No. 6 oil and No. 2 diesel). Low-speed and most medium-speed diesel engines can consume lower grades of fuel, but the high-speed engines popular in this country do not presently have this capability.

The use of lower grade fuel oils requires heating to reduce viscosity and centrifuging to remove impurities. Engines burning heavy fuels also require more maintenance than engines burning light fuel because there is more residue left after combustion. It is worth noting that although the practice of using heavy fuels is common in Europe, even motor ships with large main engines, designed to run on No. 6 oil, customarily maneuver, and operate their generators on lighter grades of fuel. The tug operators must determine if the savings in fuel costs justify the additional expense of the equipment (heater and centrifuge) and the added maintenance.

PROPELLERS

Propellers designed for towing service are usually of large diameter and relatively moderate pitch. Solid propellers are cheaper than controllable-pitch propellers, but are most efficient at one particular speed or load condition. Since they sometimes work at full speed in situations where the slip (slip refers to the potential amount of power loss between propeller speed and the ship's speed) is 100 percent, the pitch must be flat enough not to overload the engine.

A propeller's efficiency is inversely related to the number of blades it has. For this reason a single-blade (surface-effect) propeller has been used on racing boats. Two-blade propellers were (and still are) used for auxiliary propulsion on sailing vessels. The shaft is marked so that the blades can be lined up behind the deadwood to reduce drag.

The propellers of most tugs normally have three or more blades. Four and five are less efficient, but are frequently used to dampen vibration.

Controllable-Pitch Propellers. CP propellers are a maneuvering device as well as a propeller as noted above. Their principal advantage over fixed-pitch "wheels" is fuel efficiency. This is because the pitch-control mechanism can be (often automatically) adjusted to apply the *correct* amount of pitch for any condition of speed, load, or slip. The drawbacks (previously noted) include: the costs, vulnerability to damage, and some unusual handling characteristics. Additionally, there is always the possibility of fouling a working line or tow hawser in a propeller that is constantly turning if the lines are handled carelessly.

The Kort Nozzle. Both conventional and CP propellers are used in conjunction with Kort nozzles and Kort rudders. In this instance the diameter of the propeller can be smaller than might otherwise be desirable in an installation where the propeller is unshrouded.

A Kort nozzle may increase the propeller's thrust ahead by as much as 40 percent when maneuvering ahead, but the backing power is usually about half of its pushing power. The Kort nozzle is often detrimental to "light" running speed.

The propeller's tip speed is the critical factor in the efficiency of this type of installation, and should not exceed approximately 100 feet per second (actually 32 meters per second according to figures supplied by Schottel of America), since cavitation tends to erode performance at greater speeds.

RUDDERS, STERN GEAR, AND HULL CONFIGURATION

Rudders on tugs are oversize by conventional standards. This is intended to promote maneuverability. Most are of balanced or semi-balanced design, i.e., the leading edge of the rudder extends forward of the rudder post. This is done to utilize propeller flow efficiently, and for mechanical advantage to the steering gear. To compensate for the effect of the propeller's torque on steering, some rudders are fitted with a wedge at the trailing edge. (See Figs. 4-1, 4-2, and 4-3.)

Skegs are often fitted on both single- and twin-screw tugs to protect the rudder and propeller. In this case the skeg will usually provide some support for the rudder, and the bottom of the rudder post will be fitted into a bushing in an extension of the skeg.

Spade rudders are not attached to skegs and must be more stoutly constructed. They are usually combined with propellers and shafts supported by struts rather than the tug's sternpost. (See Fig. 3-5 in Chapter 3.)

The *Towmaster®* steering system is used in conjunction with a nozzle and consists of several high aspect ratio rudders behind each nozzle. This type of installation permits a rudder angle up to 60° rather than the 35° to 40° that is the limit for conventional rudders. This permits excellent maneuverability going ahead. However, for shipwork, a tug fitted with this type of steering gear would still need to use a stern line if much backing is required.

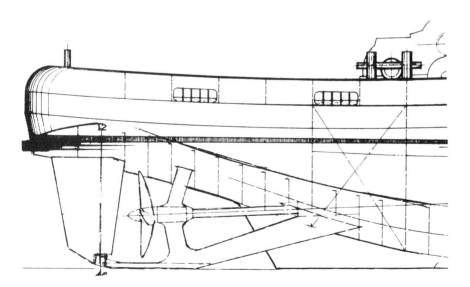

Fig. 4-2. Stern gear of a twin-screw tug with balanced rudder and skegs. Courtesy: Nickum & Spaulding.

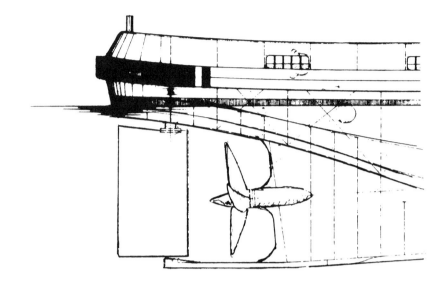

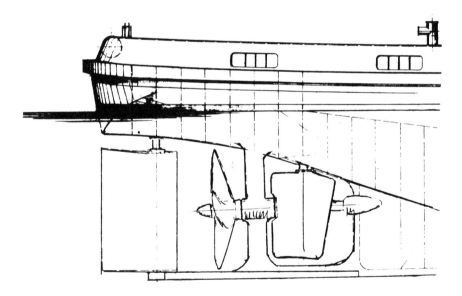

Fig. 4-3. *Above*, stern gear of a conventional single-screw tug with multichine hull. *Below*, the stern gear of a single-screw tug with controllable-pitch propeller. Courtesy: Nickum & Spaulding.

The *Kort rudder* consists of a circular airfoil-shaped shroud installed around the perimeter of the propeller. The Kort rudder is, of course, movable and is turned by the tug's steering gear (See Fig. 3-4 in Chapter 3). It is superior to conventional rudders in two respects: it improves the engine thrust *ahead*, and permits the tug to steer when maneuvering astern. The disadvantage of the Kort rudder is usually that it is slower to respond than a conventional rudder. The helm must be reversed when the engine is backed in order to continue to swing in a given direction, and the Kort rudder may reduce a tug's "light" running speed.

Flanking rudders are installed ahead of the tug's propellers. There are usually two to each propeller, and they provide steerage when the tug maneuvers astern. They are operated by separate controls, and are kept in the amidships position during normal operation ahead. They are often installed in conjunction with Kort nozzles.

Twin-screw single-rudder installations are often seen on older cruise ships. On tugs, however, this arrangement is unusual and is mostly found on vessels converted from some other service. This system of steering is not very effective, since it depends upon the vessel's forward motion for the water flow to the rudder, rather than from the propellers which are located outboard. While usable for hawser towing, twin-screw single rudders are not handy for towing barges alongside. And, since they do not have the rudder power, they are practically useless for shipwork.

Double-rudder and single-screw installations have been employed in conjunction with CP propellers. This seems a logical method of overcoming one of the unfavorable characteristics of the CPP system: the inclination to disrupt the flow of water to a rudder located behind it when in neutral pitch. This type of installation could provide good steering qualities when the pitch of the propeller is in neutral pitch as well.

The *PS (propeller-steered)* tugs mentioned in the preceding chapter differ in several respects from conventional tugs. In this case the propeller itself becomes the transmission and controls the tug's movement ahead or astern. It also replaces the rudder since the propeller is used to steer the tug. Cycloidal propellers like the VSP (Voith-Schneider propeller) control both power transmission and steering by changing the angle of incidence of the propeller vanes. The Schottel drive with SRP (steerable rudder propellers) and other similar systems transmit power with conventional propellers (often enclosed in nozzles) and maneuvering ahead or astern, and steering is accomplished by turning the propeller and directing its wash in the appropriate direction (Figs. 4-4 and 4-5).

Hull Configuration and "Stern Gear." Hull configuration, rudder design, and the size and shape of other underwater appendages such as struts, skegs, keels, and flanking rudders can all affect a tug's efficiency. Flanking rudders and skegs tend to create turbulence that has a negative effect on propeller thrust. Tunnel sterns, as well as the stern post in conventional model hulls can impede the water flow and reduce efficiency.

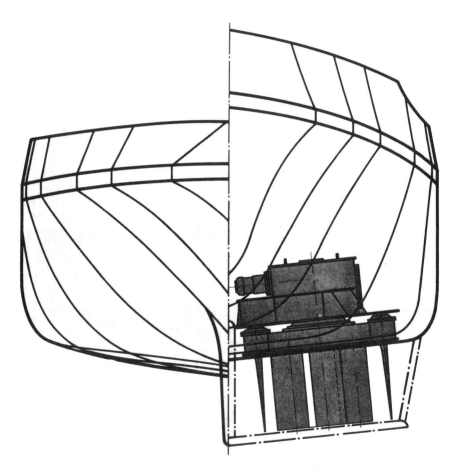

Fig. 4-4. A Voith-Schneider cycloidal rudder propeller. The angle of the vanes is changed to control steering and propulsion. Courtesy: Voith-Schneider.

Fig. 4-5. The drawing shows a Schottel rudder-propeller unit with a shrouded propeller. The propeller unit can be rotated through 360° for steering. Courtesy: Schottel of America.

The most efficient stern gear installations combine spade rudders (unattached to skegs) with the propeller shaft supported by struts, and a well-faired hull of hydroconic (double-chine) construction. This can be combined with a Kort nozzle, and a Kort rudder can be substituted for the spade rudder.

Power versus Suitability. The standard for judging a tug's ability is usually based on its "bollard pull." This is the thrust in pounds or kilograms delivered by the engine under static conditions (pulling against a dock or other fixed structure).

Bollard pull can often be predicted with fair accuracy, since tugs develop thrusts that range between 22.5 and 38 pounds per brake horsepower (bhp). This is usually consistent with the tug's hull configuration, propeller type, and whether or not Kort nozzles are installed. Bollard pull can be affected by the tug's trim, as well as the number and kind of appendages that affect the water flow to the propeller.

Bollard pull is an acceptable criterion for judging a tug's capability in some respects, but there are other factors that must be considered when evaluating a tug's suitability for shipwork. These include its maneuverability, stability, and backing power. A deficiency in any of these may limit a tug's usefulness even if its power is acceptable. Table 2 (Comparative Twin-Screw Tugboat Performances) gives values of thrust per bhp for several different propulsion and steering systems.

Table 2.
Summary of Maneuvering Systems

Type	Pros	Cons
Direct reversing	low cost and simplicity	speed range limited; engine must be stopped to reverse rotation; number of maneuvers dependent upon compressed air supply may be limited; prone to failure
Diesel electric (DE)	good speed range; fuel efficient; constant engine speed; low maintenance; very responsive; suitable for large installations	costly, vulnerable to electrical problems; heavy

Table 2. (continued)

Type	Pros	Cons
DE-SCR system	same as diesel electric but less costly; main generators can be used for ship supply	same as diesel electric
Mechanical clutches	not applicable, too small	not applicable
Hydraulic clutches	standard in U. S. towing industry for smaller engines (1,200 to 1,500 hp); quick maneuvering (4 to 6 seconds)	slow speed faster than DE or CPP systems
Pneumatic clutches	standard in the U. S. for large engines (to 4,000 hp); sometimes has "slip clutch" for slow speeds for limited time	slower maneuvering time than DE, CPP, or hydraulic clutch; slow speed faster than DE or CPP system
Magnetic couplings (two DR engines to a single output gear box)	suitable for large installation; very maneuverable with one engine running ahead and other astern with engines engaged as needed	unsatisfactory for harbor tug because maneuvering horsepower is only one-half steaming horsepower

Table 3.
Comparative Twin-Screw Tugboat Performance

Type of propulsion	Controllable-pitch propellers and twin-spade rudders	Controllable-pitch propellers and Kort rudders	Voith-Schneider propellers	Harbormasters and Kort nozzles
General outline				
Relative size of tug	Big	Big	Medium	Small
Approximate engine RPM	400	400	500-600	750
Thrust (pulling) towing power (Main engine)	25.3-27.5 lbs/SHP (11.5-12.5 kg/SHP)	30.8-35.2 lbs/SHP (14.0-16.0 kg/SHP)	22.0-24.2 lbs/SHP (10.0-11.0 kg/SHP)	33.0-37.4 lbs/SHP (15.0-17.0 kg/SHP)
Towing force when backing (as a percentage of ahead towing force)	30	30-60	90	100

Time required for an emergency stop, in seconds	39	20	18	10
Time required from full ahead to full astern, in seconds	10	10	7	7.5
Arc over which steering force can be exerted, in degrees	70	70	360	360
Steering time over full arc listed above, in seconds	15-30	15-30	15	15
Time required for 360° turn, in seconds	65-70	45-50	35-45	20-25
Turning radius, in hull lengths (L)	3-5L	1.5-2.0L	1.0-1.3L	1.0-1.3L

Courtesy: Harbormaster Division of Murray & Tregurtha Co.

STUDY QUESTIONS

1. Why has the diesel engine supplanted the steam engine aboard tugs as a source of power?
2. What effect has the diesel engine had on the design of tugs?
3. What are the principal disadvantages of the diesel engine when compared with the steam engine?
4. What methods are used to control engine maneuvers ahead and astern?
5. Describe the DR system of engine control.
6. What is the principal advantage of the DR system?
7. What are the disadvantages of the DR system?
8. Describe the DE system of engine control.
9. What are the special virtues of DE drive?
10. What are its principal disadvantages?
11. How does an SCR system differ from the conventional DE drive?
12. Are there any particular advantages to the SCR system?
13. Describe the CPP system.
14. Are systems employing magnetic couplings with two engines and one output shaft suitable for harbor tugs?
15. How are PS tugs maneuvered?
16. What is "heavy" fuel and what is its advantage?
17. What are the disadvantages of using heavy fuel?
18. What types of propellers are used in installations aboard tugs?
19. Describe solid propellers.
20. What are their advantages and disadvantages?
21. What are the advantages of the CPP system?
22. What are its drawbacks?
23. What type of transmission is commonly used on tugs doing shipork in this country?
24. What are the principal advantages of either pneumatic or hydraulic transmissions?
25. What are their disadvantages?
26. Describe the Voith-Schneider cycloidal propeller (VSP).
27. Describe other PS configurations.
28. Describe a Kort nozzle and explain its function.
29. What is a balanced or semi-balanced rudder?
30. What is a "spade" rudder?

31. What are flanking rudders?
32. What is a Kort rudder?
33. What is bollard pull?
34. Is bollard pull a fair criterion for judging a tug's serviceability for shipwork?

CHAPTER FIVE

STRUCTURAL CONSIDERATIONS

The nature of shipwork requires a tug to *push* against a ship, and to *pull* either by backing down against a head line or by coming ahead on a towline or springline. The tug must also go alongside ships that are underway and are often moving fairly fast. They may also have to work near the bow or stern of a vessel, and sometimes the flare and overhang in these areas are fairly pronounced. In order for the tug to function safely and efficiently under these circumstances there are certain structural requirements that must be met.

THE HULL

Tugs are overbuilt by conventional standards. This is done in order for them to withstand the frequent heavy contacts that are common in this employment without sustaining damage. They must also be reenforced in critical areas where the force of their propelling power is brought to bear. These areas include: the bow, the stern on tractor tugs (since they push stern first), and the deck fittings to which the working lines are secured. The tug should also be fairly "stiff" since working lines frequently lead off to the side, and this could cause a tender vessel to capsize.

THE SUPERSTRUCTURE

A well-designed harbor tug used for shipwork should have fairly low freeboard, with deckhouses (and wheelhouses) set well inboard from the rail. The bulwarks are tumbled home, and the mast should be set up in a tabernacle for easy lowering. (See Figs. 5-1 to 5-3.) Attention to these structural aspects helps prevent damage to the tug (and the ship) when the tug works under the flare of the bow or overhang of the ship's side near the stern, and when the vessels are rolling a bit.

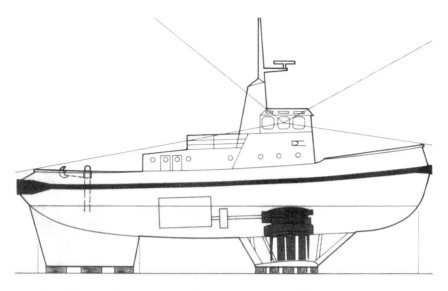

Fig. 5-1. Profile of a tractor tug showing the shape of the superstructure. Note that a heavy fender is installed at the stern. Location of tow hook is also aft. Courtesy: Voith-Schneider of America.

VISIBILITY

The operator's field of view should be as unobstructed as possible for the safety of the crew, the tug, and the ship. The new style wheelhouses incorporate additional small windows that face upwards. This is a big improvement over the old style wheelhouse, which usually had a visor that impaired the tug captain's vision, especially when working along-side large vessels with high freeboard. (See Figs. 5-2 and 5-3.) The steering and engine controls should also be placed where the operator's view will be unrestricted.

UNDERWATER CONFIGURATION

Some employment imposes limitations on the underwater portion of the hull. For example, single-screw tugs with molded hulls (round bottoms) are preferred for assisting submarines to dock and undock. The reason for this is that submarines have had their shell plating damaged by the inboard propeller of twin-screw tugs, and a chine hull (V bottom) has a sharp corner at the turn of the bilge that can also damage a sub's outer

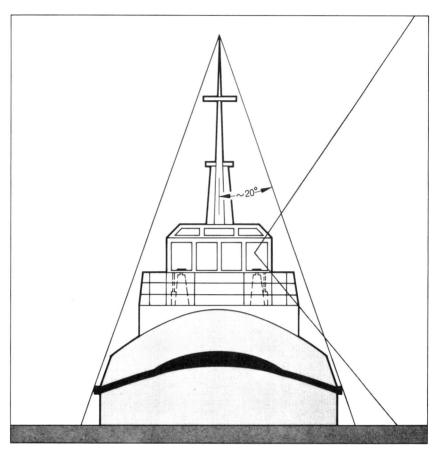

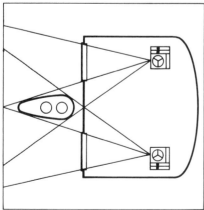
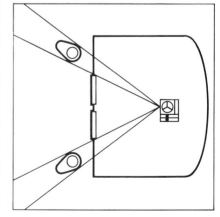

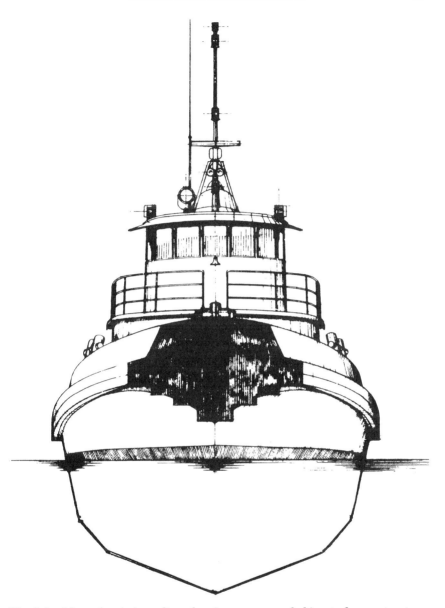

Fig. 5-2. *Above,* front view of tug showing recommended inset of superstructure and tumble home of bulwarks. *Below,* showing field of vision astern from steering station. Courtesy: Voith-Schneider.

Fig. 5-3. Front view of a harbor tug with multichine hull. Note that the forward quarter bitts "tumble in." Tug has heavy extruded side fenders. Courtesy: Nickum & Spaulding.

hull. Rolling chocks, or bilge keels, should also be dispensed with for this service. (See Fig. 5-4.)

DECK LAYOUT

The deck layout of a well-designed (American) harbor tug will have either a cruciform bitt or "bullnose" (a large closed chock) installed near the stem but far enough back so that it will not come in contact with the vessel's side when the tug is pushing. These fittings are used to lead the tug's head line or springline from a position as far forward as possible. The bullnose will have an aperture large enough to permit the easy passage of the eye and the splice of the large size working lines (or even two of them). If a cruciform bitt is used instead of a bullnose, it should be

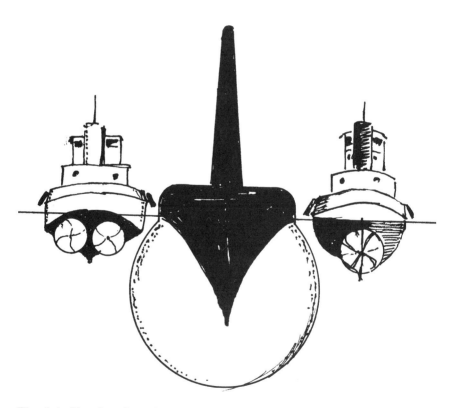

Fig. 5-4. Showing the relationship between single-screw model hull tug and twin-screw-chine hull tug alongside a submarine.

large enough to permit a wrap or two around it of whatever size lines are used, even if two lines are employed as in Fig. 5-5.

A heavy H bitt is set fore and aft in the forward deck to belay the working lines. It should be substantial enough to withstand the strains imposed upon it in this line of work.

Forward quarter bitts (Fig. 5-6) are fitted on both sides of the hull, usually just forward of the deckhouse. They are set inboard so that a line belayed to them will not be pinched or chafed when working alongside of a ship or a barge.

H type tow bitts, set athwartship, will be located aft of the deckhouse, but far enough forward of the rudders to permit good maneuverability. This distance is usually between a third and a quarter of the vessel's length forward of the stern. After quarter bitts are also installed on both sides, usually slightly abaft the towing bitts.

A capstan (if there is one) will in most cases be positioned to one side or the other of the after H bitts. Occasionally there will be a capstan forward, but usually only if there is an anchor windlass there. This can be helpful at times, but the anchor should stow so it cannot damage a ship or foul a line.

Towing hooks are not often seen on American tugs, but they should be installed if much towline work is done. They are, of course, commonplace on European tugs. The principal virtue of towing hooks is that they can be "tripped" (often by remote control) to release a hawser, even if the hawser is under heavy strain. This might avert a capsize.

The tow hook is an alternative to the H bitt, and there is one often located both forward and aft on European tugs. The after tow hook is usually located almost amidships on conventional European harbor tugs, permitting a tug to maneuver well on even a short towline, while

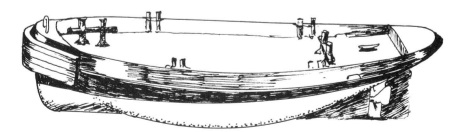

Fig. 5-5. Deck layout of a conventional American tug.

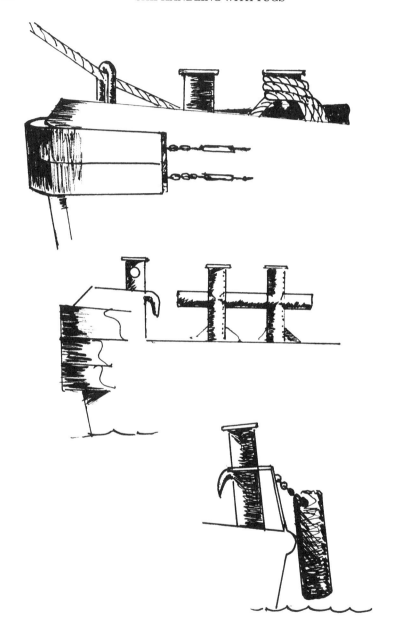

Fig. 5-6. *Above,* bullnose on tug's bow. *Center,* cruciform bitts for fair leading or securing line. *Below,* inset showing quarter bitts from the tug's side.

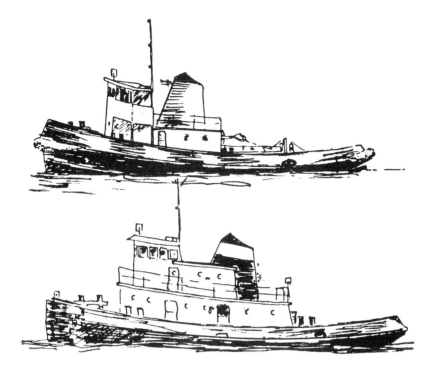

Fig. 5-7. Drawings illustrate differences between, *above,* a European harbor tug
that has a tow hook located almost midships and, *below,* an American harbor tug
with "H" bitts aft, located about one-third of the tug's length from the stern.

at the same time increasing its prospect of becoming girt or capsizing.
(See Figs. 5-7 and 5-8.)

Fairleads and cleats are frequently installed in the afterdeck to
facilitate heaving in towlines and stern lines. They may also be used to
give a better lead to a stern line even though it may be belayed on a
quarter bitt or the tow bitts.

ILLUMINATION AND MISCELLANEOUS FACTORS

There should be a searchlight mounted over the wheelhouse with the
controls in convenient reach of the operator at the handling station.
This is very handy in shipwork since the tug operator can illuminate
unlighted buoys and obstructions that otherwise would be difficult to
see at night. This is often helpful to the ship as well, as many shiphan-

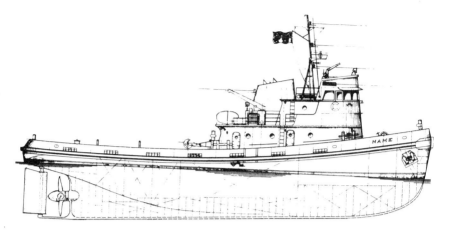

Fig. 5-8. Single-screw harbor tug with a controllable-pitch propeller. The tug is designed for use in West Australia where towline work prevails. Note the location of the towing hook and the towspans to keep the hawser from fouling on fittings on the deck. Courtesy: Nickum & Spaulding.

dlers are reluctant to use the vessel's searchlight, since they feel that it is destructive to their night vision.

The tug's decks should be well illuminated without blinding the tug captain. If there is an after control station, it should have the same facilities as the wheelhouse. There should also be a remote radio-telephone hookup, a whistle pull, and another good searchlight close at hand.

STRUCTURAL FAULTS ON SHIPS

A number of ships are very dangerous or difficult for tugs to assist. In some cases the vessel's service may require the peculiarities that make them unhandy for tugs. Submarines, for example, provide no shipside for the tug's fenders to rest against (except the underwater bow fender), and the tug will be hull-to-hull with the sub when it is lying alongside. Aircraft carriers, on the other hand, have overhanging superstructures and often many projections along the side that can be hazardous to tugs. There are usually few places on such a vessel where a tug can work safely alongside. A few passenger liners and automobile carriers have extended houses with abbreviated decks fore and aft where the chocks and bitts are located. The flare of the bow and the overhang aft may make it tough for the tug to work there. Other vessels have thoughtfully been provided with "pocket chocks" in the ship's side that a tug can make fast to. If they are the right height above the water and are located in an area where a tug can work safely, they are a real blessing! (See Fig. 5-9.) In certain cases where a vessel's purpose imposes these deficiencies, they are understandable. But in other cases, and there are many of them, such oversights are inexcusable.

Some of the new vessels with transom sterns are very wide aft to accommodate the large deckhouse. These may have most or all of their chocks located on a tiny stern deck. If there are chocks elsewhere, they usually are not far enough forward of the tremendous after overhang. Others may have the only decent chock located directly over a big "No Tugs" sign on the ship's side. Some ships are fitted with constant tension winches and use either wire rope or spring lay cable for mooring lines. Rolling chocks usually accompany these installations and are often unsuitable for the tug's working lines as their apertures are too small.

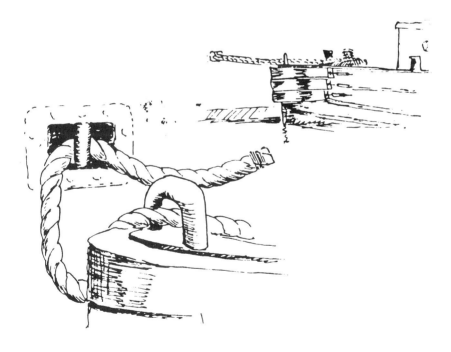

Fig. 5-9. Tug making fast to a recessed or pocket chock in the side of a passenger liner. Note how line is passed through chock and bitter end is made fast back aboard tug.

Since bitts are not used for tying up the vessel, there may be none available for securing the tug's lines.

A few ship designers thoughtlessly located the chocks aft so that when the ship is "light" the main engine cooling water will discharge on the tug's decks. In the days before sewage containment systems were required, a lot of unmentionable material from the sanitary system also landed on the tug's decks.

Not many ships have rub rails—but some of them do! I remember one of them in particular. It had a rub rail located exactly where it was guaranteed to clip most of a tug's fenders (tire casings) in half; after which the tug and ship would grind away at each other. I never figured out what purpose rub rails served beyond hanging up on the dock's fender system while the ship discharged, but it sure sold a lot of tires!

The vertical half-round pipes welded to a ship's side covering waste water and generator discharges can be a nuisance too, as they may fit between the tug's fenders and be damaged. The tire casings used for fendering can also be torn off.

Naval architects and marine engineers should consider these factors when designing a ship. After all, if tugs must conform to certain structural requirements to be effective at their trade, it is not unreasonable to expect a vessel requiring their assistance to provide chocks in suitable locations so that the tugs can indeed be employed effectively and *safely*. The safety of the ship itself may depend upon the tug's ability to function efficiently without being exposed to undue risk. Given the costs of constructing a vessel today, and the small additional cost of installing a few chocks and bitts in appropriate locations, the failure to do so is not only *inexcusable*—it is *unacceptable*.

STUDY QUESTIONS

1. Describe the important aspects of the hull of a tug used for shipwork.
2. Is the hull reenforced?
3. Why are deck structures set so far inboard on harbor tugs?
4. What is a "bullnose"?
5. Where are the bitts located on conventional American harbor tugs?

6. What are the structural requirements for the bitts and deck fittings?
7. What type of mast should be installed on a harbor tug?
8. With respect to visibility how should the wheelhouse be arranged?
9. Why are model hull single-screw tugs preferred for assisting submarines?
10. What structural characteristics of a ship can make it difficult or dangerous for a tug assisting it?
11. What are pocket or recessed chocks and why are they useful?

CHAPTER SIX

GEAR AND RIGGING FOR SHIPWORK

In my earlier work on tug operations, *Primer of Towing*, I devoted a chapter to the towing gear. It was based on the premise that a tug was no better than the gear it uses. This premise is just as valid for a harbor tug that does only shipwork and barge handling as it is for a tug engaged in offshore towing. It does not have to have as much gear, of course, but the gear it has should be in first-class shape.

The tug's gear in shipwork is not directly a concern of the pilot or the docking master; but if it fails or carries away at a critical time it could ruin their whole day! If the shiphandler feels that the tug is not properly equipped, he should let the towing company or the tug captain know— right away!

As mentioned before a tug is a floating power plant and its principal functions are to *push* and *pull*. In order for it to carry out these functions successfully, without injury to itself and to other vessels, it must have the necessary gear. This gear can be classified into the three basic categories listed below:

1. *Fender systems* to protect the tug and the ship from damage when the tug is making fast or working alongside of the vessel.
2. *Connecting gear*, the working lines (or cables), used to secure the tug to the ship.
3. *Auxiliary equipment*, the heaving lines, tag lines, goblines, quick-release straps, etc., that may be used intermittently or often but are essential to the smooth operation of the tug.

FENDER SYSTEMS

Adequate fender systems are imperative on any tug doing shipwork, especially in this country where tugs usually work alongside the ships.

Fig. 6-1. Bow fender systems.

The fenders protect both the ship and the tug from damage that would occur as a result of the heavy contact that is a normal part of this activity. (Figs. 6-1 and 6-2.)

The bow fender is of particular importance, for it absorbs and distributes the main force of the tug's engines when it pushes against the ship. The bow fenders on powerful tugs should have a wide radius for this reason. The heavy neoprene and synthetic rubber extrusions used for fenders on most tugs at the present are excellent. If they have any

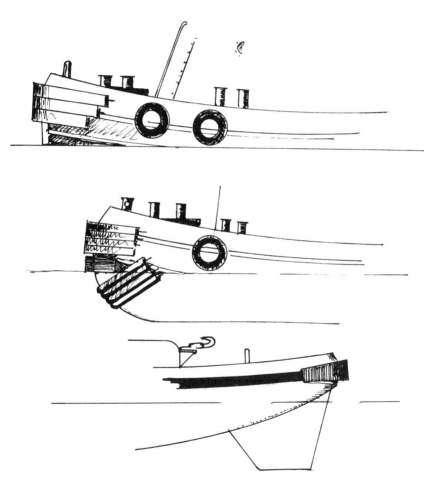

Fig. 6-2. *Above,* a typical installation on a harbor tug. *Center,* fenders for assisting submarines. These can affect handling qualities of the tug. *Below,* stern fender on a tractor tug.

fault at all, it is simply that they do not provide as much traction as the older rope fenders did with their baggy wrinkle chafing mat hanging over the fender pudding. These new type fenders have a tendency to slide down the ship's side when the tug is working at an angle without a line.

Tugs that see service working submarines must have fenders on the bow that extend below the waterline as this is the part of the stem that comes in contact with the submarine's hull. These underwater fenders can affect the tug's handling qualities too. They may not steer as well as a tug without them.

Side fenders on tugs are often made up from heavy-duty tire casings, often in their natural state. At other times the tires are cut into squares and strung on bars as a laminated fender. Occasionally, the tire casings are built up by serving them with used line which makes them bulkier and more enduring. The heaviest side fenders are placed just forward of amidships, since this is the area where the tugs usually land hardest when going alongside a ship.

Fenders can also compensate for some structural deficiencies. In a number of the older boats the deckhouse is too close to the rail; in this case the tug's breadth can be extended by using extra wide fenders (like tractor tire casings) or several of them if necessary. They are usually hung, as stated, forward of amidships—where the deck narrows and the house often stays the same width. If tugs also have wheelhouses that are a bit too wide for shipwork, roller-type fenders are often attached to either side of the bridge to protect it from damage (Fig. 6-3). When personnel are being transferred to or from a ship by a tug fitted out with this type of fender, the operator should exercise care that they are kept clear of this hazard, as they could be crushed against the ship if the vessels are rolling a bit.

Stern fenders are not often seen on American tugs as they are usually not needed (they are handy for checking the way on barges towed on a short hawser). However, tractor tugs that usually push stern first against a ship must have them.

CONNECTING GEAR

The tug's working lines are summarized as follows:

1. A good head line—about 150 feet in length with an eye spliced at each end. Sometimes another slightly smaller line with an eye at

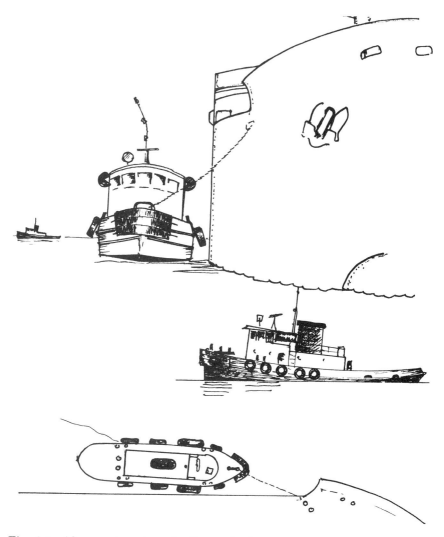

Fig. 6-3. *Above* and *center,* wheelhouse fender arrangement on a harbor tug with a wide bridge. *Below,* heavy fenders can increase the tug's breadth.

one end, and the other end whipped so that it can be rove through the chocks that are sometimes installed in the ship's side in passenger vessels and in some automobile carriers that have short forward and afterdecks (shown in Fig. 5-9).

2. A good secondary line similar to the head line that can be used as a springline.
3. A towline similar in strength to the head line and springline but of longer length (200 to 250 feet). It is sometimes desirable for this line to be of the floating type for ease of handling and to keep it out of the tug's propellers—especially the CPP which are always turning.
4. A stern line or quarter line (terms used interchangeably) if the towline is not used for this purpose. This line can be smaller than the towline because its purpose is simply to hold the tug in position while it backs against the head line. This line might also be of the floating type and like the towline must be longer than either the head line or springline.

Types of Working Lines. Except for certain ports where tugs make fast with wire ropes (ports on the Mississippi River and a few other places), most tugs use synthetic fiber working lines. Although some natural fibers, like manila, can also be used for working lines, they are more suitable for other purposes. The strength, endurance, and resistance to chafe and mildew of some synthetic fibers make them more practical for this purpose than manila. Not all synthetic lines are suitable for shipwork, and some of them are only recommended for limited applications where they are not subjected to chafe or exceptionally heavy strains. While synthetics are not vulnerable to mildew, like natural fibers, they all deteriorate from prolonged exposure to sunlight, are affected by some petroleum products like gasoline, etc., and are susceptible to damage by rust. They can also be ruined by contact with acids used for filling batteries or preparing steel surfaces for painting.

When working lines show signs of much wear, they should be downgraded to services like dock lines where their strength is less critical.

Different types of lines have particular virtues and vices that may make them better suited for one application than for another. These qualities are listed and compared as follows.

Characteristics of Working Lines.
Manila is really the only natural fiber suitable for working lines on a tug, and it was the principal cordage used aboard tugs before the advent of synthetic lines.

Pro: lowest cost, splices and ties well, is good for heaving lines, messengers, and stoppers.

Con: low strength (about a third of nylon), sinks when wet, subject to mildew and dry-rot, chafes readily.

Nylon is a name for any number of polyamide synthetic fibers. It is the strongest (and most elastic) cordage used for commercial marine purposes.

Pro: very strong (approximately three times the strength of manila), resists rot and mildew, *very elastic*, and excellent for towing hawsers and "shock" lines.

Con: sinks when wet, is damaged by sunlight and by some chemicals, *very elastic* and not suitable for working lines for shipwork for this reason, and is *murderous* when it parts under a strain.

Dacron is the trade name for synthetic polyester fiber. It is almost as strong as nylon, but is not as elastic, and is commonly used in marine applications.

Pro: very strong, does not rot or mildew, resists chafe and abrasion well, low elasticity. It is suitable for slings, mooring lines, and working lines on tugs because of these characteristics.

Con: sinks when wet, is damaged by sunlight and some chemicals, can be used but is not elastic enough for ocean towing.

Polypropylene. Pro: relatively inexpensive, light weight, and floats when wet, is suitable for stern lines, and for towlines in light work.

Con: about the same strength as manila, chafes and abrades easily, may stick when surged around bitts and capstans, is slippery when tied or spliced (splices may fail unless extra tucks are taken).

Polyethylene. Pro: about the same as polypropylene.

Con: same as for polypropylene.

Various blends on the market can be found under a variety of trade names. They may have different characteristics, but fundamentally they are compromises that use two different types of fibers that compensate for each other's deficiencies. Usually a "tough" outer shell of nylon or Dacron is laid around an inner core of polypropylene or polyethylene. The end product has greater tensile strength than either of the latter two materials, and resists chafe and abrasion. However, since the inner core is made from lighter material and floats when it is wet which is a desirable quality, it does so at the sacrifice of some of its tensile strength. Poly-Dac is a more or less typical example of good blended line and has qualities that commend it for shipwork.

Pro: reasonable strength (about double that of manila), resists abrasion and chafe, floats, is not too elastic, is suitable for all working lines, especially for towlines and quarter lines.

Con: same as for Dacron, but lighter and not as strong.

The lines described above are either of three-strand regular lay or eight-strand plaited construction. The Dacron line and blends may be laid up either way, but are usually regular lay for convenience in splicing. Polypropylene and polyethylene lines for this service should be of plaited construction as these materials are often loosely laid and have a tendency to *hockle* (develop kinks) if they are of regular lay construction.

Splices in all synthetic lines require more tucks than splices (in manila line three tucks are required). There should be four to five in Dacron and nylon, and at least as many in polypropylene or poly- ethylene lines.

Wire Rope Pendants and Working Lines. As mentioned above, tugs in some areas make up alongside ships with wire rope. In other cases wire rope pendants 15 to 25 feet in length are attached to the outboard end of the fiber working lines. This protects the "soft" line from chafe and abrasion that usually occur where the lines pass through the ship's chocks.

The wire rope pendants and working lines will have eyes large enough to fit over a ship's bitts spliced or swaged in the outboard ends. The pendant will have a small eye in the other end that attaches to the soft line. Pendants will normally only be attached to the head line and springline since the weight of the pendant would cause a towline or quarter line to sink, making them difficult to retrieve.

If wire rope is used, it should be comparable in strength to that of the soft lines used. It should be of 6 × 19 or 6 ×37 construction (6 × 37 is preferable since it is more flexible). The fiber core in six-strand cable lubricates it and permits some elasticity which is helpful. Wire rope for shipwork should be constructed from Improved Plow Steel or Extra Improved Plow Steel for strength.

The wires should be changed when they begin to show signs of wear, or when they develop "fish hooks." This is done to avoid their parting, and to protect the personnel handling them.

Line strength, wire rope strength, and appropriate sizes for working

lines used aboard tugs of various horsepower ratings are shown in
Tables 4, 5, and 6, below.

The line sizes indicated in Table 4 below are based upon Dacron, or
material of similar strength. Samson line of equivalent strength may be
of smaller circumference.

Table 4.
Working Line Sizes for Harbor Tugs

Horsepower of Tug	Size of Line
1,000 to 1,500	7" to 8"
1,500 to 2,400	8" to 10"
2,400 to 3,600	9" to 11"
3,600 to 5,600	10" to 14"

Working lines are consumable items that *must* be replaced at frequent intervals. They are subject to heavy strains, and are also liable to
chafe where they are secured to bitts and where they pass through the
bullnose on the tug and the chocks on the ship. Since these lines are
frequently respliced and "end for ended," regular lay (three-strand)
lines are usually preferred for the head line and springline which see the
most service. Plaited (eight-strand) lines may also be used, but are more
likely to be used for quarter lines and towlines.

Samson line and similar yacht braid lines (i.e., with an outer sheath-
ing and an inner core) are less popular for this service despite their
excellent strength. This is mainly due to their higher cost. They are
most often seen on very powerful tugs where their smaller sizes make
them convenient to handle, and in any situation where their strength
for a given diameter offsets the higher cost.

AUXILIARY EQUIPMENT

These items of equipment may seem inconsequential, but without them
shipwork can be more difficult or dangerous.

Heaving lines are used to pass a tug's working lines to a ship. On tugs
they are usually about fifteen fathoms long. If they are tied directly to
the tug's working line they should be at least 3/8 inch to 7/16 inch in
diameter, and preferably made of manila or some other material that is
not *slippery*. This provides a decent handhold for the seamen on deck of
the ship. If tag lines are used, heaving lines are often made of braided
line 1/4 inch to 5/16 inch in diameter. These can be thrown farther and

Table 5.

Tow Cable Strengths

6 × 19 Class Wire Rope

Breaking Strength, Tons of 2,000 lbs.

Rope Diameter in inches	Xtra Improved Plow Steel		Improved Plow Steel	
	Fibre Core	IWRC*	Fibre Core	IWRC
½"	—	13.3	10.7	11.5
⅝"	—	20.6	16.7	17.9
¾"	—	29.4	23.8	25.6
⅞"	—	39.8	32.2	34.6
1"	—	51.7	41.8	44.9
1¼"	71.0	79.9	64.6	69.4
1½"	101.0	114.0	92.0	98.9

6 × 37 Class Wire Rope

Breaking Strength, Tons of 2,000 lbs.

Rope Diameter in inches	Xtra Improved Plow Steel		Improved Plow Steel	
	Fibre Core	IWRC	Fibre Core	IWRC
½"	—	13.3	10.7	11.5
⅝"	—	20.6	16.7	17.9
¾"	—	29.4	23.8	25.6
⅞"	—	39.8	32.2	34.6
1"	—	51.7	41.8	44.9
1¼"	67.7	76.1	61.5	66.1
1½"	96.6	108.0	87.9	94.5

Source: Bethlehem Steel Co., Wire Rope Division
* IWRC (internal wire rope core)

higher than thicker lines, and can be helpful on windy days when working a ship that is "light" with a lot of freeboard.

The traditional "monkey's fist" often had a heavy bolt or nut inserted into the center for extra weight. This was acceptable, and often necessary, but the common practice of soaking the monkey's fist in red lead paint made it even heavier and harder. This practice should be discouraged as it has caused a lot of injuries.

Tag lines are lengths of line secured to the outboard end of the tug's working lines and are used to provide a handhold for the ship's deck force to pull them on board the vessel. Tag lines are attached to the bitter end of the heaving line which is passed to the vessel first. They are

Table 6.
**Fiber Rope Strengths
for Working Lines and Hawsers**

Size		Manila		Polypropylene (Monofilament)		POLY-plus		POLY-cron		Nylon		Dacron (Polyester)	
Dia.	Cir.	Tensile Strength	Lbs. per 100 ft.	Tensile Strength	Lbs. per 100 ft.	Tensile Strength	Lbs. per 100 ft.	Tensile Strength	Lbs. per 100 ft.	Tensile Strength	Lbs. per 100 ft.	Tensile Strength	Lbs. per 100 ft.
3/16"	5/8"	405	1.5	800	.70	—	—	—	—	1,000	1.0	1,000	1.2
1/4"	3/4"	540	2.0	1,250	1.2	—	—	—	—	1,650	1.5	1,650	2.0
5/16"	1"	900	2.9	1,900	1.8	—	—	—	—	2,550	2.5	2,550	3.1
3/8"	1 1/8"	1,215	4.1	2,700	2.8	2,650	3.5	—	—	3,700	3.5	3,700	4.5
7/16"	1 1/4"	1,575	5.25	3,500	3.8	3,600	5.0	—	—	5,000	5.0	5,000	6.2
1/2"	1 1/2"	2,385	7.5	4,200	4.7	4,500	6.5	—	—	6,400	6.5	6,400	8.0
9/16"	1 3/4"	3,105	10.4	5,100	6.1	5,450	7.9	—	—	8,000	8.3	8,000	10.2
5/8"	2"	3,960	13.3	6,200	7.5	6,400	9.4	—	—	10,400	10.5	10,000	13.0
3/4"	2 1/4"	4,860	16.7	8,500	10.7	8,400	12.0	—	—	14,200	14.5	12,500	17.5
13/16"	2 1/2"	5,850	19.5	9,900	12.7	10,200	14.5	—	—	17,000	17.0	15,500	21.0
7/8"	2 3/4"	6,930	22.5	11,500	15.0	12,000	17.0	—	—	20,000	20.0	18,000	25.0
1"	3"	8,100	27.0	14,000	18.0	15,000	21.5	14,000	26.5	25,000	26.0	22,000	30.5

1 1/16″	3 1/4″	9,450	31.3	16,000	20.4	17,100	24.2	—	—	28,800	29.0	25,500	34.5
1 1/8″	3 1/2″	10,800	36.0	18,300	23.7	19,300	27.0	21,000	34.0	33,000	34.0	29,500	40.0
1 1/4″	3 3/4″	12,150	41.8	21,000	27.0	22,000	32.5	24,000	39.0	37,500	40.0	33,200	46.3
1 5/16″	4″	13,500	48.0	23,500	30.5	25,000	38.0	27,000	44.0	43,000	45.0	37,500	52.5
1 1/2″	4 1/2″	16,650	60.0	29,700	38.5	31,300	46.0	34,000	55.0	53,000	55.0	46,800	66.8
1 5/8″	5″	20,250	74.4	36,000	47.5	38,300	55.0	42,000	67.0	65,000	68.0	57,000	82.0
1 3/4″	5 1/2″	23,850	89.5	43,000	57.0	46,500	65.0	50,000	80.0	78,000	83.0	67,800	98.0
2″	6″	27,900	108.0	52,000	69.0	56,500	83.0	60,000	95.0	92,000	95.0	80,000	118.0
2 1/8″	6 1/2″	32,400	125.0	61,000	80.0	65,500	97.0	70,000	112.0	106,000	109.0	92,000	135.0
2 1/4″	7″	36,900	146.0	69,000	92.0	74,000	108.0	80,000	127.0	125,000	129.0	107,000	157.0
2 1/2″	7 1/2″	41,850	167.0	80,000	107.0	86,000	122.0	92,000	147.0	140,000	149.0	122,000	181.0
2 5/8″	8″	46,800	191.0	90,000	120.0	96,000	138.0	105,000	165.0	162,000	168.0	137,000	205.0
2 7/8″	8 1/2″	52,200	215.0	101,000	137.0	105,000	155.0	—	—	180,000	189.0	154,000	230.0
3″	9″	57,600	242.0	114,000	153.0	122,000	179.0	130,000	208.0	200,000	210.0	174,000	258.0
3 1/4″	10″	69,300	299.0	137,000	190.0	144,000	210.0	163,000	253.0	250,000	263.0	210,000	318.0
3 1/2″	11″	81,900	367.0	162,000	232.0	170,000	248.0	—	—	300,000	316.0	254,000	384.0
4″	12″	94,500	436.0	190,000	275.0	200,000	290.0	—	—	360,000	379.0	300,000	460.0

Source: Wall Rope Company

especially helpful in hauling up large working lines and those lines with
a wire rope pendant attached to them. In most cases made from ¾-inch
to 1-inch diameter manila or some similar nonslippery material, tag
lines should be long enough for the ship's crew to get a hand on them
before the full weight of the hawser is felt. They are usually 30 to 40 feet
long unless the ships handled are very large.

Goblines are simply straps that pass over a towline that act as a
"preventer" to keep the towline from leading over the side and tripping
or capsizing the tug. They're secured to the afterdeck near the stern of
the tug and only permit the towline to swing through a limited arc (Fig.
6-4). Not often seen on harbor tugs in this country, goblines are frequently used on tugs doing shipwork in Europe. When used on offshore
tugs in this country, they are sometimes called *tie downs*.

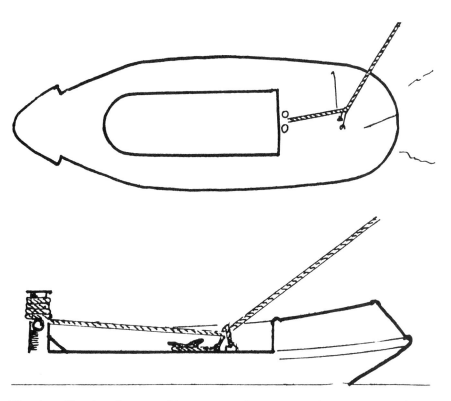

Fig. 6-4. Showing how a gobline is rigged to restrict the movement of the
towline. The gobline helps prevent the tug from being tripped or capsized when
working on a towline especially if the tug is being towed stern first.

Quick-release straps are short (six to eight fathoms) lines with an eye at one end that are used as a substitute for towing hooks. They are rove double through the eye of a ship's hawser on towline jobs and secured to the after tow bitts. This is a safety measure that permits the hawser to be cast off in an emergency with little danger to the tug's crew (Fig. 6-5).

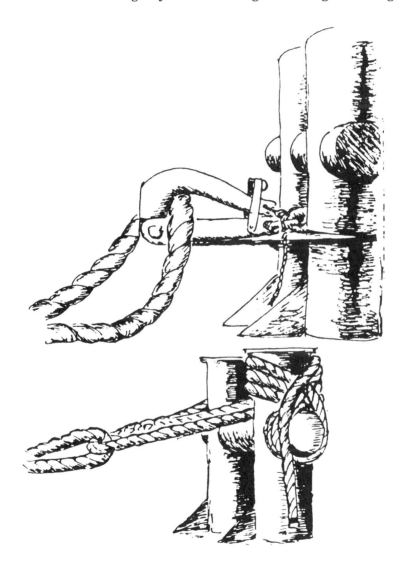

Fig. 6-5. Showing tow hook and an alternate method of using a quick-release strap for towline jobs.

There are additional items that make the tugs handier, more efficient, or safer. They include: gratings to keep the working lines dry and off of the deck, or perhaps a tarpaulin to protect against spray (in freezing weather) and sunlight; nonskid decks which make for safer footing; and a few bags of salt which will melt the ice in winter. Some large tugs have powered drums to handle and stow their working lines. These are handy and economical as they require fewer deckhands, and they are sensible since 14-inch or even 10-inch lines (especially when wet) require a lot of effort to handle. These kinds of amenities distinguish the professional operator from the Johnny-come-latelies.

STUDY QUESTIONS

1. What are the three basic components of a harbor tug's gear?
2. Describe the fender system and explain its functions.
3. What are the fenders made of?
4. Do fenders have any other functions?
5. What kind of fenders are installed on tugs that assist submarines?
6. What is meant by the term connecting gear?
7. What is connecting gear usually made from?
8. What types of synthetic lines are used in shipwork?
9. Are unblended nylon lines used for shipwork?
10. What are Dacron lines used for primarily?
11. What are polypropylene and polyethylene lines used for?
12. What are blended lines used for?
13. What purpose do wire rope pendants serve?
14. How are most working lines laid?
15. When are "yacht" braid type lines used?
16. What types of wire rope are suitable for pendants and working lines?
17. List common items of auxiliary equipment.
18. Describe the heaving lines commonly used on tugs.
19. Describe and explain the purpose of a tag line.
20. May tag lines be made of manila?
21. What is a gobline, and what is its purpose?
22. What is a quick-release strap, and how is it used?

CHAPTER SEVEN

COMMUNICATION BETWEEN SHIP AND TUG

While doing shipwork, I have witnessed and participated in occasions when the rapport between the pilot and the tug was so complete that orders were superfluous and simply dispensed with: the tugs docked the ship without instructions from the pilot. Many pilots, docking masters, and tug captains that I have talked to have had similar experiences. This kind of understanding is exceptional and for all I know, may be some heretofore unrecognized form of ESP. The occasions, however, when this type of mutual understanding occurs are rare enough that you would be foolish to depend upon them, and more conventional means of communication should be employed in order for those of us not gifted with clairvoyance to understand the pilot's orders. If a tug is to carry out a shiphandler's instructions effectively, it must first receive them.

In the past, communication between ship and tug was carried out with whistles. The vessel usually used the ship's whistle to direct the after tug, while the pilot would use a policeman's whistle to signal the forward tug. The tugs would respond with their own whistles, or sometimes one tug would use a smaller "peeper." This was done so that the pilot or docking master could distinguish one tug from the other. This can be important in the middle of the night, and can help avoid some confusion about "who is doing what."

In some ports, notably New York, a fairly lengthy dialogue could be carried out between vessels using whistle signals and there was an extended, if complicated, vocabulary in general use there and in some other areas. This form of communication proved practical and remains in use to a certain extent to this day. In general, however, communication today is by VHF radiotelephone and the handheld walkie-talkie.

This is just as well. You can imagine the difficulties a tug might have in understanding signals given on a mouth whistle from the wing of the bridge of a "stern winder" the length of two football fields away! Compound this with a few other complications, which seem humorous in retrospect but which are not so funny at the time. Whistle signals (both the ship's and the tug's) have a tendency to echo off of tall buildings located close to the waterfront. There are docks that are particularly difficult to work for just this reason. That is not the only problem. A police officer directing heavy rush hour traffic on a busy thoroughfare near a wharf can create a panic with his whistle, confusing the tug as well as the pilot or docking master. In any event, the VHF radiotelephone has resolved most of the problems of communication, provided that the shiphandler and tug can find a common channel free from the distraction of idle chatter. It is, however, still appropriate for the tug to acknowledge on its whistle, whenever this is more convenient, than answering on the radio.

Even if radiotelephone is the normal medium for communication between ship and tug, it is still a good idea to have some basic signals understood in case of a radio failure. Probably the simplest are the ones generally understood and found in use just about everywhere. They consist of the following signals:

One short blast means "come ahead on your engines" if stopped.
One short blast means "stop" if you are going *ahead* or *astern* on your engines.
Two short blasts means "back your engine."
Three *very* short blasts is a signal for "more speed."
One prolonged blast is a signal for "slow speed."
One long blast followed by two short blasts is a signal to "let go" or "shift" the tug.

Instructions to the tug on the VHF radiotelephone should be precise. The tug should be identified first at each command, and the orders given should be as brief and direct as possible. The tug acknowledges the pilot's orders using the whistle, or by responding on the radiotelephone.

The use of slang should be avoided. A command "Tug *Dorothy*, come full ahead," and "Tug *Mary W.*, back slow" are much preferred to "let'er rip, Louie," and "rear back on her, Sam." In addition to the obvious, the latter commands will sound rather silly at a hearing should an accident take place.

STUDY QUESTIONS

1. What methods of communication are used to pass orders to the tugs?
2. How does the tug acknowledge an order?
3. How can the pilot tell if the right tug has received his order?
4. What danger is associated with using whistle signals?
5. What does one short blast mean?
6. What do two short blasts mean?
7. What do three short blasts mean?
8. What does one long blast mean?
9. What do one long and two short blasts mean?

CHAPTER EIGHT

HANDLING THE "LIGHT" TUG

My purpose in this chapter is to provide some instruction in the fundamentals of handling various types of tugs. While this material is directed to beginners, seasoned operators may find it useful for reference when they are required to handle equipment that they are not familiar with. In order for the novice to understand the characteristics of various types of tugs, a still air, no-current situation is assumed, and certain typical situations are outlined below.

SINGLE-SCREW, RIGHT-HAND PROPELLER

The tug is dead in the water. When the engine is engaged ahead with the rudder amidships, it will move ahead and start turning slowly to port as a result of the propeller torque—unless the rudder is fitted with a compensating wedge on its after edge. In the same situation, if the engine is engaged astern, the tug will move astern and will back to port because of the propeller's torque.

To stop or reverse the direction of movement the engines are simply engaged in the opposite direction until the desired effect is achieved. If the tug's rudder is turned right or left with the engine engaged ahead, the tug will immediately begin to turn in the same direction as that of the helm. The rate of turn will depend upon the amount of rudder angle used and the engine speed. The tug will usually turn in a smaller circle at slow speed, but this depends upon the tug (Fig. 8-1).

After they have sufficient sternway for the rudder to take effect, some tugs will steer when backing and moving astern. These tugs will usually continue to steer when moving astern with the engine stopped until steerageway is lost. Many tugs, however, do not respond well when backed. They can only be controlled by "kicking" the engine ahead from time to time, with the rudder turned in the proper direction. In this

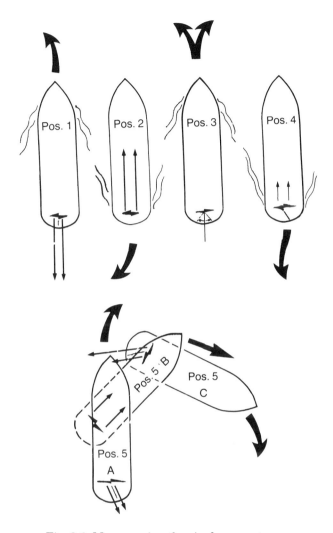

Fig. 8-1. Maneuvering the single-screw tug.
Position 1: tug moves ahead amidships with torque turning bow to port. Position 2: tug moves astern with rudder amidships, and stern kicks to port. Position 3: tug moving ahead turns right or left according to position of the rudder. Position 4: when tug astern, stern will first kick to port, but tug *may* steer astern after it has sternway. Position 5A: tug moves ahead with hard right rudder. Position 5B: tug backs engine which slows tug and kicks the stern to port. Position 5C: tug comes ahead again to complete the turn. In this figure, and similar, later figures, the thin arrows indicate the direction of engine thrust; that is, if an engine is moving ahead, the arrow points astern, and if the engine is going astern, the thin arrow points ahead.

instance the sternway is maintained, and the engine is only used ahead enough to assist the steering. When a single-screw tug is required to make a hard turn in a confined space, the helm is put over in the required direction, and the engine is engaged ahead. After the tug has started to swing "smartly," but before it gathers too much headway, the engine is backed just enough to kill the headway without reducing the swing. The helm is usually left untouched since its position is immaterial until the tug has sternway. This maneuver may have to be repeated several times until the tug has completed the turn. A tug with a right-hand propeller will turn much more readily to starboard since the torque of the propeller will assist by "kicking" the stern to port when the engine is backed.

Note: This does not apply to tugs with controllable-pitch propellers since the rotation is the same ahead or astern. It is also worth noting that some tugs with Kort nozzles may not react to the torque effect.

SINGLE SCREW WITH FLANKING RUDDERS

When a tug fitted with flanking rudders maneuvers ahead, it responds much like its conventional counterpart. However, it differs from a conventional tug in maneuverability when backing its engine. The flanking rudders are installed ahead of the propeller (there are usually two for each propeller) and are used to direct the propeller wash when the engines are operated astern. This permits the tug to be controlled when maneuvering astern, as well as when maneuvering ahead.

The flanking rudders are maintained in an amidships position when the tug is operating its engine ahead; otherwise the rudders might have a detrimental effect on the tug's handling qualities. If the tug is to be turned in a confined circle (by backing and filling), the flanking rudders are turned in the same direction as the regular rudder when the engine is backed (Fig. 8-2).

SINGLE SCREW WITH KORT RUDDER

A single-screw tug with a Kort rudder will have characteristics similar to those of a tug fitted with flanking rudders. It will respond to its helm when moving ahead, much as any single-screw tug. The exception is that it may not *dead stick* (i.e., steer with the engine stopped) as well as a conventional tug. It will also steer well when maneuvering astern. In practice, however, it is a little slower to handle than a tug with flanking rudders since the engine must be stopped when maneuvering from

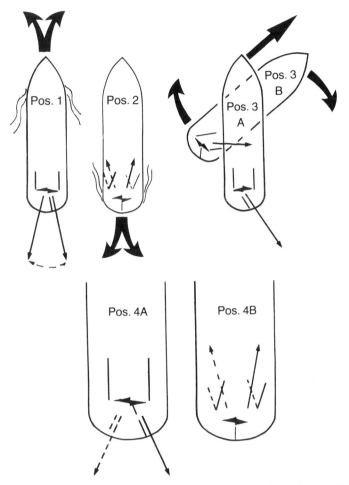

Fig. 8-2. Maneuvering the single-screw tug fitted with flanking rudders. Position 1: tug moves ahead and turns right or left according to rudder. Position 2: tug moving astern backs to right or left according to direction of flanking rudders. Position 3A: tug moves ahead with rudder hard right and flanking rudders amidships. Position 3B: tug moves astern with flanking rudders to the right to continue the turn. Position 4A: rudder directs propeller flow going ahead. Position 4B: flanking rudders control propeller flow moving astern, and are kept midships when the tug is moving ahead.

ahead to astern until the rudder angle is changed (to amidships or reversed). Otherwise, the tug will swing in the opposite direction to the one it was in if the engine takes effect before the helm is changed (Fig. 8-3).

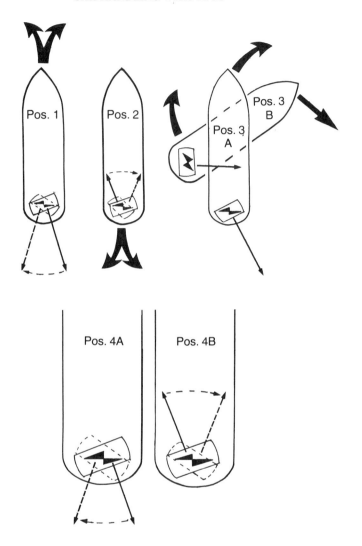

Fig. 8-3. Maneuvering the single-screw tug fitted with a Kort rudder.
Position 1: tug moves ahead and turns to the right or left according to the
direction of the Kort rudder. Position 2: tug moving astern backs to right or left
according to direction of Kort rudder (note with left rudder, tug will back to the
right, and with right rudder, tug will back to the left). Position 3A: tug moves
ahead with hard right rudder. Position 3B: tug *must* stop engine and change
direction of rudder to the left *before* going astern in order to maintain the swing.
   Position 4A and 4B: show details of steering effects of Kort rudder.

TWIN SCREW

If the tug is dead in the water and both engines are engaged ahead, the tug will move forward. If the engines are engaged astern, the tug will back. In both instances, if the speeds of the engines are equal, the tug will move in a straight line (Fig. 8-4).

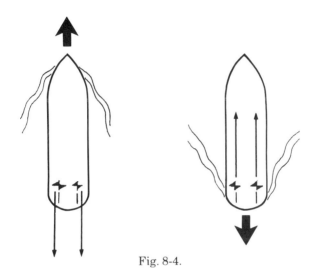

Fig. 8-4.

To stop or reverse the direction of movement, the engines are simply engaged in the opposite direction until the desired effect is achieved. If the tug's rudder is turned left or right with the engines engaged ahead, the tug will immediately begin to turn in the same direction. The rate of turn will be determined by the amount of rudder angle used (degrees) and the engine speed. If the engines are engaged astern, the tug's stern will begin to turn in the direction of the rudders after the tug has sufficient sternway (Fig. 8-5).

STEERING WITH ENGINES ONLY

If the tug is dead in the water and one engine is engaged ahead or astern, with the rudder amidships, the tug will respond by moving ahead or astern and turn toward the side of the stopped engine (Fig. 8-6). If the tug is moving ahead or astern with both the engines engaged (rudder amidships) and one engine is stopped, the tug will also turn toward the stopped engine. This is caused by the resistance of the stopped propeller and the off-center location of the thrust from the other propeller.

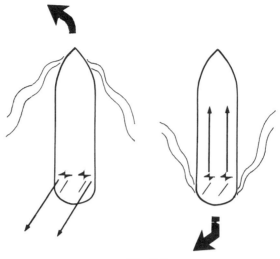

Fig. 8-5.

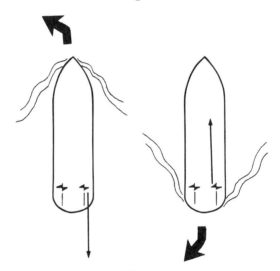

Fig. 8-6.

If the tug is being operated on one engine alone, it can be steered straight ahead or turned either right or left. Compensating rudder angle must be carried to correct the effect of the offset propeller. If the engine is backed, the stern will respond to the effect of the propeller rather than to that of the rudder. Some tugs *may* respond to the rudder when enough sternway is gained (Fig. 8-7).

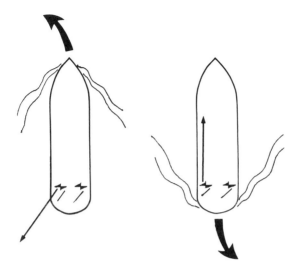

Fig. 8-7.

TWIN-SCREW EFFECT

None of the situations outlined above take advantage of a twin-screw tug's exceptional maneuverability. In order to do this, the operator must be proficient in using the engines in opposition to each other.

If the tug is going ahead on both engines with rudder amidships and one engine is backed, the tug will both turn toward the backing engine and lose speed. If the tug is going astern on two engines, rudder amidships, and one engine is engaged ahead, the stern of the tug will be cast toward the side of the propeller turning ahead (Fig. 8-8). As an operator you have the option of applying as much rudder angle or engine power as you choose. The tug can be made to turn quickly or slowly, and can turn while moving ahead or astern. It can even be turned end for end while remaining virtually stationary. The variations are endless, but the dynamics are obvious (Fig. 8-9).

Flanking is a term used to describe moving a tug sideways. This is a variation of using both engines in opposition (one ahead, one astern) to turn a tug, but in this case the controls are reversed. For example, if the operator wishes to move the tug laterally to starboard, the port engine is engaged ahead, the starboard engine astern, and the rudder is turned to the left. In flanking, you turn the rudder in the opposite direction from

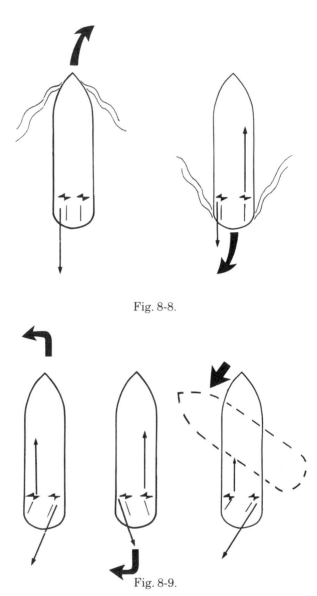

Fig. 8-8.

Fig. 8-9.

which you want to go. The effect of the port engine ahead with the left
rudder would normally turn the boat to port, but backing the starboard
engine cancels the turning effect and the movement of the tug ahead.
The paddle wheel effect of both propellers turning in the same direction
while the boat is dead in the water assists in this maneuver (Fig. 8-10).

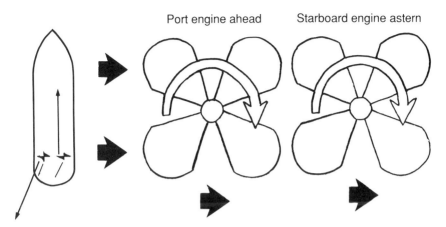

Fig. 8-10. Flanking and paddle wheel effect; inboard turning propellers.

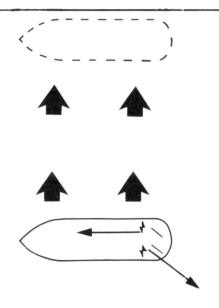

Fig. 8-11. Flanking.

The amount of rudder angle and engine power required to accomplish this will depend on the trim of the tug and the wind and current (Fig. 8-11).

TWIN SCREW WITH FLANKING RUDDERS

The characteristics are essentially the same as those noted above, except that the tug *will* steer astern on one engine, and the tug can be flanked in several different ways.

PROPELLER-STEERED TUGS

Their characteristics differ markedly from conventional tugs, and they are much more maneuverable. Propeller-steered pusher tugs most resemble conventional tugs in their handling qualities since the stern is steered *away* from the direction of the turn when moving ahead. When backing, of course, the stern is steered in the *same* direction as the turn. They can turn in one spot and steer astern. If they are of twin-screw configuration, they can be flanked (Figs. 8-12, 8-13, and 8-14).

The propeller-steered tractor tugs have their propellers located forward and steer the bow of the vessel *toward* the direction of the turn. Conversely, when they back, the bow is steered away from the desired direction. They are highly maneuverable, and the twin-screw tractor tugs can be flanked (Fig. 8-13).

HANDLING THE LIGHT TUG

The tug's stock-in-trade is its maneuverability and power. The effectiveness with which these are employed depends upon the ability of the tug's captain. Learning to handle them is a hands-on process, either by actually handling a tug or practicing on a simulator. This is a hands-on process because there is no convenient rule of thumb for estimating a tug's turning rate or stopping distance. Even sister ships may differ. These factors depend upon the tug's rudder power and engine power, both ahead and astern. The stopping distance, for example, can be affected by the time that is required for the engine controls (or engineer in the case of direct-reversing engines) to respond. Seasoned handlers know this, and they can feel out an unfamiliar tug very quickly. However, most of them will try a few maneuvers with a strange tug before working in close quarters. As a newcomer to tug handling, you would do well to follow this example, and should practice handling the tug in an unrestricted area until you develop a *feel* for it, along with a judgment of distance and the stopping and turning characteristics of the tug. Sometimes it helps to work close to a reference point (a buoy or the corner of a dock) to sharpen your perceptions. Touch and go landings are also helpful in developing this proficiency.

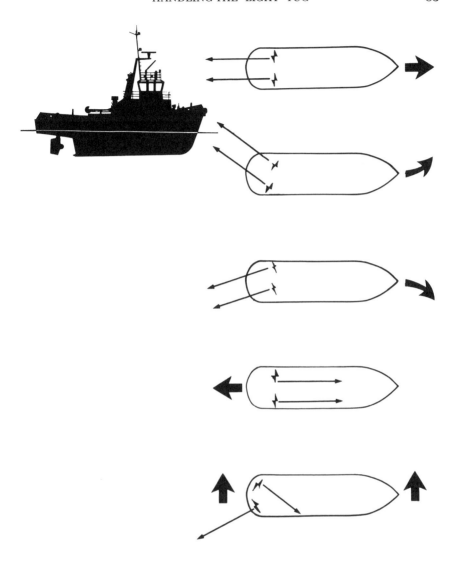

Fig. 8-12. Steering maneuvers with twin SRP stern installation. Courtesy: Schottel of America.

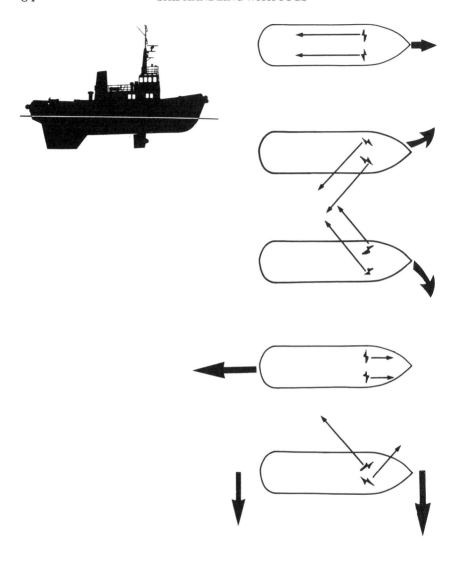

Fig. 8-13. Steering maneuvers with twin SRP bow installation. Courtesy: Schottel of America.

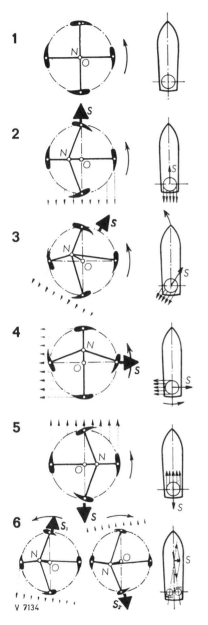

Operation of the VSP

The pivoted propeller blades project from a circular rotor casing which is flush with the ship's bottom and which rotates at constant rpm about an axis which is generally vertical. Links which lead to the steering centre N are fitted on the blade shafts inside the rotor casing. When this steering centre is moved from the centre O of the circle, the blades perform an oscillating movement about their axes and a propeller jet is produced with a thrust acting in the opposite direction (see sketches).

Assume that the propeller rotates in the direction of the arrow. In sketch **1**, the steering centre N is located in the centre O of the circle. While rotating, the blades remain tangential and no thrust is developed (**'idling' of the propeller**).

In sketch **2**, the steering centre N is shifted to port, and the blades are so controlled that the verticals to the chords of the blade profile intersect in the steering centre N. Each blade then performs an oscillating movement about its axis. The leading edge of the blade is directed outwards in the forward half circle and inwards in the rear half circle. Thus, in the forward half, water is thrown into the blade orbit, and, in the rear half, away from the orbit, though in the same direction. In this way, a water jet astern is produced and, as reaction, thrust S, which provides forward propulsion: **the ship moves forward.**

The thrust is at right angles to the line O-N, and its magnitude is proportional to the distance O-N. Because of the rotational symmetry about the axis of the propeller, similar considerations apply to any other location of the steering centre N.

In sketch **3**, the steering centre is shifted to port and simultaneously forward. Propeller jet and thrust S are again at right angles to the line O-N; in addition to a longitudinal component, the thrust includes an athwartship component, or in other words, the propeller provides a steering force: **the ship turns to port.**

When the steering centre, as shown in sketch **4**, is shifted forward, a pure thrust athwartships to starboard is produced: **the ship turns on the spot.**

If the steering centre N is shifted to the right, as shown in sketch **5**, the resulting conditions are opposed to those shown in sketch 2; the thrust is directed astern: **the ship moves astern.**

If, in a ship equipped with 2 Voith-Schneider Propellers, one propeller is given a forward oblique thrust and the other an astern oblique thrust with both thrusts directed to the same side (sketch 6), then the resultant of the thrusts S1 and S2 is a transverse thrust S which acts about midships. **The ship moves transversely.**

For clearness' sake, the schematic links inside the Voith-Schneider Propeller are simplified in the sketches. Actually, the movement of the blades is controlled by linkage systems (kinematics) of which one is shown on page 4.

Fig. 8-14. Operation of the Voith-Schneider propeller. Courtesy: Voith-Schneider.

TRIM WIND AND CURRENT

There are several other factors that can have a fairly pronounced effect on the handling qualities of a tug. When a tug's fuel and water tanks are full, it will be slower to respond to its engine and helm than when it is less heavily laden with stores. It will also be less affected by wind, but vulnerable to the effects of current. Conversely, a tug light on stores will be more affected by wind, less so by current.

Fore and aft trim can be important also. If the tug is light aft, the propeller may cavitate, reducing its efficiency, especially when backing. Steering may be erratic if trimmed by the head. When trimmed too much by the stern, the bow will have a tendency to blow off in fresh winds, and the tug will have to use more engine power to compensate for this factor.

DOCKING AND UNDOCKING

After you, as a beginner, are proficient at operating the tug in open waters, and have had a chance to develop your judgment of distance and a feeling for the tug's responses (i.e., turning rate and stopping distance at various speeds) you are ready to undertake the next step—this involves docking and undocking the tug. Tugs are responsive and usually "forgiving," but it is best to practice these maneuvers at slow speeds and in slack tide situations at first.

Of the two maneuvers, undocking is normally easier. The tug will usually (but not always) undock in the opposite fashion from that in which it docked. This means that it will most likely back clear of its berth. A single-screw tug will usually cast off all of its lines, except its bow springline. It will then come ahead easily into the springline with its helm turned toward the dock. When the stern has opened up enough, the tug will cast off the springline and back clear of the dock (Fig. 8-15). A twin-screw tug may undock the same way, but it may also cast off all lines, come ahead on its outboard engine, and back the inboard engine, with the helm turned toward the dock until the stern is open enough to back clear. It can also "flank" off the dock by backing the outboard engine while coming ahead on the inboard engine with the helm turned toward the dock. Unconventional tugs like those fitted with flanking rudders and Kort rudders, or propeller-steered tugs of the pusher type can easily steer out, moving astern. Tractor tugs will probably maneuver out, bow first.

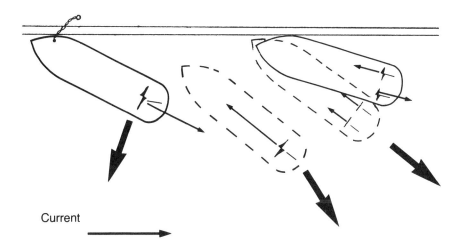

Current

Fig. 8-15. Undocking.

Docking is easiest in still water or in a moderate head current. A single-screw tug will normally approach the dock slowly at a 15° to 20° angle, stop its engines when it is close to the dock, and then "bear off." It can back its engines when it is close alongside, put out a forward springline, and then work easily ahead on the springline until it is in position alongside. If the tug makes a fast approach to the dock and then backs hard to check its way, there is one side effect (other than torque) that must be expected if it is a solid dock. The propeller wash will drive down between the hull of the tug and the dock and push it away from the face of the dock. This same type of thing occurs with ships too (Fig. 8-16).

A twin-screw tug can make the same kind of approach, but can also lie parallel to the dock and then flank alongside.

In a fair current the tug should not approach the dock too steeply as this will make it difficult for the tug to spring alongside. If the tug must dock with a strong fair current, it is best to bring the tug in flat to the dock, back smartly, and then put out a stern line from the after quarter bitts (Fig. 8-17).

The new generation of harbor tugs that steer astern will have no problem in a fair current situation. They will simply back into the current as if they were docking bow first. The line-handling procedures will also be different since these tugs will most likely put out a short stern line or back spring.

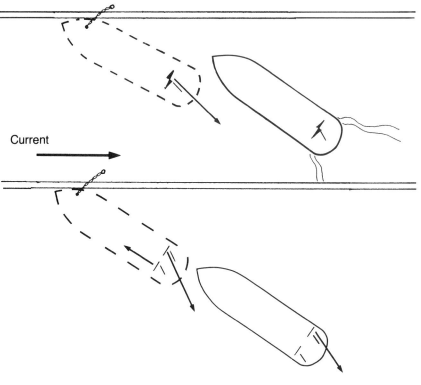

Current →

Fig. 8-16. Docking the single- and twin-screw tug.

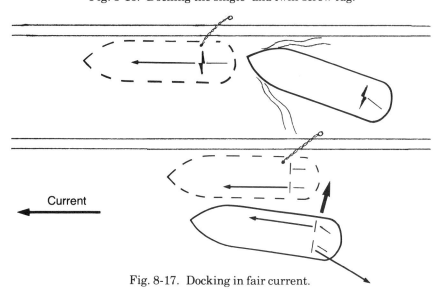

← Current

Fig. 8-17. Docking in fair current.

STUDY QUESTIONS

1. Describe the handling characteristics of conventional single-screw tugs.
2. How is a single-screw tug maneuvered when it is necessary to back for some distance?
3. How is a single-screw tug turned in a short distance?
4. Will a single-screw tug turn more readily in one direction than the other?
5. What is the principal advantage of flanking rudders or a Kort rudder on a single-screw tug?
6. Are Kort rudders as effective as flanking rudders?
7. Will a twin-screw tug steer ahead on one engine?
8. Will a twin-screw tug steer astern when backing on one engine?
9. What is meant by the term "twin screwing"?
10. What is meant by the term "flanking," and how is it done?
11. Can a twin-screw tug with flanking rudders steer astern on one engine?
12. Can twin-screw PS tugs be flanked?
13. How do the dynamics of the steering system on PS tractor tugs differ from conventional and PS pusher type tugs?
14. How do conventional tugs usually undock?
15. How does a conventional tug normally dock in still water or in a head-current situation?
16. Can a twin-screw tug be flanked alongside?
17. How should a conventional tug dock with a fair current?
18. What is the best way to get the "feel" for handling a tug?

CHAPTER NINE

BASIC TUG HANDLING
FOR SHIPWORK

Although I write this chapter primarily for the benefit of the tug handler who is a newcomer to the field of shipwork, I am sure it will also be of interest to the pilot or shiphandler who has not had experience operating tugs. There are several reasons for this. First of all, it will give the pilot or shiphandler an insight into the actual *mechanics* of a tug's operation, and a better understanding of what the tug's captain *must* know in order to assist the ship to best advantage. This kind of knowledge can be especially helpful in situations where the tug's handler is a little inexperienced at shipwork.

THE FUNDAMENTALS OF SHIPWORK

Shipwork, like barge work, is the final test of the tug handler's ability. It is more challenging than most other handling activities since often both vessels (ship and tug) are underway. When this is the case, it is an exercise in relative motion (for the tug, of course). But that is not all. The tug's captain must also continue to control the tug in spite of the effect of the other vessel's wake and propeller wash.

Coming Alongside. If you are just breaking in as a mate on a harbor tug, you will probably discover that the most difficult part of shipwork is putting the tug alongside an inbound ship moving at a good rate of speed. If you are careless or try to accelerate the maneuver, the tug might land alongside the ship hard enough to do some damage. This is especially likely to occur if you fail to anticipate the hydraulic forces that will have an increasing effect on the tug the closer it gets to the vessel.

When a tug approaches a moving ship to *make up,* it should shape a course parallel to the vessel for a bit and adjust its speed to that of the vessel. The tug should then ease gently in and compensate as necessary for the effect of the vessel's wash (Fig. 9-1). If the tug is going to go alongside the quarter of a ship, the suction caused by the vessel's passage will have a tendency to pull the tug into the vessel. Usually pacing the vessel with the tug's helm turned slightly away from it will utilize this suction to pull the tug alongside the ship easily. As soon as the tug comes against the ship the helm should be put over towards the vessel with the engines kept running ahead until the lines are fast.

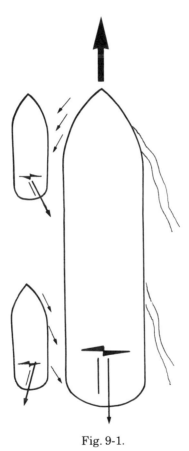

Fig. 9-1.

Ideally, the tug should land alongside the ship about its own midships or a bit aft of that. The bow is then gently swung in toward the vessel as the helm is put over. Sometimes the suction near the stern of the ship is very strong, and will pull the tug in quickly. If this is the case, the tug's captain can land the tug farther forward where there will be less suction, and can then let the tug slide back into position. Many ship captains will grumble about this "messing up the paint job," but it is preferable to a dent.

It is generally less hazardous to come alongside a ship forward, but it still requires care. The tug is most often pushed away from the ship by the bow wave, especially if the vessel's entrance is hollow. The problem here usually stems from overcontrolling when coming alongside. Pacing the ship for a bit will, in most cases, give an indication of what to expect, and will probably solve this problem.

When a tug is approaching a ship to go alongside, and its speed is too fast, it can stop its engine in order to slow down if necessary. It should *not back down,* however, as it can easily lose steerage and might take a dive toward the ship. If the tug crosses a ship's wake while overtaking the vessel, its propeller might cavitate, especially if it is backing its engine. A failure to anticipate this could lead to an accident.

Towline Work. Working on a towline is probably the most dangerous employment that the tug will engage in. This is particularly the case if the master or pilot is excitable and relies too heavily on the use of the ship's engine. In this instance it can easily overpower the tug, causing it to *girt* or to *trip.* Either circumstance can lead to a capsize (Fig. 9-2).

The most hazardous part of towline work occurs when a tug is required to take a towline from the bow of a vessel that is underway. The tug must pass close aboard the bow so that the vessel's head line can be lowered to the tug's deck. If the tug's quarter lands against the ship's side, the tug may not be able to steer away from the ship, and the tug might get caught crossways ahead of the vessel and capsize. This type of accident is called *stemming* (Fig. 9-3). In this situation, about the only thing the tug can do is come full astern with the helm midship and try to back out of danger. Tractor tugs (which are designed for towline work) have an advantage over conventional tugs in this respect since their steering will remain unaffected (Fig. 9-3).

When a tug is performing a towline job (except when working ahead of the ship), the tug's captain will normally be at the after control station where he can keep an eye on the tug's deck force, the lead of the towline, and the ship's wheel wash. The ship's wheel wash will often give a clue as to the amount of power the ship's engine is using, and the tug can be

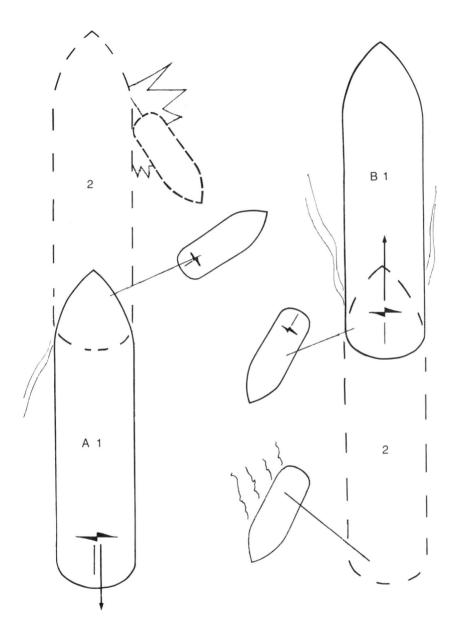

Fig. 9-2. Tug in Position A is being tripped. Tug in Position B is girt and may be capsized. The action is called girting.

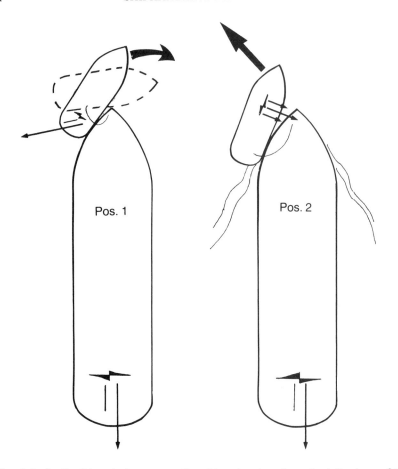

Fig. 9-3. In Position 1 the conventional tug is pinned against the bow of the inbound vessel. Tug *cannot* steer away from the ship since its stern is against the vessel. It must "power" out of danger by coming full astern with rudder midships or risk capsize. Position 2 tractor tug *can* steer away from ship.

maneuvered to compensate for this. The tug's towline should be leading toward the direction of the vessel's anticipated direction of movement.

If it seems that the ship is going to move rapidly ahead or astern, the tug should attempt to get parallel to the ship and run with it in order to avoid a capsizing situation. If this is not possible, the tug should stop engines and put the helm midship. The tug will then most likely be towed stern first by the ship and might land heavily alongside, doing some damage. However this is preferable to being rolled over (Fig. 9-4).

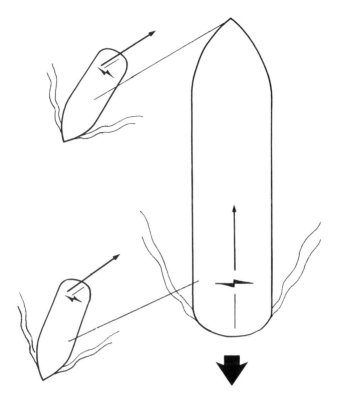

Fig. 9-4.

Should the ship be either dead in the water or moving slowly there will be no problem, and the tug can be used to best effect. Towline length is normally 100 to 150 feet. A short towline restricts a tug's maneuverability. A longer towline is sometimes inconvenient, but will permit the tug more freedom of movement.

SOME *DO'S* AND *DON'TS* OF SHIPWORK

There are a number of do's and don'ts that should be brought to your attention as a beginning handler so that you can avoid some bruises and bumps, especially to your self-esteem. While this kind of advice is helpful, it must be qualified by experience.

1. Do not back full ahead on a slack head line, or come ahead hard on a slack towline. The combined force of the tug's momentum and the power of its engine can easily part any line. The tug should

maneuver easily (ahead or astern) until the line comes tight, at which point power should be gradually increased. Most synthetic lines indicate when they are approaching a breaking strain by "twitching" or vibrating. Their diameter will also be much reduced. Nevertheless, with short leads they can part very quickly.

2. When backing full astern on a head line and you receive an order to stop the engine, drop the tug to slow speed astern first and then stop the engine. The tug handler must still be ready to check the tug's headway should the elasticity of the working line propel the tug toward the ship too rapidly.

3. When approaching the dock, never let the tug get caught between it and the ship. This makes long, skinny tugboats! Stay in position as long as it is safely possible, then notify the pilot of the situation and remove the tug.

4. When a tug is coming alongside a ship that is underway, you, as the tug captain, should not allow yourself to be distracted. The situation can change so quickly that even a moment's inattention can cause an accident.

5. Whenever your tug is going to work near the bow of a ship without putting up a line (especially at night), it is a good idea to give a "toot" on the whistle to let the mates on the bow know the tug is there, so they don't unexpectedly drop the anchor.

6. Remember also that when a tug crosses a ship's wake, the propeller has a tendency to cavitate. A little care when overtaking a ship in this circumstance is appropriate to avoid an accident.

7. When the after controls are to be used, you, the tug's captain, should ascertain beforehand that the covers are off the controls and that they are in *neutral* position. The reasons are obvious. You should not have to fumble with the control cover in the middle of the night. The controls should definitely be in neutral position before shifting over from the wheelhouse as some types of controls will engage (if they are in the ahead or astern position) as soon as the switching lever in the wheelhouse is changed. This has led to some serious accidents.

8. Nylon lines should *never* be used for shipwork. They are much too elastic and can be murderous if they part.

9. When a tug is working alongside a ship with a head line up, the line should be long enough so that the tug can lie flat alongside the vessel. If the head line is too short, the bow of the tug will be

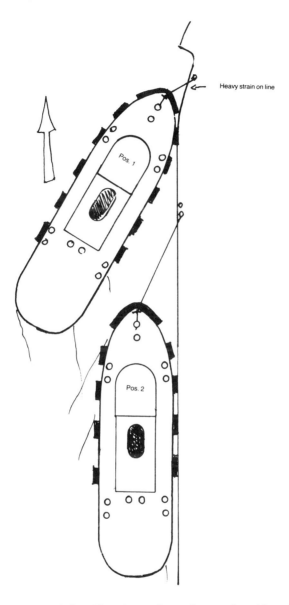

Fig. 9-5. Position 1: this tug's head line is much too short and could part easily under the strain of the ship's forward motion or from the tug's engine being backed. The tug is also susceptible to capsizing if the ship is moving rapidly. Position 2: this tug's head line is the proper length and is not likely to part during normal maneuvers on the part of the ship or tug. The tug is also less likely to capsize if the ship is moving rapidly.

snubbed in toward the vessel, and the resultant strain could part the line if the ship is moving too fast or if the tug backs. The tug would also run the same risk if the vessel is moving rapidly (see Fig. 9-5).

SOME COMMON HAZARDS OF SHIPWORK

Most marine casualties can be attributed to one or more of the following causes: weather, mechanical failures, and human error (negligence). In shipwork (as far as the tugs are concerned) the percentage of casualties caused by weather is negligible, so the rest must be chalked up to the last two factors.

Mechanical Failures. Most mechanical failures can be attributed to a breakdown of the steering gear or the propulsion system. If the engine fails to back, or the steering gear does not respond, then the ship or the tug is likely to be damaged. Occasionally a line parts or a fender on the tug is carried away, resulting in injury or damage. These failures may be *unexpected* but they are rarely "acts of God," and some attention beforehand might have avoided the accident. Regardless of this, the percentage of accidents attributable to breakdown is insignificant when compared to that charged against *negligence.*

Negligence or Human Error. Negligence is the single major contributing factor in accidents occurring in shipwork. Its principal constituents are:

1. Excess speed.
2. Poor handling (either ship or tug).
3. Careless line handling (ship or tug).
4. Careless handling of equipment.
5. Faulty communication.

When excess speed is the cause of an accident, the tug is often the victim. It is usually no match for the ship in size or power. As mentioned before, tugs on towlines are easily overpowered, and can be dragged alongside the ship and damaged or capsized. Tugs using quarter lines are also threatened with a capsize if the ship moves too fast. Most dangerous of all is the risk of stemming to a tug picking up a head line from a fast moving ship. This is illustrated in Fig. 9-3. But even tugs working alongside a ship secured only by a head line have been rolled over when the ship was operated or maneuvered at excessive speed.

Ships are victims also. A tug coming alongside too fast may get caught in the vessel's wash (forward or aft) and take a dive toward the ship. A tug overtaking a ship may try to back down in the fast water of its wake, and the propeller cavitates with the same result.

A ship making a bend may not be responding well to its helm, so the shiphandler decides that more power is the answer and rings for more speed. This renders the tug completely ineffective. The ship may go aground, hit a dock, or worse yet, strike another vessel.

In the case of faulty ship and tug handling the ship is often the injured party. A tug hits an inbound ship while coming alongside. *Haste* is as much to blame as speed, because the tug's skipper failed to feel the vessel out.

Backing full on a slack head line or coming ahead hard on a towline can part it. This, too, has been mentioned before. This kind of occurrence is more likely to injure personnel than damage the ship, which is even greater cause for concern.

Ships are not blameless either. Should a vessel come ahead unexpectedly while a tug is working the stem with a line up, the tug could be easily caught under the flare of the ship's bow and damaged. Similarly, if a tug is made up dead astern, it can be caught under the aft overhang if the ship backs hard enough to pick up sternway. In these instances the only thing that the tug can do is cast off or cut its line.

Quite a few accidents occur as a result of negligence with respect to the *careless* handling of lines, both the tug's and the ship's. When a tug is let go, the lines should be slacked back to the tug instead of let go on the run. This avoids having a line strike the deckhand, fall in the water, or perhaps foul one of the vessel's propellers. Tug crews should also tend their lines carefully, especially the quarter lines and towlines which can easily get caught in the wheel, and in particular controllable-pitch propellers which are always turning.

Ships should stop their engines when casting off a tug's towline aft since it is easy for the propeller to pick up such a line. This is especially true if the vessel has sternway.

In the careless-handling-of-equipment category, dropping a ship's anchor unexpectedly has led to some serious accidents. Shifting the controls from the wheelhouse of a tug to the after control station, or vice versa, on some tugs can be dangerous. Some types of controls will engage (ahead or astern) if they are not in neutral when the transfer lever is moved, and the engines may take off before the tug's captain can get to the controls.

Faulty communication can stem from poorly understood orders, radio failures, or radiotelephone transmissions garbled by overriding traffic. Whistle signals can be misinterpreted; and echoes off of high buildings can be misleading. Signals from nearby ships can misdirect or confuse the tug's handler.

There are no ready remedies in this situation. It is *not* recommended, but seasoned tug captains will sometimes rely on their own instincts when everything else fails. They should, however, *know* what is required since their actions (no matter how well intended) expose the tug to legal liabilities if damages occur.

Shipwork can be a tricky business, and the safety of all concerned is dependent upon the awareness and vigilance of those who direct and handle the ships and tugs involved. The hazards discussed in this chapter are mentioned elsewhere in the text, but in this case the repetition can be justified if it alerts the newcomer to the dangers associated with shipwork. (See Appendices 1 and 3.)

STUDY QUESTIONS

1. What is likely to be the most difficult part of shipwork for a newcomer to tug handling and why?
2. How does the hydraulic effect caused by the ship's passage through the water affect the tug?
3. How should the tug handler compensate for these effects?
4. What problems can occur during this maneuver, and what are the best ways to avoid them?
5. Should a tug ever back its engine when coming alongside a ship?
6. How should a tug be handled as it comes alongside a vessel?
7. Why should a tug back easily on a slack head line?
8. Why is towline work dangerous?
9. How can the tug handler best avoid this type of situation?

10. What other danger is associated with towline work, and how does it occur?
11. What may happen when a tug crosses a vessel's wake?
12. How can this endanger a tug crossing a ship's wake?
13. What is the principal cause of accidents involving tugs doing shipwork?
14. Of the causes cited which is the most common, and why?

CHAPTER TEN

THE *HOWS* AND *WHYS*
OF SHIPWORK

In order to understand the hows and whys of shipwork, you must examine the dynamics of the relationship between the ship and the tug. As previously noted, a tug can only push, pull, or apply resistance passively. But it is also an *external* force. It can apply these forces (subject to limitations) to the ship independently, in conjunction with, or against the other forces affecting a vessel. These include wind, current, the ship's own momentum, and propelling and steering forces. If these forces are applied intelligently, the tug can turn the vessel, assist it to steer, move it laterally, or check its way. Shiphandlers know that if a ship is dead in the water (no current, no wind assumed), two small tugs can do anything they want with it (Fig. 10-1).

The ship in this instance is like a lever, and its pivot point will correspond to its CLR (center of lateral resistance). This is simply the geometric center of the area presented by the center of the submerged portion of the ship's side (Fig. 10-2).

If a tug is used to turn the vessel, the farther it is forward or aft of the pivot point, the more effective it will be. Conversely, if the tug is to move the vessel laterally, the closer it is to the pivot point, the better it will carry out this task (Fig. 10-3).

Vessels are seldom "dead in the water" except when they are docking or undocking. They are usually moving ahead or astern, and the *pivot point* will shift *forward* or *aft* toward the direction of the vessel's movement. The exact location of the pivot point will depend upon the vessel's trim, but it will be toward the bow when the vessel is going ahead, and will move aft to a point near the stern when the vessel gathers sternway. This still applies even if the vessel is not making way over the bottom but is breasting the current. As before, the tug that is pushing or pulling

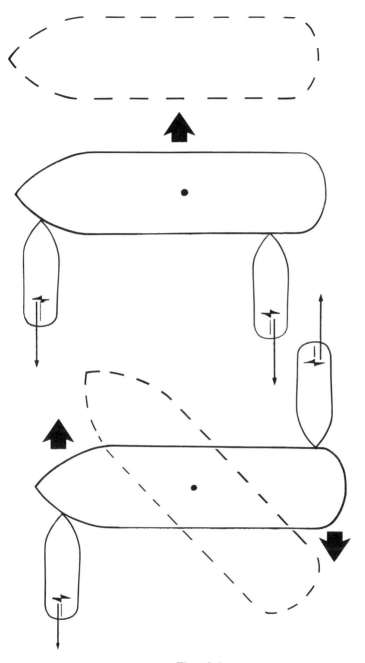

Fig. 10-1.

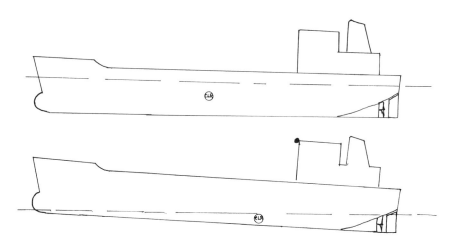

Fig. 10-2. Change in CLR (center of lateral resistance) due to trim of vessel.

farthest from the pivot point will have the most turning effect, and the one closest to the pivot point will tend to move the vessel sideways (Fig. 10-4).

However, the dynamics change when the ship is moving. Under this circumstance the tug *modifies* the ship's behavior, and the tug is frequently used in *conjunction* with or in *opposition* to the vessel's steering gear and engine instead of independently as it would be if the ship were stopped. When the vessel is moving, the function of the tug is to *assist* the ship to carry out the maneuver, rather than to handle the vessel as if it were a barge, and carry out the whole maneuver by itself.

STANDARD MANEUVERS

The tug's basic function is to provide assistance in the maneuvers listed below:

1. Propelling. (Refer to Chapter 15.)
2. Steering.
3. Turning.
4. Moving the vessel laterally.
5. Checking the vessel's way.

When the tug assists a vessel to steer, to check its way, or to propel it, it is presumed that the ship is moving. When the tug is used to turn the vessel or move it laterally, the vessel may be either moving or stopped.

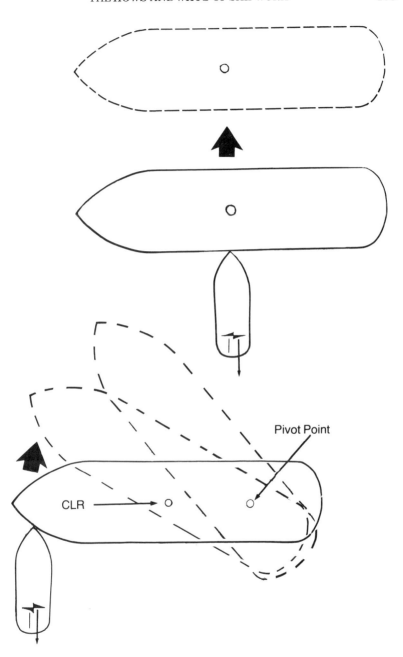

Fig. 10-3. Note that with a single tug pushing, the vessel will not pivot about its CLR but at a point at the opposite end of the ship from the tug.

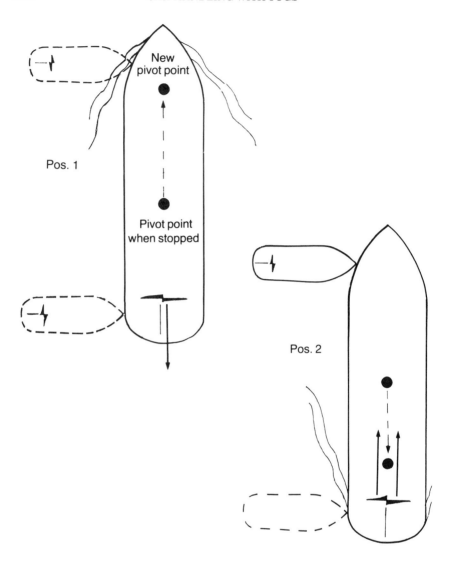

Fig. 10-4. Position 1 illustrates shift in pivot point when vessel moves ahead. Position 2 shows shift of pivot point aft as vessel moves astern. In both cases tugs farthest from the pivot point will have the greatest turning effect, and those closest to it will have less turning effect and some tendency to move the vessel to the side.

The average "docking job" is likely to involve any or all of these functions at various stages of this operation.

One tug forward, inboard side of the turn: tug *backs* which checks vessel's headway and cants bow toward the tug. This resistance acts like a springline and increases the effectiveness of the ship's rudder. (Note: the ship's rudder will move the stern *away* from the direction of the turn.) Tug's effectiveness: good.

One tug forward, outboard side of the turn: tug *pushes* which forces bow in direction of turn. Ship's rudder forces stern in *opposite* direction. If vessel's speed is too great, it reduces tug's effectiveness since tug will not be able to maintain a good angle (60° to 90°), and tug will have a tendency to push the vessel ahead as well. Tug's effectiveness: good to fair, depending upon vessel's speed.

Steering (Vessel Moving Ahead). One tug forward on towline: tug can steer the bow well, *but* the ship must not *overtake* the tug. Tug's effectiveness: good.

One tug after quarter, inboard side of turn: tug pushes, and compounds effect of ship's rudder in moving vessel's stern *away* from direction of turn. Tug can also be used *hipped up.* This is explained below. Tug's effectiveness: good, unless vessel is moving too fast.

One tug aft, outboard quarter: tug is ineffective unless "hipped up" (explained below). Tug's effectiveness: nil.

One tug dead astern: tug can push on either side of the stern. By pushing on inboard side of turn, this tug compounds the effect of the ship's rudder in pushing stern *away* from direction of turn. Tug's position is farthest from pivot point. Tug's effectiveness: excellent (Fig. 10-5).

Steering (Vessel Moving Astern). This situation is much the same as when the vessel is moving ahead, except the ship's rudder will not have much effect unless the vessel's engine is "kicked" ahead. The tug farthest from the pivot point (working against the stem) will have the best advantage (Fig. 10-6).

Checking a Vessel's Way (Ahead). Tugs placed forward will check a vessel's headway when backed. If only one tug is used, the bow will cant toward the tug. As a vessel slows, a tug may respond to the torque of its own propeller and swing out from the ship and have a turning effect.

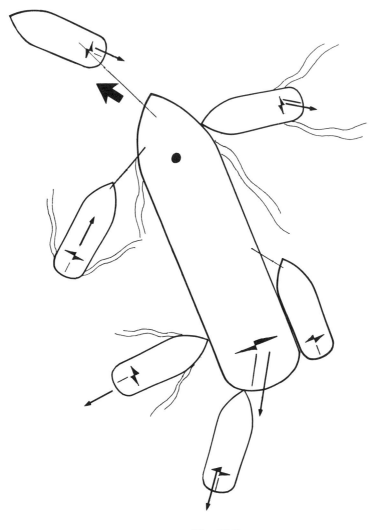

Fig. 10-5.

Tugs secured aft will react in the same manner *until* the ship backs. Then the propeller wash will tend to blow the tugs out to the side. Tugs dead astern on a head line can back or *cock* at an angle to work as a drogue (Fig. 10-7).

Turning a Vessel. The situation is very much like steering a vessel, except that the ship is moving very slowly or is stopped. Using tugs to

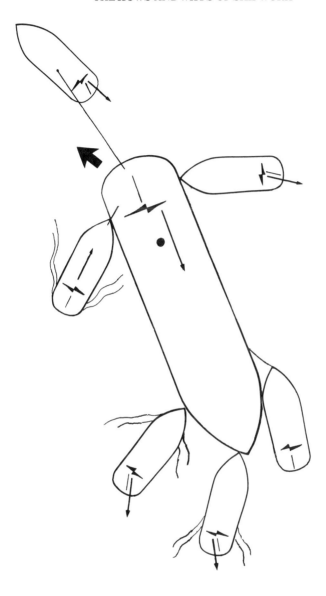

Fig. 10-6.

push at opposite ends of the vessel in opposite directions is the most effective way to accomplish this maneuver. The ship can be turned about in one ship length. When only one tug is used, the vessel will

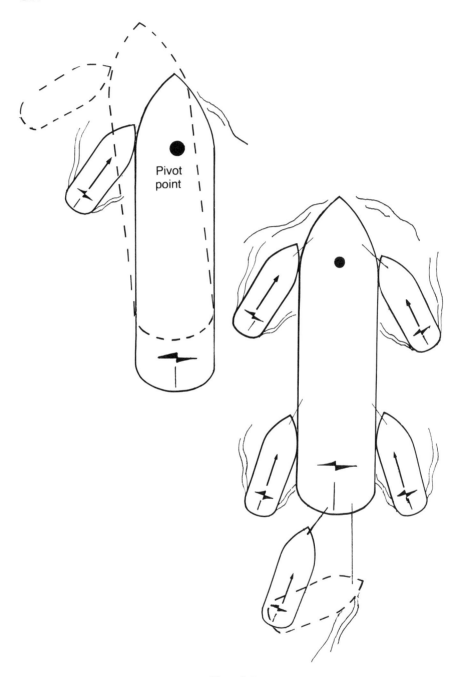

Fig. 10-7.

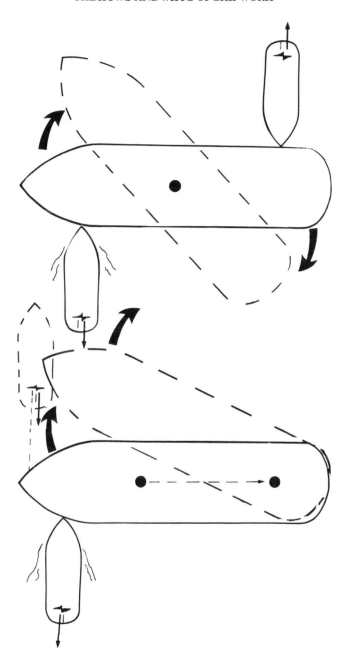

Fig. 10-8

actually pivot at a point near the other end of the vessel. This will require almost two ship lengths unless the vessel helps the tug by backing and filling. In this case, it is usually best to place the tug forward where it will be clear of the ship's wheel wash (Fig. 10-8). Tugs using towlines can also be used in this maneuver.

Moving a Vessel Laterally. One tug forward pushes against the bow. The ship comes ahead easily with helm turned toward tug to *lift* the stern. One tug pushing midships, or two tugs fore and aft can also move the ship sideways, as mentioned before. In addition, towlines can be used (Fig. 10-9).

Using Tugs on the Hip. On the hip or *hipped up* are terms used in the towing industry to indicate that the tug is solidly lashed to a vessel, often a barge. The correct terminology for this practice is *breasted* or *alongside* towing. The tug is securely lashed alongside the barge or ship, usually with a minimum of three lines: head line, springline, and stern line. Wire rope is sometimes used for this purpose.

When a tug is hipped up aft, the vessel is maneuvered as if it were a twin-screw ship. A tug on the inboard side of a turn will back its engine while the ship comes ahead with the helm turned toward the tug. A tug on the outboad side of the turn will come ahead with its helm toward the ship while the ship backs its engine (Fig. 10-10).

The tug should be secured *flat* (parallel) to the ship rather than *toed-in* (as it would be if it were handling a barge). In this way the tug will retain the steering advantage of its off-set position.

When a tug is hipped at the bow of a vessel (facing aft), it can assist the vessel to turn or steer as the vessel moves astern, or it can move the vessel laterally. Turning is accomplished by having both ship and tug maneuver ahead with their helms turned in the same direction (both either right or left). Moving the vessel laterally is accomplished by having both vessels maneuver ahead with their helms turned in opposite directions (right to left or left to right) (Fig. 10-11).

Using the Tug as a Passive Force. A tug as a passive force can be surprisingly effective. This is particularly evident when a tug is forward and fast alongside a ship in ballast and with very little forward draft. Although the tug's presence will act as a drogue and tend to cant the bow

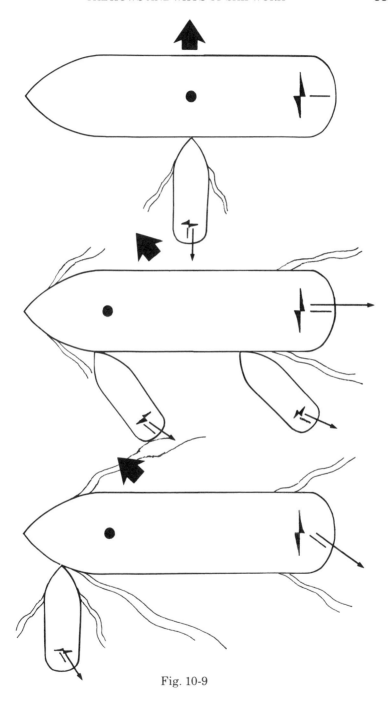

Fig. 10-9

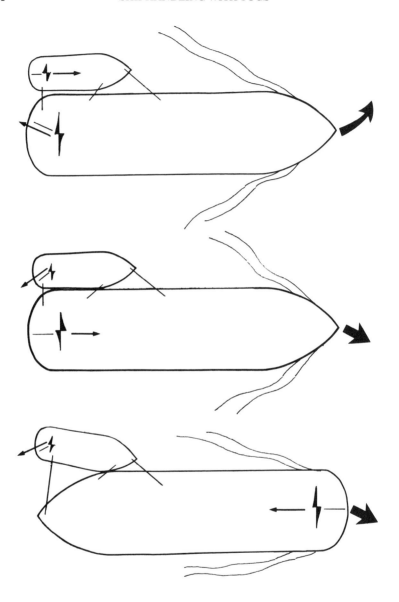

Fig. 10-10.

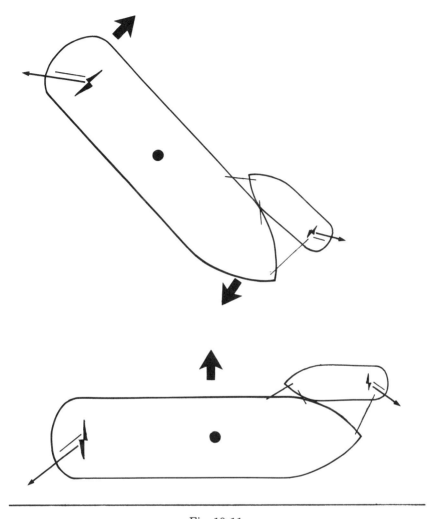

Fig. 10-11.

to the side the tug is secured to, the tug will still have a tendency to
stabilize the bow (directionally). This is especially apparent on windy
days and when the vessel is proceeding at slow speeds (Fig. 10-12).

A vessel under tow may often be assisted by a *tailboat* that is secured
to the stern by a head line rigged singly or led out like a bridle to chocks
on either quarter. The purpose of the tailboat is to assist the towing
vessel to steer by backing whenever the ship takes a sheer or is hard to
turn. Quite often, however, it is unnecessary for the tailboat to back as

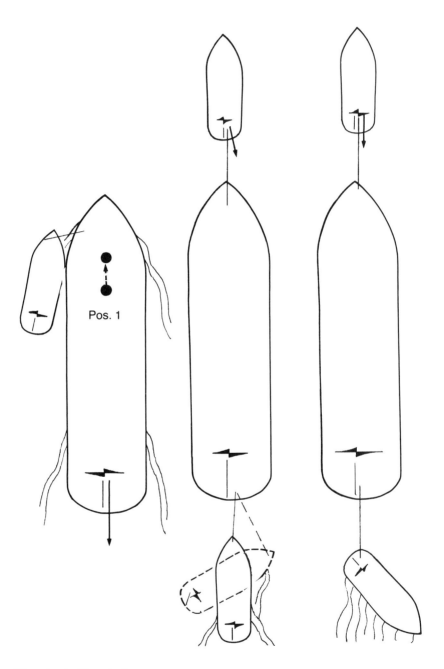

Fig. 10-12. Note in Position 1, the pivot point shifts forward and improves the
vessel's steering qualities.

the effect of its presence will provide enough drag to keep the ship under control of the lead tug. In addition to this, the tailboat can often steer the stern of the ship without using its engine simply by sheering the tug to one side or the other by putting its helm over. This type of operation is described more fully in Chapter 19.

Occasionally when ships are worked European fashion with tugs on towlines fore and aft, one of the tugs may be towed backwards for a bit. As often as not, its passive resistance may be all that is required to keep the tow in shape or reduce the vessel's momentum, aided only by an occasional touch ahead on the tug's engine. At times a tug will be towed along almost sideways for maximum braking effect. This must be done with great care to avoid capsizing the tug.

Tug Placement. The seasoned shiphandler is likely to have anticipated the sequence of events in using the tugs. As a result, certain priorities will dictate where the tugs are placed and how they will be used. For example, assistance steering the ship while approaching the dock may be wanted. A tug dead astern will do this nicely. Also, the tug can be used to move the ship laterally and in this case the tug should be placed where it can both assist with steering and with moving the vessel sideways. The placement of the tug will probably be forward (Fig. 10-13). By the same token, a tug on a towline can control the bow of the ship quite well, but if the tug is to breast the ship to the dock (unless it is a tractor tug) it will usually have to let go and shift positions.

Aside from the dynamics involved in placing the tug, other considerations come into play. With aircraft carriers the top hamper overhangs the shipside and affords few places where a tug can work safely alongside. Other vessels such as car carriers and container ships as well as ships of European design may have only a few chocks about the deck for making up the tug, and these may be badly placed. Passenger liners also may suffer from similar deficiencies. Many have their chocks and bitts located so far forward or aft that a tug must be extremely careful in order to avoid damage. If such a vessel is being handled and the shiphandler has any doubts about placing the tug, it may be wise to check with the tug captain for a safe place to spot the tug.

The shiphandler must keep other factors in mind as well. For example, if one of the tugs must shift, it is a good idea to put the most maneuverable tug in this position. The most powerful tug will usually be placed where it is needed. This is usually forward on a deep-loaded

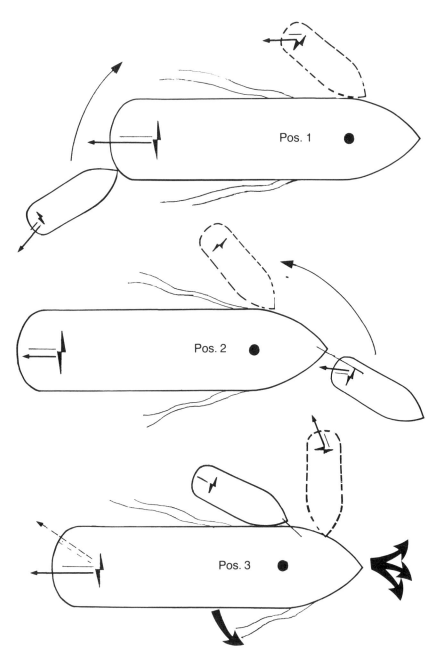

Fig. 10-13. Tugs in Positions 1 and 2 must shift to move vessel laterally. Tug in Position 3 can, without shifting positions, assist vessel to steer or move laterally.

ship, but it might be of more service aft on one that is in ballast. If tugs with flanking rudders, or with the Voith-Schneider or Schottel drive, are to be used, it would be best to place them in positions where the tug would have to back a lot. Handy tugs (those with a low profile) can be useful working near the ends of ships and under overhanging structures.

To the casual observer, the tug's position may seem inconsequential. However, those who are familiar with shipwork understand that securing the tug a few feet farther forward or aft, or at the angle at which a tug lies when it pushes or pulls, can have a remarkable effect on how the ship responds.

Shipwork with tugs is, as one docking master observed, "like judo. It's much more important where you grab 'em than how big they are." Ships come in all sorts of sizes and shapes, and unless they are sister ships, few will be alike. Nevertheless, there are a few general rules that apply. Subject to the structural limitations of the vessel and the location of the chocks and bitts, these rules are:

1. On large, deep-draft vessels, tugs are most effective working as far forward or aft as is safe or practicable.
2. On smaller vessels or those of light draft forward, the bow tug may function better if it is secured farther aft than would be proper for a larger or deeper vessel.
3. On large, deep-loaded ships the more powerful tug is usually placed forward. When the bow of a ship is light, it is probably better to place the stronger tug aft.
4. If one of the tugs is required to shift positions, it is best to use the more maneuverable one for this purpose.
5. Tugs that can steer astern (Kort rudders, flanking rudders, etc.) should be used in positions where backing is required.

STUDY QUESTIONS

1. What forces can a tug bring to bear on a vessel?
2. How are these forces applied?
3. What are the tug's forces used for?

4. When a ship is dead in the water, where is the pivot point located?

5. Where is the pivot point when the vessel is moving?

6. Where will the tug be most effective in turning a vessel?

7. Where will the tug be most effective in moving the vessel laterally?

8. If one tug pushes (or pulls) at 90° one end of a dead ship, will the vessel pivot about its center of lateral resistance (CLR)?

9. How much space will it require to turn a ship about with one tug?

10. How are tugs used to move a vessel laterally that is dead in the water?

11. How can one tug move a vessel laterally when the vessel is moving?

12. How can a tug made fast forward assist a ship making a bend?

13. Can a tug on a towline assist a ship making a bend?

14. How can two tugs fast aft assist a vessel making a bend?

15. Can a tug made up astern of the ship assist a vessel making a bend?

16. How can two tugs fast forward check a vessel's way?

17. Can a tug dead astern help check a vessel's way?

18. Is the placement of a tug important?

CHAPTER ELEVEN

WORKING TUGS ALONGSIDE

Until fairly recently, the employment of tugs alongside was almost exclusively an American practice. Tugs in other ports throughout the world followed the European custom of working on a towline. This latter method is convenient for assisting ships through narrow waterways, and it can be employed in most circumstances. But there is a hazard associated with towline work that does not normally apply with tugs made fast alongside properly. However, discounting the element of risk involved in towline work, there are certain other advantages in using the tug alongside. These are the convenience of making fast and the relatively short time required for the vessel to respond to the tug's efforts. In most instances the ship will provide its own propulsion ahead and astern. There are exceptions that will be discussed elsewhere in the text. As previously mentioned, the tug's principal functions are to: assist a vessel to turn; move a vessel laterally; provide steerage; check a vessel's way; and hold it in position against a dock while it is making fast or letting go lines. The dynamics involved have been discussed in Chapter 10 and most are fairly obvious. Nevertheless, certain other elements should be considered. These include:

1. The conventional single- or twin-screw tug is more effective maneuvering ahead than when backing. The reason for this is that the propeller thrust is less when going astern than when going ahead, and the tug may not respond to its rudder when backing during shipwork.

2. If a tug (except a propeller-steered tug and one fitted with flanking rudders) is required to back for an extended period of time, it will often fall out of position because of the vessel's movement ahead or astern, because of the effect of wind or current, or because of the effect of the torque of its own propeller.

3. A tug's effectiveness is seriously diminished if the vessel is traveling at excessive speed or uses its engine rashly. If the vessel has much way on and the tug is required to back, it could easily part the head line. If the tug is required to push under these same conditions, it might not be able to work out to enough of an angle to affect the vessel to any great degree. A vessel maneuvering ahead or astern, under full power, may make the tug's efforts futile and even jeopardize its safety.

4. There is an element of delay when a tug's engines are maneuvered from ahead to astern more or less in proportion to the length of the head line. For example, if the ship is high out of the water, the tug's head line will be longer than if the ship were deep loaded with little freeboard. A tug must back easily until all the slack is out of the head line before applying full power. Otherwise, there is the risk of parting a line. The pilot or shiphandler should anticipate this delay when giving orders to the tug.

5. The tug's maneuverability is a factor that must also be considered when shifting from port to starboard or from forward to aft on the ship. A handy twin-screw tug can change positions more rapidly than a single-screw tug (especially if it is an old-timer with a direct-reversing engine). If the delay is not anticipated, it could be a critical factor should the vessel be swinging heavily or setting down on the dock.

MAKING THE TUG FAST

Practices vary in different parts of the country. In some ports tugs normally make fast with only one line. In this case there may be only one deckhand on board to handle lines. In other ports tugs fulfilling the same function may carry a crew of two or three on deck and often automatically put up two or three lines, even when not necessary (head line, springline, and stern line) (See Fig. 11-1).

Pilots or docking masters should bear this in mind. If they are working a port where one deckhand is the normal complement, and they are anticipating the need of a quarter line or stern line, they should advise the towing company of the need for additional personnel. Failure to do so could impose an impossible burden on one deckhand and result in a delay that could cause an accident.

When coming alongside a ship to make up, a tug will usually send up its hawser with a heaving line. Should the ship be high out of the water,

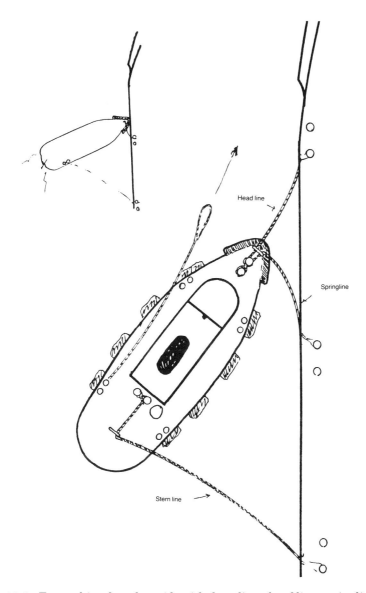

Fig. 11-1. Tug making fast alongside with three lines, head line, springline, and stern line. If another stern line is required forward, it can be led up to the deck of the tug and secured aboard the ship. Slack can be heaved up when the tug comes ahead on its engine. The springline, if used, should always lead out of the bow chock on the tug, even if the head line must be made fast elsewhere. Sometimes it is only necessary for the tug to put up a head line. Stern lines or quarter lines are only necessary if the tug must back its engine.

and if the wind is blowing, time can be saved if the vessel's deck crew passes its heaving line to the tug.

On some aircraft carriers and cargo ships transporting vehicles, a deckhand would have to have the arm and eye of a big league pitcher to throw the monkey's fist through the proper chock. (Some of them do!) In this case, it will save time to have a messenger or heaving line led out through the chock for the tug to pick up. It is not unusual to suggest to the masters of these vessels beforehand that these steps be taken.

Springlines on tugs doing shipwork are usually led from a position as far forward as practical on the tug. This will be the bullnose or bow chock if the tug has one. This is done to permit the tug to pivot freely. If a springline is made fast farther aft by the forward quarter bitt, the springline will keep the tug from turning as much as it may need to get into position (45° to 90° to the ship's centerline). The head line (frequently referred to as the backing line) is sometimes made fast farther aft if both lines will not fit through the bow chock (Fig. 11-1).

Stern lines or *quarter lines* are terms that are used interchangeably in this text, and refer to lines that are led from the after quarter bitt or stern of the tug to a position on the ship that will maintain the tug approximately at right angles to the ship. This is done to counteract the effect of the torque of the tug's propeller or the effects of the ship's movement ahead or astern. Quarter lines are also used to counteract the effect of wind and current.

If the ship is moving ahead, the quarter line will be led forward along the outboard side of the tug and passed aboard the ship. The ship will have to steer a little wide to allow the tug to come ahead with the rudder turned hard over in order to get in position and to take the slack out of the quarter line. If the quarter line is to be led aft, it can be passed aboard from the inboard side of the tug and slacked as needed. It is important to remember that when the quarter line or the stern line is in use, excessive way on the ship is dangerous as this can part the line or even capsize the tug.

Torque refers to the tendency of the propeller to cast the stern of the vessel in the direction opposite to the normal rotation of the propeller when the engines are backed. The effect of torque is readily apparent when you realize the large diameter and pitch of the propellers that are installed on most tugs. Using this effect in shipwork is discussed in Chapter 13.

MAKING A BEND

Vessels approaching a bend may have tugs on both bows to facilitate controlling the ship. If the vessel is light forward, the tugs can be useful even if the vessel is moving fairly fast (5 to 6 knots). If deep laden, the vessel should move slow enough (3 to 4 knots) to enable the tug on the outboard side to push at an angle of 45° or more to the ship. Otherwise it will have little turning effect and may increase the ship's speed. A tug on the inside of the bend can be used effectively backing, as this will cant the bow in the direction of turn. The resistance of the tug will retard the vessel's advance. The ship's rudder will also be more effective working against this resistance. In this instance the ship's speed is fairly critical to the tug. If the vessel is traveling too fast, the weight of the tug being towed alongside may impose such a severe strain on the head line that it might part if the tug backs hard.

On the outboard quarter of a ship, a tug can do very little unless it is hipped to the ship. In this case the tug can come ahead with its helm turned toward the vessel; if the vessel backs, it will have a twin-screw effect. A tug on the inboard quarter can assist by backing if it is hipped up, or by coming ahead if it has only a head line up. However, it will be more effective pushing if the bend is sharp. Here again the vessel's speed should be slow enough for a tug to maintain at least a 45° angle to the ship (Fig. 10-5).

STEERING SHIPS

A tug at the bow of a ship can steer the ship very effectively as the vessel moves astern by pushing on either side of the stem. It may not be necessary for the tug to put up a line, but if it does, the line should be cast off beforehand if the ship moves ahead. When the ship has a bulbous bow that is exposed, has extreme rake to the stem, or excessive flare, a tug may not be able to work in this position.

A tug on the stern of a vessel can also assist the vessel to steer as the tug moves ahead by pushing on either side of the stern. Since the tug is working behind the propeller, it should have a head line up through the center chock aft in order to maintain control. The propeller wash from the ship will naturally have a tendency to wash the tug away when going ahead, and will suck the tug into the ship when it backs. In any event, the tug will need the restraint of a head line as a tug will sometimes behave erratically because of disturbed water around the

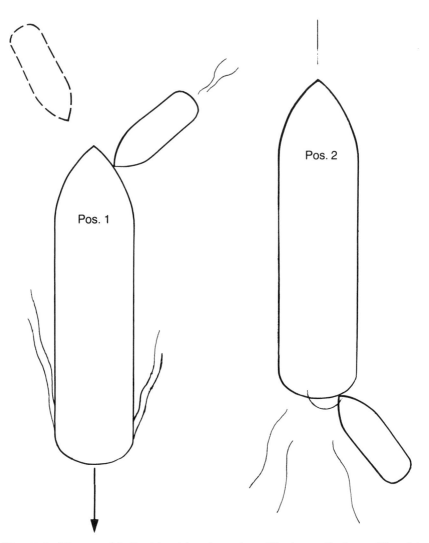

Fig. 11-2. The vessel in Position 1 is going astern. The tug on the bow will assist the vessel to steer by pushing against the appropriate side of the bow near the stem. The tug may not put up a line, but if it does the line should be cast off before the ship comes ahead to avoid having the tug damaged by the flare of the bow. If the ship has excessive flare, rake to the stem, or a bulbous bow, the tug may not be able to work safely in this position.

The vessel in Position 2 is being assisted by a tug on the stern (aft of the propeller) as it comes ahead. A tug in this position can work effectively on either side of the stern. The tug should put up a line in the center chock aft in order to maintain control in the wheel wash from the ship.

stern. Since this method is often used in making an approach to a dock, the advantage is that the tug can be used to push the stern of the ship towards or away from the dock. Tugs can normally be used in this fashion on vessels with a cruiser stern that are deep in the water and they can also work on some transom sterns. They cannot work in this position when a ship is of light draft, or where the stern is of such a configuration that the overhang would damage the tug (Fig. 11-2).

WORKING INSIDE

There are occasions when it is convenient for the tug to work on the inboard side of a ship when docking or undocking. This is most commonly done at tanker berths where openings between piling clusters leave enough space for the tug to work safely (Fig. 11-3).

When a vessel is docking, a tug may be stationed on the inshore side. This is to prevent it from landing heavily when coming alongside as a result of the effect of wind or current. Undocking from such a berth is similar. The tug stations itself where it can work safely between the dolphins, and then breasts the ship clear of the dock.

Ships can also be breasted clear of cargo docks that are continuous. The stern of the vessel must be sprung open enough for a tug to get inside, between the ship and the dock. A single-screw tug working in this position will probably have to put up a head line to avoid sliding down the ship's side because of the acute angle. Refer to the diagrams which show the mechanics and progressive steps of these maneuvers (Fig. 11-4).

COMPENSATING FOR DRAG

Tugs may cause drag that can affect a ship's steering qualities. This is most noticeable on smaller ships when two tugs are fast on the same side of the vessel. If the shiphandler finds this bothersome, he can advise the tugs to keep their head lines slack. This is easily done by coming ahead enough to relieve the tension on the head line without pushing the ship.

SHIFTING THE TUG

If a tug is required to shift from forward to aft or from one side to the other, to avoid delays, it is preferable to assign the most maneuverable tug to that position, unless other considerations such as horsepower make it impractical. The shiphandler is often involved in a fairly intricate maneuver, but his concentration should not cause him to overlook

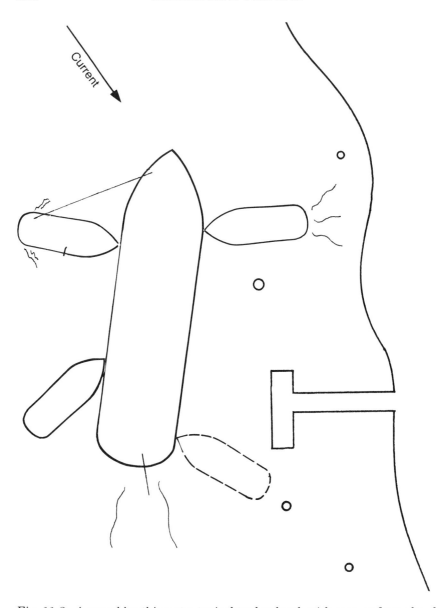

Fig. 11-3. A vessel berthing at a typical tanker berth with current from ahead setting the vessel on the dock. A tug can be effectively employed on the inboard bow to keep the vessel from landing heavily as it comes alongside. A tug on the off-shore bow would require a quarter line in order to accomplish this by backing. A tug may be used on the inshore quarter aft, but the ship can usually keep the stern from coming in too fast by using the rudder to hold the stern up.

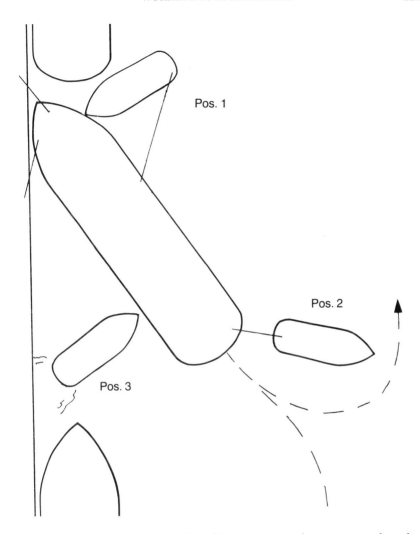

Fig. 11-4. The ship is being undocked by tugs using three commonplace, but different methods to achieve the same results. In Position 1 the tug will breast the bow of the ship to the dock and open up the stern by pushing against the ship forward of the turn of the side. The tug can then steer the ship as it backs clear of the dock. In Position 2 the tug is towing the vessel off the dock. This requires a little care in order to avoid having the bow of the ship drag down the dock. An inshore head line should be held until the ship is well opened and then the tug can tow the vessel off, straight astern, until it is clear. In Position 3 the ship will heave its head line while holding the forward springline so that the tug can work its way between the ship and the dock. A single-screw tug will probably put up a head line, a twin-screw tug may not have to.

factors that can affect the tug and may, as a result, also affect the ship.

If a ship is being turned through the wind and is light, the shiphandler may want to shift the tug to the other bow of the ship. Once the bow has passed through the eye of the wind, the tug should back enough to check the vessel's swing before letting go. This will give the tug time to shift to the new lee bow without having to race around to the other side, perhaps losing time in maneuvering. Another hazard is the possibility of hitting the ship due to the speed of its turn. Experienced pilots are aware of this (Fig. 11-5).

If a tug must shift from one quarter to the other, it is helpful if the ship can avoid backing hard until the tug is fast. Otherwise the ship's wheel wash might carry the tug almost to the bow. This can also delay the process of getting into position to work, and may lead to an accident. Some shiphandlers have difficulty in handling transitions from steering to turning, to moving the vessel laterally, etc. In this case it is best to break the maneuvers down into steps like:

1. Stop ship.
2. Turn ship.
3. Shift tugs.
4. Breast vessel to dock.

SHIFTING THE SHIPS

In some cases the ship's position alongside the dock is fairly critical. This often occurs at tanker berths and RO-RO facilities. Tugs can usually shift a vessel ahead or astern easier than if the ship uses its own engines. If two tugs are used, the tug at the opposite end from the direction of the shift can lie nearly flat alongside, pushing the vessel forward or aft. The other tug should stay at approximately 90° to the ship, coming ahead and "pinning" it to the dock when in position.

If only one tug is used, it can push at a slightly steeper angle to the ship (15° to 30°) and shove it ahead or astern until the ship is in position and its movement has been checked by its forward or after springline (Fig. 11-6).

TYPICAL MANEUVERS

No two maneuvers are exactly alike. Subject to the varying forces of wind and current, size and trim of the vessels, and unexpected occurrences, most maneuvers in a given situation are similar. Some are illustrated in Figs. 11-7, 11-8, 11-9, and 11-10.

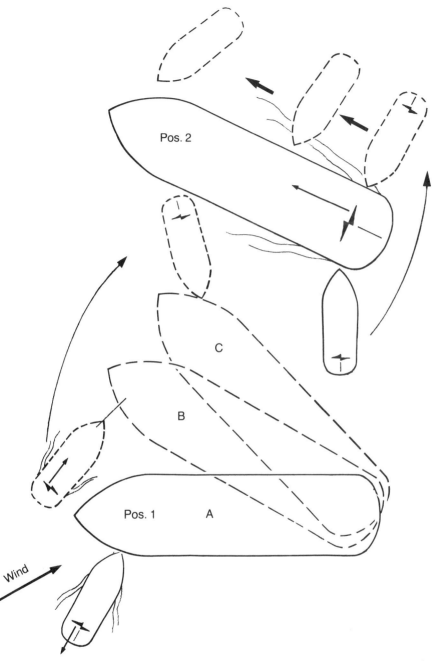

Pos. 2

C

B

Pos. 1   A

Wind

Fig. 11-5. Position 1 tug backs to check the vessel's swing before shifting to lee bow. In Position 2 if the ship backs before the tug shift is secured, the tug could be washed up on the side of the vessel.

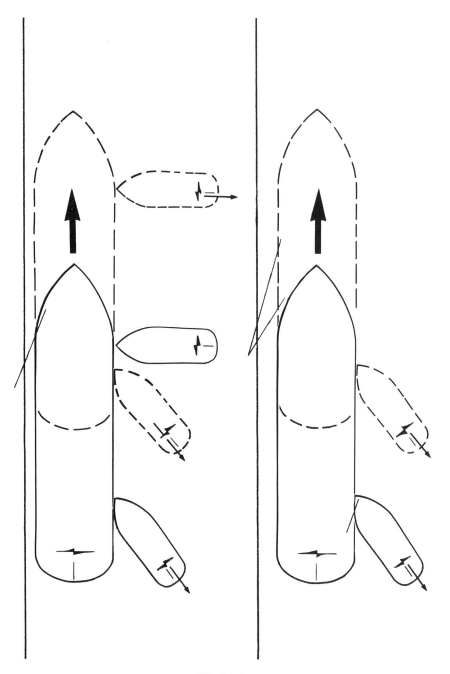

Fig. 11-6.

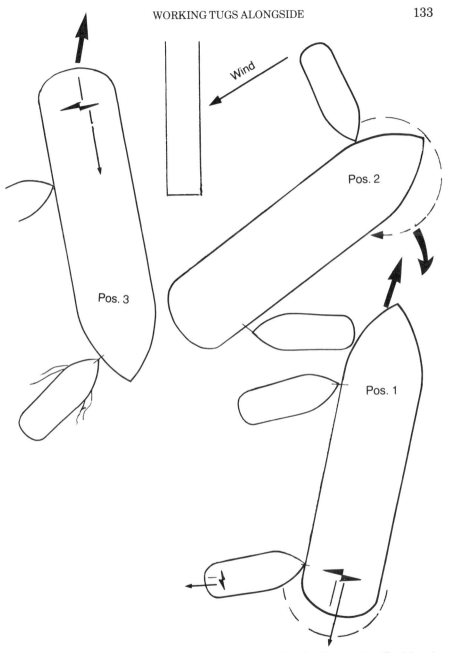

Fig. 11-7. Vessel berthing stern in on the leeside of a finger pier. Position 1 vessel slows and tug aft shifts to starboard quarter. Position 2 vessel stops and forward tug shifts to starboard bow. The vessel can then back easily until it is in position with tug assisting as needed.

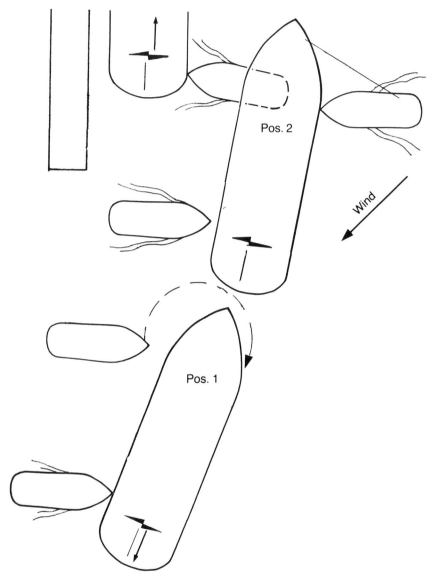

Fig. 11-8. Position 1: ship is proceeding slowly ahead with forward tug shifting to starboard bow. A quarter line or stern line should be put up if the wind is strong or the ship is light forward. Position 2: forward tug will push or back as required. After tug will let go its line but continue to push as needed on the port quarter as long as it can stay alongside the ship. Position 3: ship is now "dead in the water" with both tugs fast on the starboard side. Tugs can push or back to berth the vessel.

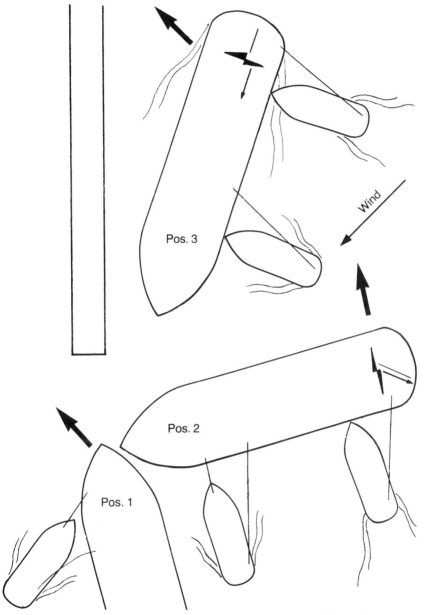

Fig. 11-9. Vessel docking on weather side of dock stern in. Both tugs fast on port side with quarter lines up. The transition from Position 2 to Position 3 is obvious with the tugs backing and pushing as required while the ship maneuvers with its engine ahead and astern.

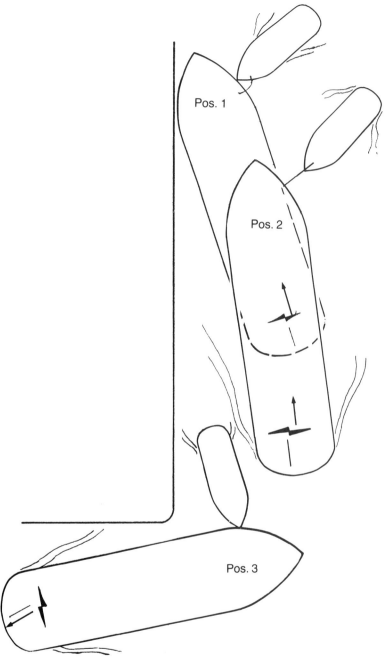

Fig. 11-10. Position 1: tug breasts bow of ship to the dock to open the stern. Position 2: tug backs bow of ship clear of dock as the vessel goes astern. Position 3: tug has let go its head line and shifted to port bow of vessel to help it complete the turn.

STUDY QUESTIONS

1. What is the advantage of using a tug alongside?
2. Does a tug alongside propel the ship?
3. Why does a conventional tug use a quarter line?
4. How many lines does a tug normally put up?
5. Where are springlines led from on the tug?
6. Is it sometimes helpful for the ship's crew to pass a heaving line or a messenger to the tug?
7. If the tug is going to use a quarter line leading forward, what must the ship do?
8. Explain how steering the bow or the stern of a ship is done.
9. Can a tug work in this fashion on all vessels?
10. Will the tug require a line?
11. Is it possible for a tug to work on the inshore side of a ship docking and undocking?
12. How should a tug's lines be cast-off?

CHAPTER TWELVE

WORKING TUGS ON A TOWLINE

Using tugs on a towline for docking a ship is seldom done in this country, though it is the prevalent method in Europe. Nevertheless, this method is quite useful for undocking and for several other applications (Fig. 12-1).

In situations where employing tugs alongside or on a towline are good alternatives, the choice will usually depend upon local custom. There are occasions when one method is more appropriate than the other, or where it is the only practical way to employ the tug. In towline work this would apply when the ship is obliged to transit narrow bridges, locks, and channels and where the width of the waterway would prohibit using tugs fast alongside. Compared with the alongside method, there are certain disadvantages. One is the danger of the tug capsizing if the ship's engines are used rashly. Another is that towline work is generally more time-consuming—when the tug is used along-side and where the ship will respond more quickly to the tug's efforts.

The mechanics of towline work appear fairly obvious. The tug pulls the ship (or the end of ship to which it is made fast) in the direction the pilot wishes. This seems straightforward enough, but there are a number of factors to be considered if the tug is to be used effectively and safely.

HAWSER LENGTH

Normal hawser length for towline work is usually between 100 and 150 feet, but if the ship must be maneuvered in a confined space, the towline length may be restricted. The difficulty here stems from the fact that the tow bitts on American tugs are usually located about a third of the length forward of the stern which limits their maneuverability quite a bit on a short towline. They also have a tendency to skid sideways to

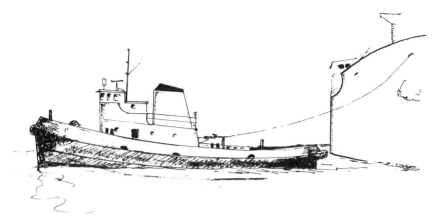

Fig. 12-1. A European harbor tug.

some degree when the helm is turned to change their heading. When the tug is pulling a ship from ahead (towing), there is a tendency for the bow of the vessel to be set in the opposite direction of the intended turn at first, an effect most apparent on a small or light draft vessel and less noticeable on a heavily laden ship. This tendency is not all bad for if anticipated, it can be useful. Tug skippers use this effect all the time and often *snap* their barges by applying power in a turn to swing them clear of obstacles (Fig. 12-2).

TUG'S WHEEL WASH

The tug's wheel wash is another factor that must be taken into consideration, as it sometimes has a noticeable effect on the handling qualities of a ship. This may be of little consequence if the vessel is simply being pulled off the dock or turned. However, if the vessel is being towed through narrow channels or bridges, this can have a detrimental effect on the vessel's steering. It is usually more pronounced on deep draft ships, but it can cause the bow of light draft ships to oscillate a bit. The remedy in most cases is to increase towline length. If this is not possible, a reduction in the speed of the ship may be necessary.

TOWING ASTERN

It is not commonly done in this country, but there are occasions when tugs may work on a towline on each end of a vessel, and one will be towed stern first. If a tug working in this fashion is going to be towed astern, even for a short distance, it is a wise precaution to rig a gobline. This is

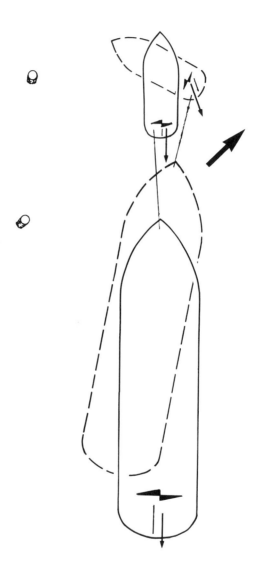

Fig. 12-2.

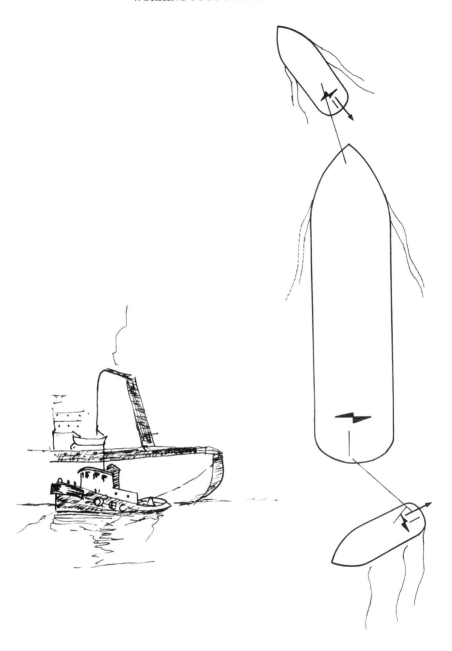

Fig. 12-3.

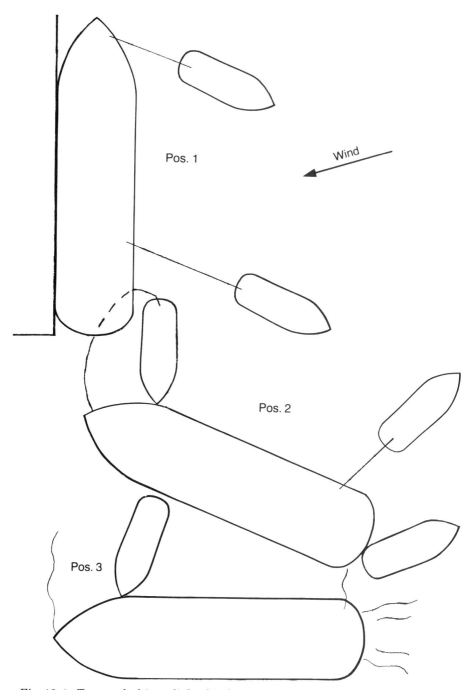

Pos. 1

Wind

Pos. 2

Pos. 3

Fig. 12-4. Tugs undocking a light ship from a weather berth using towlines. The tug on the bow must stay in position so that it will be ready to push the bow of the vessel when it is clear of the end of the dock.

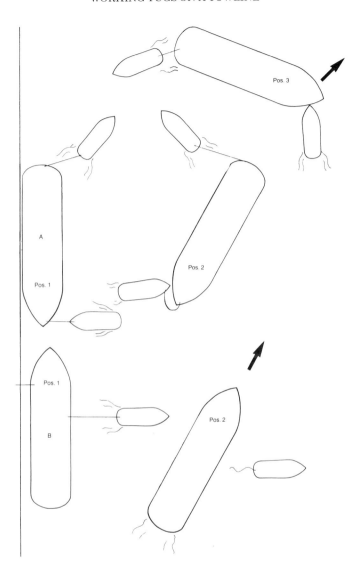

Fig. 12-5. Vessel A is being undocked with two tugs. In Position 1, vessel A is being backed off the dock by the forward tug while the stern of the vessel is towed off by a tug on a towline. Positions 2 and 3 illustrate progressive steps in the maneuver as A is turned. Vessel B is undocked with one tug pulling on a towline fast just forward of midships. The breast line is held and slacked as needed to lift the ship evenly off the dock until the stern of the vessel will clear when she comes ahead on her engine.

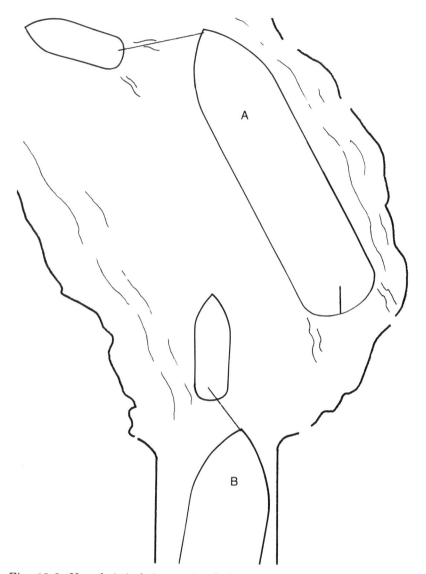

Fig. 12-6. Vessel A is being assisted through a sharp turn by a tug on a moderately long towline. The ship should avoid overtaking the tug as this might trip it. On very hard bends it is sometimes necessary to back the ship's engine in order for the tug to work to best effect.

Vessel B is being assisted through a narrow lock by a tug on a very short towline. With a loaded ship it is best to have a tailboat or a tug lashed up on the quarter. A light ship might dispense with the tailboat, but should avoid using its engine ahead as this can destroy the tug's effectiveness.

simply a preventer that is passed over the hawser which restricts its arc of movement so that the tug will not be *girt,* or pulled sideways, as it is towed stern first (Fig. 12-3).

FURTHER PRECAUTIONS

There is another difference between towline and alongside work. If towing the ship, the tug will be supplying much of the power required to propel the vessel. The ship should be careful not to override the tug as this can destroy the tug's effectiveness or endanger it. Another word of caution is appropriate here: when the tug is let go, the pilot should allow sufficient time so that the tow hawser (whether the tug's or the ship's) can be kept clear of the ship's propeller. The diagrams in Fig. 12-4, 12-5, and 12-6 show common ways of employing the tugs.

STUDY QUESTIONS

1. What is the advantage of towline work?
2. What are the disadvantages of this method?
3. Is the towline often used for docking ships in this country?
4. How does it differ from using tugs alongside?
5. What is the normal towline length in this country?
6. What is meant by the term *snapping a tow*?
7. How is this used to advantage?
8. What hazards are associated with towline work?
9. How can these hazards be avoided?

CHAPTER THIRTEEN

USING TORQUE TO ADVANTAGE

In previous chapters, the subject of torque was mentioned briefly and it was noted that a single-screw tug (or any single-screw vessel) is subject to the effects of torque. It was also noted that this effect is apparent when the tug's engine is turning ahead, but that the rudders, which direct the thrust from the propeller, can compensate for its effect. When the tug is backing, however, unless it has flanking rudders to direct the propeller wash, the stern of the tug will cast to one side or the other, depending on the pitch of the propeller. With a standard right-hand turning wheel, the tug's stern will move to port when its direction of rotation is reversed to back the tug. Tugs that are fitted with a Kort nozzle may not respond in this fashion.

If a tug is fast to a ship with only a head line, in still water with no wind and no way on the vessel, lying at approximately 90° to the ship, the stern will move to port (assuming a right-hand propeller) when the tug backs its engine. This is often referred to as the "paddle wheel effect." It is obvious that if the shiphandler wishes this tug to maintain its angle of 90° without having the tug put up a quarter line, then the ship must move in the same direction and at the same speed that the stern of the tug is moving. As long as the vessel's direction and speed of movement conform to the effect of the torque on the tug, the tug will stay in shape.

Now, you may think, "If it's this much trouble why bother? Have the tug put up a quarter line instead." The answer, of course, is that it is less complicated than it seems. There are occasions, especially if the ship's chocks and bitts are poorly located, or when the tug may only be required to back for a short time, that it is appropriate and convenient to use the tug this way. If the tug has only one line up and will be required to shift, it will have only one line fast which can be cast off quickly.

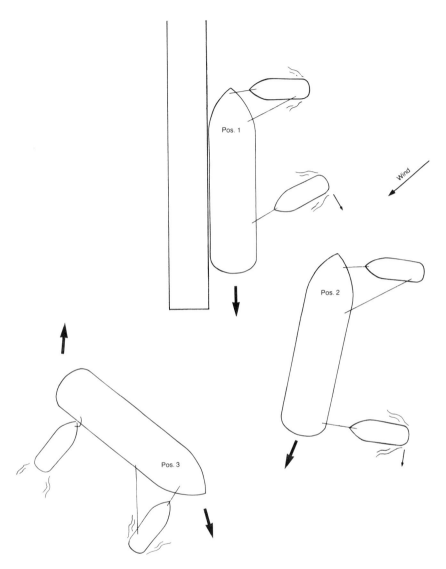

Fig. 13-1. An in-ballast tanker departing its berth.

The forward tug will only back intermittently, and so must use a quarter line to stay in position. The after tug uses a longer head line and positions itself at an angle so that it will be able to back the ship off the dock enough for it to go astern before the tug's torque moves it out of position. Once the ship has sternway the paddle wheel effect of the after tug's propeller will keep it in shape provided that the speed of the ship astern closely approximates the effect of the torque on the tug.

If a tug is breasting a ship against the dock while it lets go its dock lines and then is required to back, it might fall out of position before the ship has enough way on it to compensate for the paddle wheel effect. In this case, if the tug pushes at an angle so that it will have a little extra time before it falls out of position, the ship may be far enough off the dock and have enough way on to keep the tug in shape (Fig. 13-1). It may also help to gain a little bit of time if the tug slacks its head line a bit, so that the stern of the tug must then swing through a longer arc before it is out of position. If the pilot and tug's captain work well in this situation, the ship can usually be maneuvered so that the tug maintains the proper angle to the vessel.

Torque can also be useful when the ship is making a sharp bend. If the vessel slows down enough, provided the tug's torque is consistent with the vessel's direction of movement, it will gradually swing the tug out until it is at a right angle, or nearly so, to the ship as it backs. This will have the maximum turning effect on the vessel.

This probably seems more complicated than it actually is in practice, for the position of the tug itself indicates the effect of torque. If a pilot is interested in using this effect but is wary of the outcome, it might be best to try some of these maneuvers in noncritical situations to become familiar with the tug's responses under different conditions.

STUDY QUESTIONS

1. What effect does torque have on the single-screw tug when it is backing?
2. How can the tug's angle be maintained when backing if no stern line is used?
3. Why is this useful?
4. How can the tug stay in position longer if it is required to back more?

CHAPTER FOURTEEN

USING TUGS IN CURRENT

Most harbors, except those isolated by locks, are tidal. Often a river may feed into an estuary or bay where a harbor is located. In other instances the harbor facilities are built along a river's edge and may be many miles from the river's mouth. Ships using this facility will be subject to the effect of the river's current. In any event, current is an everyday reality for most pilots. The current direction and velocity may change with the ebb and flow of the tide; or it may be a river current whose direction is constant, but the velocity will change according to the height of the river. Whatever the cause of the current, it adds another dimension to shiphandling.

It is usually assumed that a vessel breasting a head current enjoys the advantage of being able to maintain steerage while moving with little or no headway over the bottom. Conversely, a vessel with a fair current may actually be dead in the water and still be moving rapidly over the bottom. In this circumstance it would have, at best, a very limited ability to steer. Often ships docking in a head current will dispense with tugs unless the current sets obliquely across the channel, or onto the dock. If the ship is docking with a fair current, it is almost a certainty that tugs will be required to assist the vessel. The problem when using tugs in this situation arises from the fact that tugs are subject to the same forces that affect the ship. Tugs must be "made up" to the ship in such a fashion that any maneuvering they might do to compensate for the current will not *adversely* affect the vessel. Or, they must be secured to the vessel in a manner that will *eliminate* the need to maneuver to stay in shape. The tugs may be used in many different ways: as *free agents* (i.e., with no lines); with a head line only; with two or three lines (head, stern, and perhaps a springline); on a towline; and hipped up.

Upon reflection it will occur to the reader that there are really only three basic situations involving current: current ahead, current astern, and crosscurrent. This seems simple enough, but the ramifications can be extensive. Current ahead can be "dead" ahead, setting on the dock, or setting off the dock. The crosscurrent situation can be equally complex. This usually occurs in slipways where berths lie roughly at a right angle to the current, and there is probably still water between the docks. The approach can be from up current or down current, and the ship may berth on the leeside of the current or with the current pressing the vessel against the dock. Vessels entering and departing these berths may have to cope with current working against either bow or stern while the rest of the vessel is in still water. Furthermore, it must be understood that docking and undocking, in many situations, are not *reciprocal* movements. Tugs may be used in fashions that may not be often seen in no-current shipwork. This might include docking on a towline and the use of the tug hipped alongside the ship forward or aft.

Towline work is suitable for docking and undocking in current ahead and astern, with the current "on" or "off" the dock. The use of another tug or the anchor may be required when docking. (See Figs. 14-1, 14-2, 14-3, and 14-4.) This method is sometimes used in crosscurrent situations, but not if space is limited.

Tug alongside (head line only) is a method used with current ahead, astern, or across. With current on the dock it may require the assistance of another tug (Figs. 14-5, 14-6, and 14-7).

Tugs with quarter lines are often used in "fair" current situations and when backing into or leaving slips with crosscurrent at the head of the dock (Figs. 14-8 and 14-9).

Tugs with no lines (free agents) are only used *pushing*. They can assist in head, stern, and crosscurrent situations. They frequently work inside and do not put up a line in order to be able to clear out quickly (Fig. 14-10).

Tugs hipped up on the quarter (Mississippi River style) are used for docking and undocking in head current situations (Fig. 14-11).When the tug is fast, the vessel is maneuvered as if it were a twin-screw ship, with the tug functioning as the outboard engine. Tugs hipped up forward can be used in stern current situations for *undocking*. The lashed up tug backs against the springline to work the bow toward the dock. The ship's rudder is put hard to port, the ship having sternway relative to the water moving past the rudder will move the stern away from the

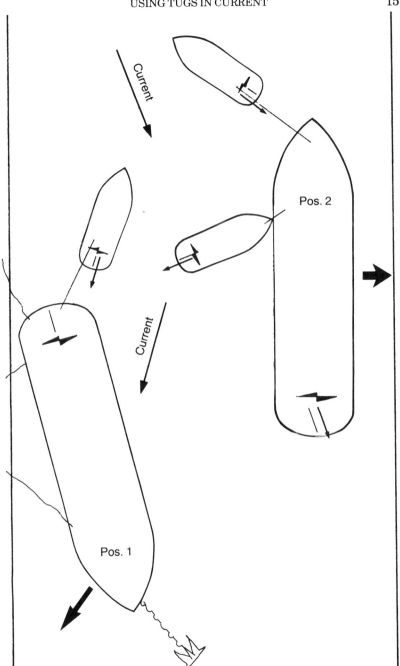

Fig. 14-1.

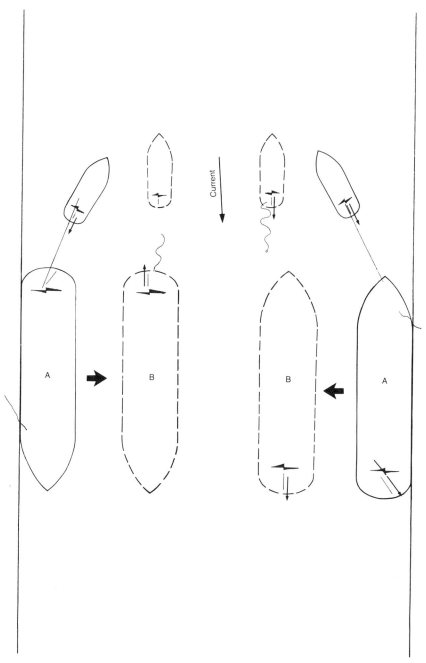

Fig. 14-2. Undocking.

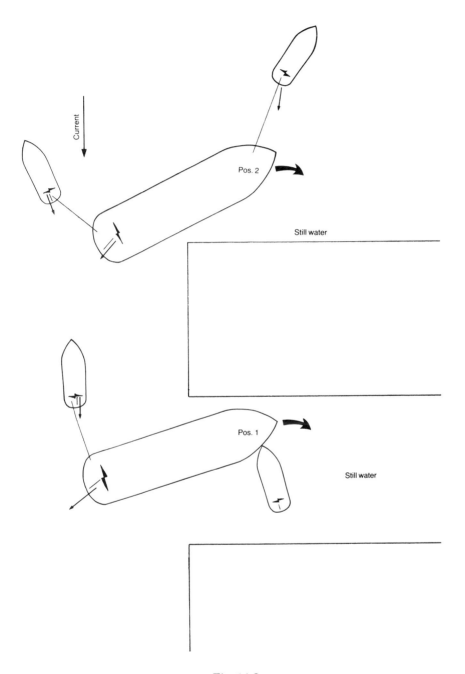

Fig. 14-3.

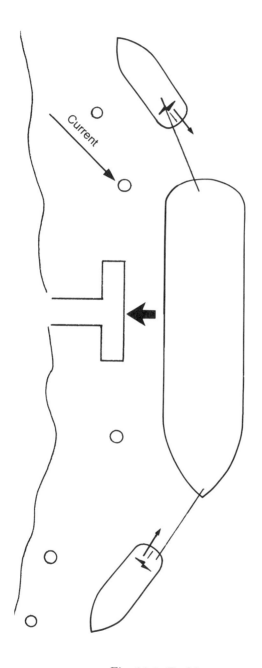

Fig. 14-4. Docking: two tugs on towlines.

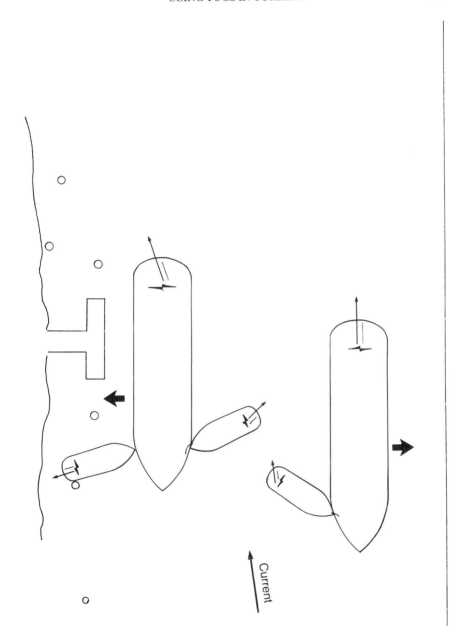

Fig. 14-5.

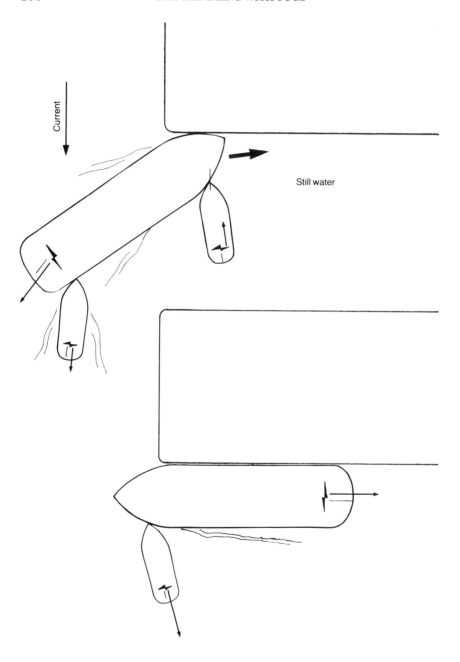

Current

Still water

Fig. 14-6.

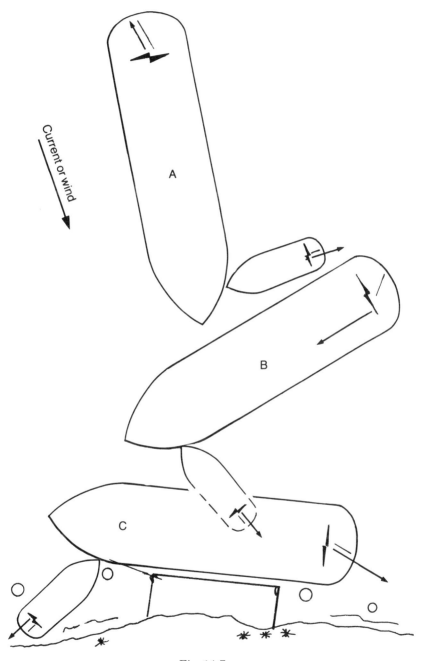

Fig. 14-7.

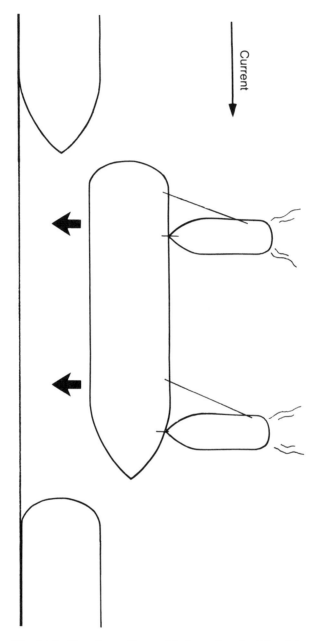

Fig. 14-8. Tugs breasting a ship into a berth with a fair current.
Quarter lines keep the tugs in position while the ship backs its engine as needed
to stem the current.

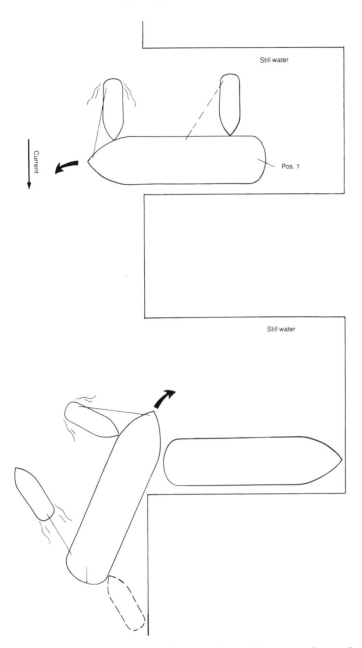

Fig. 14-9. Ship departing berth may only require one tug forward.
Ship entering berth will require two tugs if current is strong. After tug may be
used either pushing or pulling as shown.

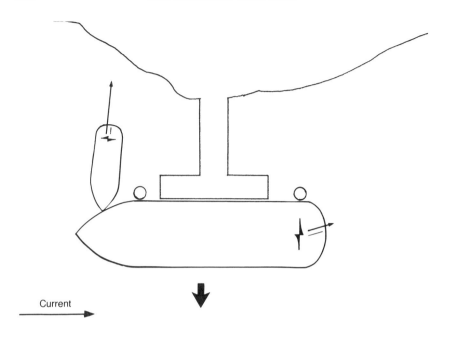

Current

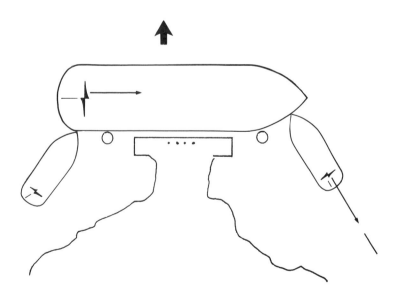

Fig. 14-10.

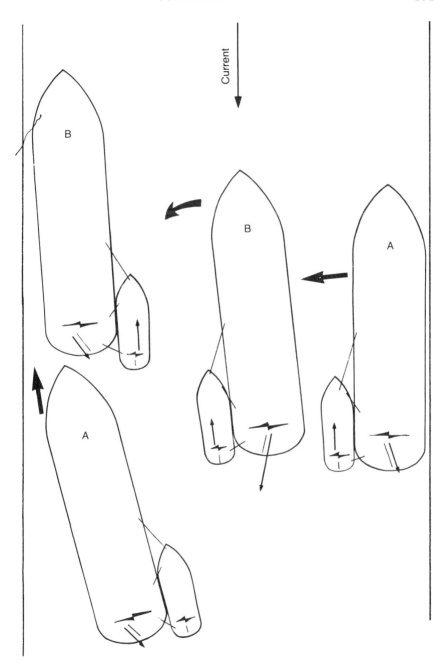

Fig. 14-11. Docking and undocking with tug on "hip," Mississippi style.

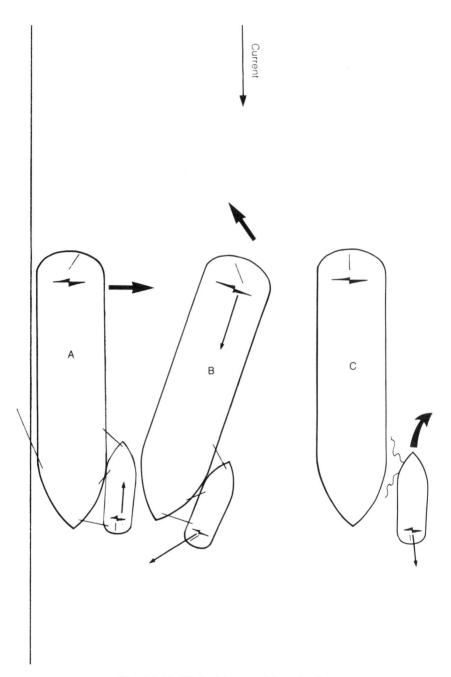

Fig. 14-12. Undocking: tug hipped to bow.

dock. When the current gets between the ship and the berth, and strikes the ship along its starboard side, the ship moves bodily away from the berth. The tug comes ahead with port rudder to move the bow away from the dock and simultaneously straighten the ship in the channel while the ship's engine comes astern against the current (Fig. 14-12).

STUDY QUESTIONS

1. Can a ship berthing in a head current dispense with the services of a tug?
2. Can a ship with a fair current berth without a tug?
3. What is the principal problem for the tug assisting a ship in a current?
4. How is it made up to the ship?
5. When would a tug normally work without a line?
6. When a tug is hipped up to the ship, where is it made fast, forward or aft?

CHAPTER FIFTEEN

HANDLING DEAD SHIPS

Sooner or later it falls to every pilot's lot to shift a dead ship with tugs. If he's familiar with the process, then, of course, there is no problem. The dynamics of towing a dead ship are quite different from handling a powered vessel, and there are a wide range of makeups that are possible.

One example illustrates this proposition quite well. I was taking a small freighter out of lay-up and one tug was ordered to shift the ship from the lay-up berth to the fuel dock. The pilot, thinking in conventional terms, had the tug hipped up on the quarter. A great deal of maneuvering was required to undock, shift, and dock the vessel, simply because the pilot failed to analyze the dynamics. The bow of the ship was light and vulnerable even to a light breeze, and the single-screw tug had to turn the vessel 180° in a narrow channel. This involved a lot of backing and filling. As a result, a job that should have taken a little over an hour, took more than three hours.

What the pilot should have done was to have the tug made up alongside the bow of the vessel. This is what a tugboatman would have done. It would then have been a straight shot to the fuel dock, and the tug's position forward would have stabilized the bow of the ship against the untoward effect of wind and cut the maneuvering time in half. It all worked out in the end, but it could have been done much easier.

There are basically about three different ways of handling dead ships:

1. With tugs alongside;
2. With tug and tail boat;
3. With tug alongside and lead boat.

When tugs are used alongside and the ship is small, it may require only one tug. After all, tugs handle quite sizeable barges unassisted and can handle a ship of comparable size just as well. If the pilot has any doubts about where the tug ought to make fast, he should first consider which side of the ship goes to the dock, and also where the bow or stern of the vessel goes. He should also consider the kind of turns that the tug will be required to make with the ship in tow alongside. With the tug on the hip (especially if it is a single screw) it is best for the tug to be fast on the inboard side of a turn if a hard turn is to be made. The reason for this

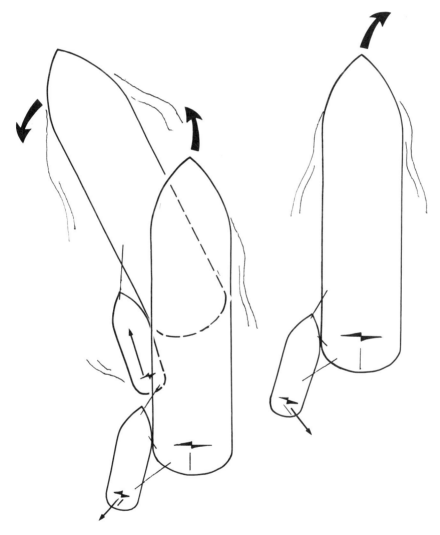

Fig. 15-1.

is that if the tug backs its engine it will accelerate the swing without adding headway to the tow. In fact, it will be able to back and fill as necessary even in a very sharp turn or in confined quarters without losing control of the tow. If, however, a tug is on the outboard side of a turn and backs, it will kill the swing and so it must continue to power throughout the turn. This could lead to a mishap if the approach to the turn has been misjudged (Fig. 15-1).

Both ships and barges towed with the tug alongside tend to skid or set to the side more than a ship operating under its own power would do. This is caused by the large angle of rudder required for the tug to keep the ship under control and to compensate for the tug's off-center location. This will be more apparent in light draft vessels than in those that are deep loaded. Having the tug hipped up with its bow inclined in toward the ship will reduce the amount of helm it will have to carry to keep the vessel under control (Fig. 15-2).

Larger vessels will require additional tugs to shift. In some ports, three tugs are required as a minimum for shifting dead ships. In this case, one tug will hip up aft to provide propulsion. The other tugs will be secured forward on either side of the bow with a head line to assist steering the vessel.

Very large ships may require four or more tugs to be used in a shift, with two tugs fast alongside aft and two tugs forward, one either side, to steer. The reason for employing so many tugs has more to do with maintaining control over the vessel than the need for the propulsion (this assumes that the tugs are well powered). Tugs so far from the centerline on very wide ships have a limited ability to steer the vessel and are frequently used as if they were machinery components of a twin-screw ship, using one tug's engine ahead and the other's astern at times for the twin-screw effect.

When tugs are used alongside, it may be just as convenient to move the vessel stern first as it is to move it bow first, though a little more care may be necessary in docking stern first to avoid damage to the rudder and the propeller (Fig. 15-2).

Tug and tailboats are often used for shifting dead ships, especially if locks, bridges, and narrow channels must be navigated. In very close quarters, I have seen gate lines used successfully, though a short towline might do just as well. The tug at the stern must be particularly alert and check the way of the ship so that it does not gather enough way to overpower the lead tug. If one of the tugs has flanking rudders, it would be best to have this act as tailboat as it can slow or steer the vessel while backing down. In instances when the after tug is working stern first, a gobline should be rigged to prevent this tug from being tripped.

On lengthy shifts, it is sometimes practical to use a tug fast alongside on the quarter of the ship and a tug ahead of the ship with a towline to the bow. This is a particularly effective way to utilize two tugs with moderate power to move sizeable ships and to be able to use their power

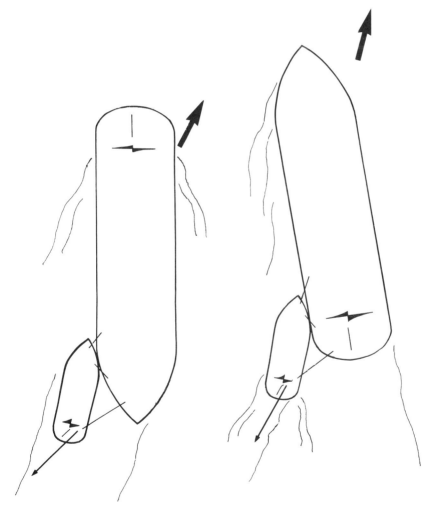

Fig. 15-2.

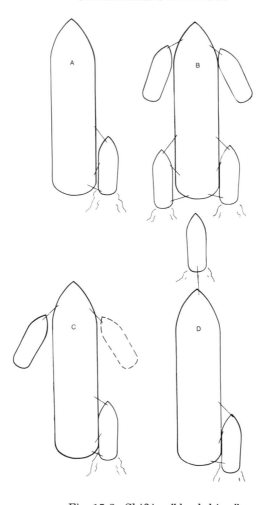

Fig. 15-3. Shifting "dead ships."

Vessel A is a small ship (less than 5,000 DWT), and it is being handled by a single tug of 1,600 horsepower "hipped up" on the quarter.

Vessel B is a large vessel requiring four tugs. The forward tugs assist by steering. The after tugs are principally for propulsion.

Vessel C is a ship of moderate size (less than 20,000 DWT). The tug forward assists with steering. This tug can be placed on either bow but is more effective on the side opposite the propelling tug which is hipped up aft.

The tug configuration used in moving vessel D is the most efficient method since both the tugs are propelling the ship. The forward tug both tows and steers the vessel. The after tug mainly supplies the propulsion, but it can also steer and more importantly, also back its engine when it is necessary to slow or stop the ship.

to best advantage. The tug on the stern can stop the ship by backing, if necessary, and the tug on the bow can overcome the ship's tendency to swing toward the backing tug by pulling to offset this effect, if it is desirable to do so. When the ship is moving ahead, both tugs are propelling the vessel and controlling it (Fig. 15-3).

STUDY QUESTIONS

1. What is the difference between handling a dead ship and assisting a powered vessel?
2. Is one tug ever used to handle a small- or medium-sized ship by itself?
3. If only one tug is used and a hard turn must be made, where should the tug be?
4. Does a ship propelled by a tug on the hip have a tendency to skid sideways?
5. When a larger ship is shifted, are more tugs required?
6. Are vessels ever handled stern first?
7. What does the term *toe-in* mean, and what purpose does it serve?
8. Describe several hookups for handling dead ships.
9. Why is the use of a tug on a towline forward and a tug hipped up aft an effective way to use tugs?
10. How are tugs fast aft on beamy vessels used most effectively for steering?

CHAPTER SIXTEEN

SALVAGE AND
EMERGENCY SITUATIONS

Approximately 90 percent of all marine casualties occur in pilotage waters. Since tugs are usually readily available, they are often called upon to assist vessels in salvage and emergency situations. The terms *salvage* and *emergency* are not necessarily synonymous, nor are they mutually exclusive. The distinction often hinges on legal technicalities that are not material to this text. To avoid confusion these subjects are dealt with separately in the balance of this chapter.

SALVAGE SITUATIONS

Exclusive of acts of war or fire, marine salvage normally falls into one of the three following categories: sinking, grounding or stranding, and rescue towing. Marine salvage can be a very complicated business and for this reason much of it is beyond the scope of this book. Our interest is confined *only* to that category most likely to confront the pilot or docking master—*grounding*.

Vessel Aground. It is almost inevitable that every pilot will on some occasion have to deal with a grounding. If you put the vessel aground, it is highly likely that you will be expected to attend to the process of refloating it. Of course, if the vessel is too hard aground or stranded, the services of a professional salvor may be required. In any event the pilot or shiphandler should know something about the forces that must be overcome in order to refloat the vessel and the *remedies* (methods used to overcome them). Once a vessel is aground there are basically four different factors that can affect it and the efforts to free it. These are the following:

    1. High winds that can have a considerable effect, especially on

light-draft vessels with a lot of exposed freeboard. They can cast a vessel ashore and keep it there. Conversely, if the wind shifts it might free the vessel.

2. Strong currents that have their greatest effect on deep-draft ships and like heavy winds can beach a vessel and work it even farther ashore. They can also cause a heavy buildup of sand or mud around a vessel (usually around the up-current side) that can complicate refloating it.

3. Heavy seas that can put a vessel ashore and force it harder aground. They can also frustrate rescue efforts and cause serious damage. But paradoxically, heavy seas can also work to the salvor's advantage. They may help break the suction of sand or mud bottom, grind down a coral bank, or (if the vessel is pitching) "pump" clear the loose material beneath a vessel and help free it.

4. Ground effect that is the amount of the vessel's lost displacement and the actual weight of the vessel that is borne by the material that it rests upon. This can be determined if sea conditions permit by comparing the vessel's draft before and after grounding. The vessel's immersion scale will provide the necessary information to calculate the amount of ground effect in tons.

The friction or resistance that must be overcome to refloat the vessel is a coefficient of this weight (ground effect) and ranges from 30 percent to 150 percent or more depending upon the nature of the bottom. Salvors calculate this percentage at 30 percent to 40 percent for soft sand or mud; about 50 percent for hard sand or gravel bottom; 50 percent to 100 percent for coral bottom; and 80 percent to 90 percent up to 150 percent for rocky bottom.

Vessels can be refloated in several different ways. If a vessel is grounded at low tide and the tidal range is sufficient, it might float off on the succeeding high tide. But if the ship went aground at or near high tide, it might have to wait until the next spring tide—and then only, if there was a sufficient difference in the tidal range, would the vessel be refloated.

A vessel might be able to lighten up enough by discharging ballast or cargo, or perhaps by jettisoning enough cargo (the ultimate sacrifice), to refloat itself. But if these methods fail or for some reason they are not feasible, the remaining alternatives will probably involve the use of beach gear, or assistance from tugs.

Salvors, of course, will employ any and all of these methods—singularly or collectively if necessary to refloat a ship. Each method has its merits and deficiencies. Waiting for the tide is cheapest if the ship doesn't have to wait too long for a high enough tide. But even in this case, it might be wise to have a tug standing by to avoid having the vessel broach when it is free of the bottom.

Discharging ballast if it is prudent or practical is the next simplest method. The salvor should consider the effect this will have on the vessel's stability since the ship will already have suffered a loss of GM (metacentric height) because of the shift in the center of buoyancy.

Discharging cargo is an acceptable method of lightening ship, but sea conditions may not permit the necessary lighters and barges to lie alongside. Furthermore, usually only break-bulk freighters and tankers are likely to have the necessary gear aboard to carry out the discharge unassisted. The jettison of cargo is a last resort—and in the case of a tanker loaded with crude the financial penalties and costs of the cleanup are likely to exceed the value of the ship and its cargo.

Beach gear or tugs are often employed in conjunction with other efforts and are almost certain to be used when other alternatives have failed. Beach gear, of course, is the traditional method of refloating stranded ships. It consists of heavy wire rope falls attached to a strong cable that in turn is secured to an anchor and several shots of chain for weight and is set offshore of the ship. Sometimes the gear is laid out on the deck of a barge fitted with winches, and is attached to the ship by heavy cables. In other instances the ship may use one of its own anchors attached to a cable and rig tackles on deck. The falls in this case have sometimes been contrived from the vessel's own cargo gear. The average set of beach gear can develop 40 to 60 tons of pull and often several sets of gear will be used to provide sufficient power to pull the vessel off. Beach gear rigged on barges is still often used but many modern salvage tugs are fitted with powerful winches and heavy anchors (usually Eell-type anchors) that can exert up to 100 tons of pull on the anchor cable. The salvage vessels will usually set out their anchors and then pass their tow cable to the stranded ship. This arrangement has the same function as conventional beach gear but is much easier to set up.

Tugs are usually the first vessels called to assist a ship that has grounded. But until fairly recently (within the last generation) their power was comparatively limited—usually less than 1,600 horsepower. This was often insufficient to refloat a large ship that was hard aground.

For this reason tugs often served in an auxiliary capacity or handled the barges fitted with beach gear. But things have changed in recent years. There are now plenty of 3,000 to 5,000 horsepower tugs around, and some tugs have up to 9,000 horsepower. Many have Kort nozzles and hydroconic bottoms and can generate bollard pull in excess of 200,000 pounds. These powerful tugs can provide a competitive alternative to standard salvage operations using beach gear. One reason for this is that beach gear generates a static pull in the direction that the anchor is placed. The tugs, on the other hand, can move about and pull from different directions. When this is done, tugs can "twist" the vessel from side to side which helps break the grip of suction from the bottom. If the vessel is aground at one end, or in one area of its bottom, the overhanging portion of the ship becomes, in effect, a giant lever that the tug can pull against and which can greatly increase the tug's effectiveness.

As noted above, tugs are usually the first vessels called to assist a ship aground, since they are nearly always available on short notice. "Like ants at a picnic," as one disgusted salvor noted when he arrived too late with his salvage vessel. In this case a pilot or salvage master can be grateful for any experience he might have had with tugs in this kind of operation.

There are certain elementary steps that should be taken as soon as possible after a vessel goes aground:

1. Determine if the vessel is holed.
2. Check the vessel's draft to determine how much it is aground.
3. Take soundings around the vessel to determine where it is aground.
4. Note the state of the tide when the vessel grounded, and determine whether the range is increasing or decreasing.

The reasons for taking these measures are self-evident. If the vessel is holed, for example, and the ship is making more water than its pumps can control, it would be prudent to leave the vessel aground until the leak is repaired or more pumps are available. The difference in draft before and after grounding would give some idea of the amount of ground effect, and soundings around the perimeter of the ship will locate the portion of the ship that is aground and perhaps indicate the area of the vessel's bottom where damage is likely to have occurred. This may also be a good indicator of how the tugs can be most efficiently employed. Vessels aground all along the bottom in soft sand or mud usually come off best in the direction opposite to the one in which they went aground. Of course, twisting the vessel some helps break the suction of the bottom against the hull—which may be a large component of the resistance necessary to overcome.

Sometimes it helps to spot the tugs so that their wheel wash helps dredge away material from the side of the vessel. This is best accomplished by making the tugs fast on a short towline at various stations along the ship's side and moving them progressively from one position to another if this action is effective.

If the vessel is aground on one side only which sometimes occurs when a pilot overshoots a bend, it is often possible to have the tugs push against the inshore side of the ship, providing there is enough water there. It is probably best to have the tugs concentrate their effort near the stern so that the vessel can back clear as it comes off without damaging the stern gear (rudder and propeller) unless the bottom is quite soft (Fig. 16-1).

Vessels that ground on a lump or a bank and are only aground in one place (fore, aft, or midship) usually respond best if they can be swung from side to side. On sand or mud bottom this tends to flatten the lump, and on coral or limestone bottom it has a tendency to grind down the material until the vessel comes free. Vessels that are aground on steep-to, firm mud banks or rounded cobble stones can come off with very little warning 't is a good idea for both the ship's crew and the tug's crew to anticipate this possibility.

The kind of groundings that a shiphandler is most likely to encounter usually occur in protected waters. This makes salvage efforts easier and safer. But occasionally ships go ashore in areas exposed to heavy seas or wave action, often just outside the breakwater or harbor entrance.

If a vessel does ground in an exposed area and a tug can come alongside safely, it may be wise to have it spot the ship's anchors to weather to prevent it working farther ashore. The anchors, however, are not likely to be much help refloating the ship if the vessel drove ashore bow first since the lead of the chain will be foul in the hawse, unless it is a stern anchor. Anchors can, however, be detached from their chains and connected to cables that can be heaved with falls laid out on deck of the ship like beach gear (Fig. 16-2).

In the event it is not possible to set the anchors, the vessel should ballast down if the sea makes up to avoid going harder aground. In this

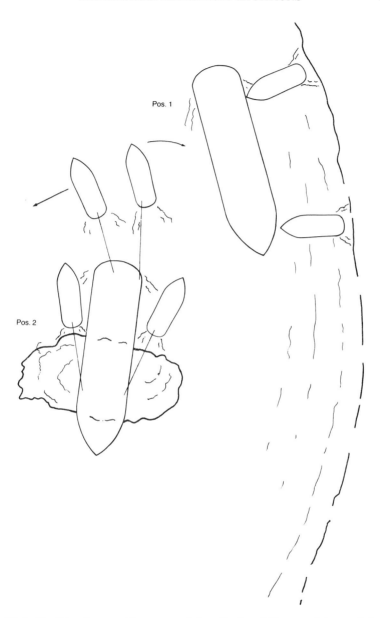

Fig. 16-1. Position 1: vessel has grounded on the bend. Tugs pushing on inboard side will probably be most effective in refloating vessel. Position 2: vessel may find it advantageous to have tugs pulling from alongside to dredge material away from shipside. Tugs pulling on stern should swing from side to side to "twist" the vessel as this will help break the suction.

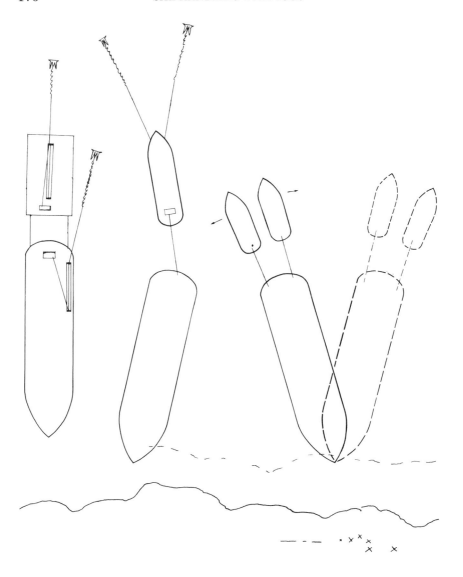

Fig. 16-2. Different aspects of refloating a vessel by traction are shown: beach gear rigged on a barge; beach gear rigged on the vessel; a salvage vessel with the anchor cables led to winches; and the tugs. The tugs can pull from different directions to twist the vessel.

instance even if only one small tug arrives on the scene, it should put up a line and take a strain, until more help arrives. This may prevent the ship from "climbing the beach" or broaching. If a vessel broaches on a rocky shore more hull damage can occur. On sand beaches there is a tendency to "swallow" the ship (remember Cape Hatteras?). On a coral or limestone shore the vessel will have a tendency to dig itself in and will be much harder to refloat.

Tugs should be ready to make their maximum effort at the peak of the flood tide. Fuel and ballast should be shifted or discharged if it is helpful to lighten or trim the ship beforehand. The pilot or salvage master should be in constant radio contact with the tugs when they are working. If the vessel comes off suddenly as vessels sometimes do, the results can be disastrous if communication is not maintained. I saw this happen once with nine tugs working on towlines. The ship came off as though it were propelled by a giant slingshot. The confusion was unbelievable. Fortunately, only one tug was seriously endangered and its hawser parted saving it from a probable capsize. No two salvages are ever exactly alike, but there are certain fundamental rules that apply:

1. You should make maximum effort to refloat the vessel at high tide.
2. You must place the tugs where their wheel wash will dredge away material if the bottom is soft and the vessel is aground fore and aft.
3. If tugs are working close together on towlines have them adjust their hawsers to the same length. If the tugs come together they are usually well fendered and no damage is likely to occur. However, if one tug strikes another's hawser it is likely to part and do severe damage or injury.
4. If the vessel starts to move at all, even from side to side, have the tugs maneuver to sustain the motion.
5. Realize that even if a vessel can refloat itself with its own engine, it may require a tug to assist in steering until it reaches deeper water.
6. As the salvage master you should stay alert and maintain contact with the tugs the entire time they are working.

USING TUGS IN EMERGENCIES

Most emergencies affecting vessels in pilotage waters fall into one or more of these five categories: (1) fire; (2) holed or sinking; (3) stranded (discussed above); (4) loss of power; and (5) loss of steering.

As noted, tugs are suitable for assisting in most of these situations since they are powerful and maneuverable. If they are fitted with fire-fighting gear, as many are (especially at oil terminals), their capabilities in an emergency may be enhanced.

Fire. While fire may not be the most common emergency it is potentially the most dangerous of those listed. It is often essential, especially in the case of tankers, to remove the tankers from their berths. In this case this is likely to be the tug's first priority. Ships normally have "fire wires" hung over the side, fore and aft, for tugs to make fast to—for this purpose. Before approaching the ship, the tug should have its towing gear ranged (towline or cable, shackles, etc.), fire hoses led out and tended, and the crew should be dressed in oilskins or fire-fighting gear.

The tug will normally back up to the ship to take it in tow astern. Fire hoses can be played upon the ship to reduce the heat and protect the crew while they are securing the towline to the fire warp. Other vessels can also help by directing their fire monitors or hoses in such a fashion that they will cool the area. The tug should slack 200 to 250 feet of hawser or tow cable before taking an *easy* strain in order to avoid parting the fire wire (Fig. 16-3).

If the tugs are secured at both bow and stern of the ship, they can control the vessel fairly well. However, if only one tug is used, it is probably best secured forward (unless the vessel is trimmed heavily by the bow) as the ship will be easier to control. It will still tend to sheer away from the side that the tug is secured to, but this tendency will normally be less pronounced if the tug is forward than it would be if the tug were aft. In either case, if a tug can get alongside at the opposite end of the vessel and push against the same side that the towing tug is on, it can assist in maintaining control over the ship (Fig. 16-4).

Once the vessel is clear of the dock, it is often convenient to ground it. This should be done in an area where the bottom is flat and soft so that the ship will not be unnecessarily damaged when the tide drops. If the tug is required to assist at fire fighting, it will usually be directed by professional fire fighters.

Vessel Sinking or Holed. If the ship is sinking or holed, it will need the tug to assist in putting it aground (as quickly as possible) although tugs

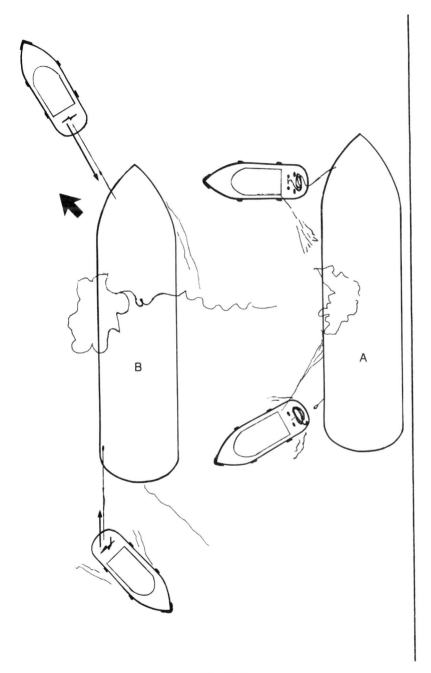

Fig. 16-3.

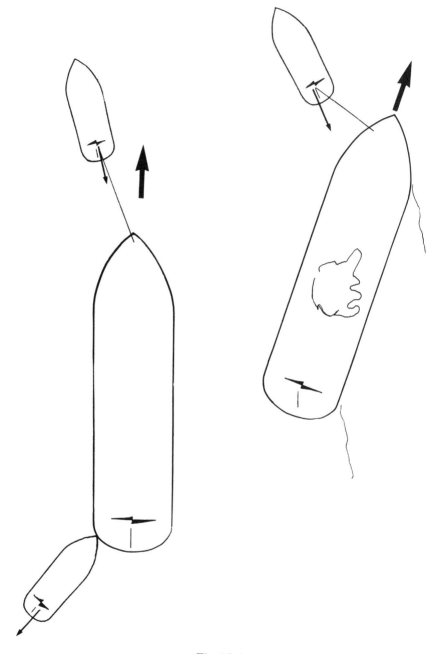

Fig. 16-4.

have been used to breast a vessel that had been holed against the dock to keep it from capsizing or sliding into deeper water. In this instance, the vessel was resting on a slanting bottom that deepened from the dock outward.

If a tank vessel is holed and leaking flammable products, the tug should stay clear of this area, as it is likely to be gassy. The fumes could cause a galley or an engine room explosion. In this instance the tug may only be able to approach the vessel from the weather side, and even this might be hazardous (Fig. 16-5).

Loss of Power. This is a dead ship situation as described in Chapter 15. By use of a towline, a small tug can handle a very large ship that would be impossible to handle on the hip. If it only has a short distance to tow and is having trouble controlling the ship made up to the bow, the tug can take the vessel in tow stern first while the ship drags one of its anchors for directional stability. (See Chapter 18.)

Loss of Steering. A tug can readily assist a vessel with loss of steering to steer. It can work nicely on a towline ahead of the vessel especially if the vessel is light forward. The vessel should steam ahead *slowly* to avoid tripping the tug.

The tug can also steer the vessel by making up alongside forward, where it can control the ship at moderate speeds by pushing or backing. It can also hip up on the quarter of the vessel and employ the tug's engine in opposition to the ship's engine (ahead and astern) for a twin-screw effect. The tug's rudder can also be helpful in this instance.

The tug can also steer the stern of the vessel when circumstances permit by making up dead astern of the vessel and pushing on either side of the stern as needed, or, in the case of a smaller vessel, sheering the stern as is sometimes done with tailboats. (See Chapters 11 and 19.)

Some Priorities. Tug masters should be aware of the order of their responsibilities. Their first priority is the safety and welfare of their crews. Their next most important concern should be for their own vessel. Then their final considerations will be the vessel they are assisting. They might be justified in risking their crews to save lives, but they must weigh the risk carefully before exposing their personnel to undue hazard to save property. Those who employ a tug master's services should also be aware of these responsibilities.

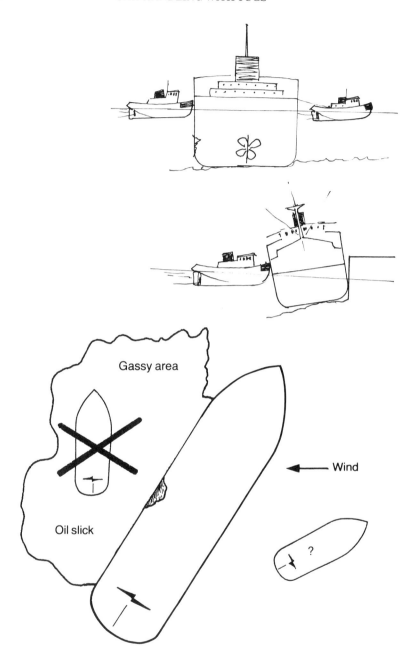

Fig. 16-5.

STUDY QUESTIONS

1. When a vessel goes aground, what forces must be overcome to refloat it?
2. What procedures are used to refloat a vessel?
3. Which is the least desirable method?
4. What are the first steps to be taken after a vessel goes aground?
5. If a vessel is holed, should it be refloated?
6. What is one of the effects of current?
7. What effects can heavy seas have on a vessel aground?
8. What should a vessel do to avoid being washed farther aground?
9. If the vessel can refloat itself, why is it sometimes prudent to use a tug?
10. How may a small tug assist a ship that is aground?
11. What is "beach gear"?
12. Are tugs sometimes more effective than beach gear?
13. What type of emergencies might a tug have to respond to?
14. How should a tug take a ship in tow that is on fire?
15. Can one tug control the ship?
16. How can a tug assist a ship that has a power failure?
17. How can a tug assist a vessel that has lost its steering?
18. If a tank vessel is holed and the area is gassy, what should the tug do?
19. List a tug captain's responsibilities in order of importance in an emergency.

CHAPTER SEVENTEEN

USING TUGS IN EXPOSED WATERS

The increase in the size of ships that has taken place in the last genera-tion has sometimes created problems in berthing for many of these vessels. Some of them are so large that few harbors can accommodate them. Consequently, they must often load and discharge their cargos at moorings and berths located in open roadsteads. As in other circum-stances, tugs will be required to assist these ships to maneuver, and to dock and undock in safety. On other occasions, ships may require tugs to make fast alongside in open waters when they are approaching harbors with narrow channels, particularly if there is a heavy current set across the channel. In both instances, the ship and the tug are subjected to a risk of damage caused by heavy contacts due to sea conditions that do not exist in ordinary shipwork. It is apparent that the tug should be especially well fendered for this type of service. The bow fender must be ample, and very well secured to avoid having it come adrift if the tug pitches heavily when it pushes against the ship. For this reason some tugs, like the one shown in Fig 17-1, have heavy pneumatic wheel type fenders that will roll up and down the ship's side as the tug pitches. This is a definite improvement over conventional fenders for working in exposed waters.

While fendering is important, there are also other considerations. Working lines should be of a larger size than normal. They should also be given a longer lead to prevent them from parting as they come under heavy strain during the rise and fall of the tug in the swells. Deep-loaded ships are usually fairly stable platforms, and tugs can often make up safely in their lee in fairly rough seas. Ships in ballast often roll quite a bit, and special care must be taken as the tug comes alongside since considerable impact can result from the ships rolling against each other. I have seen damage occur in these circumstances, even with

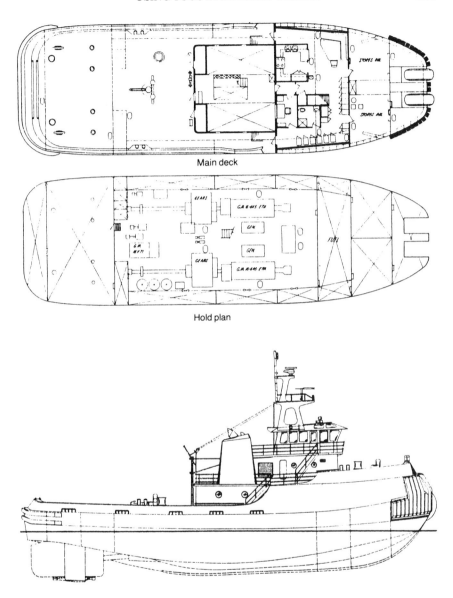

Main deck

Hold plan

Fig. 17-1. An interesting twin-screw tug of 5,700 horsepower designed for docking VLCCs and ULCCs in exposed areas. The tug is fitted with Kort nozzles and flanking rudders. The bow-fender system includes two heavy pneumatic tires that permit the tug to roll up and down the shipside in a seaway. It also has a quick-release towing hook. Courtesy: Atlantic Marine Inc.

well-fendered tugs. The fenders simply did not extend far enough down to protect the ship's side.

Tugs respond more slowly to their engine and rudders in a seaway than they do in quiet water. You, the operator, regardless of your skill, will not be able to maneuver with the same degree of finesse in rough water as you would in calm conditions. The pilot or docking master must anticipate this negative effect on the tug's maneuverability under rough weather conditions.

Towline work is particularly suitable for shiphandling in exposed waters, if it is practicable, as it minimizes or eliminates contact between the ship and the tug. Here again, the hawser length should be increased, in order to moderate the effect of the swells on the strain of the towline. Prudence dictates the handling of the vessel at slow and moderate speeds to avoid damage. If damage does occur as a result of contact between the ship and the tug in a heavy seaway, it is not likely to be minor.

Occasionally a tug will be used to assist a vessel making fast to an SPM (single-point mooring). The conditions here are what you would normally expect to encounter in any unsheltered area. The large vessel that normally loads or discharges at this facility must make an extended approach to the mooring buoy. This is a delicate balancing act between the forces of wind and current and the vessel's often-limited maneuverability at slow speed. And, it is often a protracted process since it takes a while for the vessel's headway to dissipate and to make the final approach with bare steerageway. Unless the current is running strongly, bare steerageway will be lost as soon as the vessel backs its engine to stop. At this juncture the vessel must be close enough to the buoy and remain in this position long enough for the mooring gear (usually chain or cable) to be passed aboard and secured.

In a situation where wind is no factor, a vessel with a right-hand propeller would approach the buoy from down current with the buoy dead ahead or fine to port so that it would clear the buoy as it responded to the torque of the propeller when it backed—but still be close enough to pass the lines. This is a ticklish maneuver, but not necessarily dangerous (unless the SPM is a structure). However, a lot of time can be lost if the shiphandler misjudges the situation, or the vessel handles poorly. A tug can provide some welcome assistance in this instance by helping the vessel to steer—particularly during the final approach, and especially keeping the vessel in shape when it backs. This can be quite helpful when the wind is at odds with the current, and if the ship has a tendency to *weathervane* (to head or to back into wind) as soon as the engine is rung astern.

A tug is best employed alongside forward, and clear of the chocks where the mooring gear is to be passed. A tug on a towline might interfere with the mooring operation (Fig. 17-2). Since the ship is moving very slowly and must of course stop to pick up the mooring, a tug of relatively moderate power can be useful in this situation. Many SPMs are unattended by tugs, but if tugs are available, they should be used to avoid unnecessary delays and to eliminate the uncertainties that are common when large ships are handled at slow speeds.

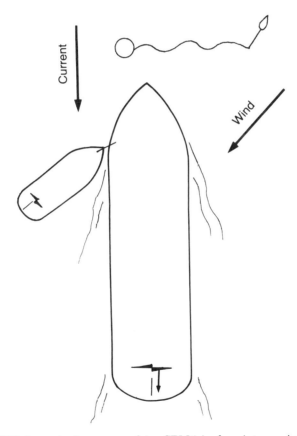

Fig. 17-2. With large tanker approaching SPM (single point mooring), tug may be required to back or push to keep the vessel in shape when it backs its engine to stop.

STUDY QUESTIONS

1. What additional considerations must be given to a tug assisting ships in exposed waters?
2. What is a roller fender and is it suitable for this type of shipwork?
3. In addition to the use of roller fenders, what other precautions should be taken?
4. Does a tug handle the same in a seaway as it does in protected waters?
5. How does a tug assist a vessel mooring to an SPM?

CHAPTER EIGHTEEN

TUGS AND ANCHORS

An extended discussion on the use of anchors per se is beyond the scope of this volume. Our concern here is confined to applications where anchors are used in conjunction with tugs for shiphandling. If you are interested in other aspects of this subject you should refer to books listed in the Bibliography.

When an anchor is used as an accessory to shiphandling, it is often referred to as a "poor man's tugboat." This is an interesting if not altogether accurate analogy. It is true that when anchors are used judiciously, they sometimes allow the shiphandler the option of dispensing with the services of a tug. There are also occasions when the use of anchors might be preferable to using a tug. However, anchors function differently from tugs—they are essentially *passive* devices. They can neither push nor pull like a tug can unless they are being heaved in after they have been dropped. When the vessel is docking or maneuvering, the principal function of the anchor is to act as a restraint. For example, the anchor can be used to stabilize the light bow of the ship on a windy day if enough chain is slacked to allow the anchor to drag along the bottom. If the bow continues to blow off, then more chain is slacked—carefully—until the vessel responds.

When the proper amount of chain is slacked out (usually a shot to a shot and a half at the water's edge—depending upon the depth of the water and the nature of the bottom), the resistance of the anchor dragging through the material on the bottom can help a vessel maintain steerage at very slow speeds with the engine working ahead. The ship may not even have to back its engine to stop when docking, since the resistance of the anchor may be sufficient to check its way when the engine is stopped.

This is all very useful. Nevertheless, the only time that the anchor can be used to pull is when it is used as a brake to check a vessel's way and as a *deadman* (or a kedge) to heave against. It cannot *push* at all.

When the anchor is used in conjunction with a tug, it continues to function passively except when it is used as a deadman. It may be used to restrain the vessel's motion (ahead or astern). It can also be used to stabilize a vessel's direction of movement. It can fix (subject to the amount of chain used) the position of the bow (or the stern—if a stern anchor is used) of the vessel while a tug maneuvers the other end of the ship. When it is used as a deadman, the bow (or the stern) of the vessel can be maneuvered by heaving while a tug pushes or pulls the other end of the vessel as required. For example, it can be very handy for undocking a ship (Fig. 18-1). The anchor can also be used to provide directional stability to a vessel being towed stern first by a tug or, when that vessel is backing with a tug made up on the quarter, to steer the stern.

There are a number of more or less typical maneuvers somewhat like the Mediterranean moor where the vessel is turned through 180°. The tug is used to assist the vessel through the turn while the anchor stabilizes the bow (Fig. 18-2).

Whenever tugs and anchors are being used for shiphandling, you, as the pilot, should be sure that you exercise the same degree of control over the anchor that you do over the tug, and that the mate on the bow understands his orders. If, for example, the anchor is dropped prematurely or too late, the ship could be left poorly positioned to complete the maneuver. If too much chain is slacked, it may not be possible for the anchor to be heaved back aboard the ship once it is berthed (if this is desirable). Conversely, if too little chain is slacked, it may not have desired effect, and the vessel will not respond as expected.

Sometimes the anchor is used as a deadman and the chain must be heaved in when the vessel is unberthing. If it is heaved too fast, the anchor can cause the vessel's bow to swing more than is desirable, making the vessel difficult to control. Some maneuvers typical of the use of anchors with tugs are shown in Fig. 18-3.

Some ships are also fitted with stern anchors. They are common on passenger liners, and are occasionally seen on other types of vessels. They can be very useful, especially when the vessel is required to anchor in confined areas, or when it is desirable to keep the vessel from swinging too much. They are also used for holding the ship in position to make a lee when embarking and disembarking passengers from launches.

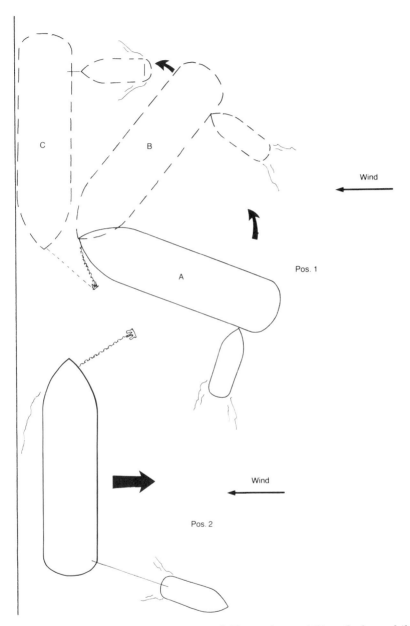

Fig. 18-1. Position 1: vessel is being turned. The anchor stabilizes the bow while the tug pushes the stern around. The anchor will prevent the bow from landing heavily on the dock. Position 2: vessel is using the anchor to heave the bow off the dock while the tug tows the stern clear.

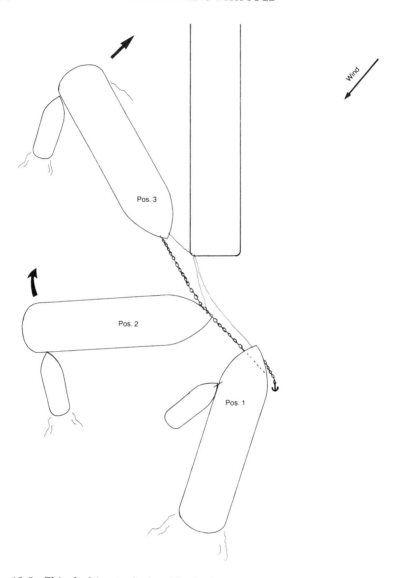

Fig. 18-2. Ship docking to the leeside of a finger pier with a single tug and using the anchor.

Position 1: tug is placed forward until the anchor is dropped and a head line has been passed to the end of the dock. Position 2: tug has shifted to the opposite quarter and will turn the ship. Position 3: tug is breasting the ship to the dock and also pushing it easily astern. The wind is holding the bow of the vessel off the dock. The anchor chain must be slacked judiciously, and the head line tended on the capstan.

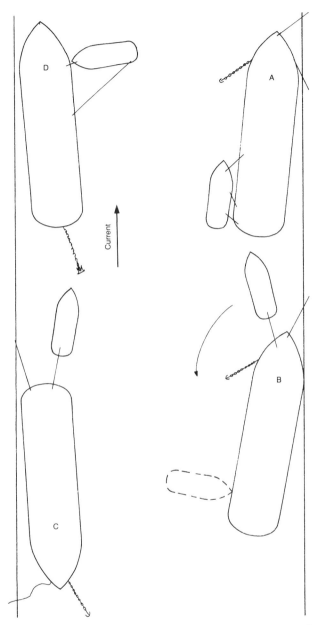

Fig. 18-3. Tugs being used in conjunction with anchors to berth ships.
Tug handling vessel B may have to shift to breast the stern of the ship alongside
the dock, depending upon the direction of the wind. Tug handling vessel C is
towing the vessel stern first into its berth.

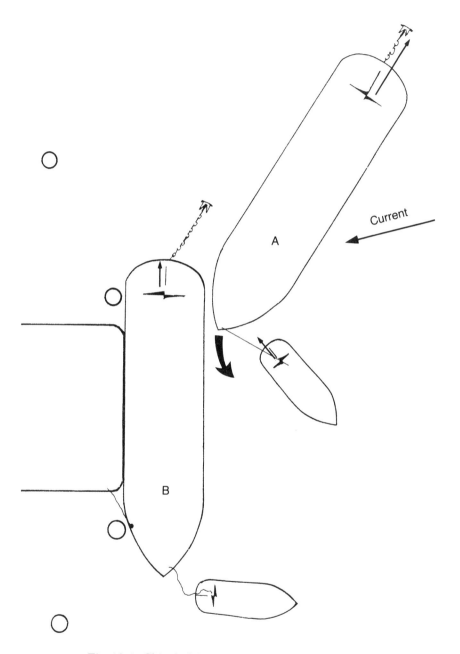

Fig. 18-4. Ship docking with fair current on the dock.

Stern anchors are most useful when docking and undocking in fair current situations (Fig. 18-4). The pilot though should use a great deal of caution when stern anchors are used, and make sure that the chain is always leading astern, for if the vessel does override the chain when backing or maneuvering the rudders and propellers could be damaged.

STUDY QUESTIONS

1. Why is an anchor called a "poor man's tugboat"?
2. How does using an anchor differ from using a tug?
3. When a vessel is maneuvering, how is the anchor used?
4. In what other ways is the anchor used?
5. How is the anchor used when tugs are also employed?
6. How are stern anchors used?
7. What danger is attendant in heaving a stern anchor?

CHAPTER NINETEEN

TUGS AND TAILBOATS

Those who decry the decline of our maritime skills should watch some of the shiphandling operations that are carried out under demanding circumstances. It might cause them to revise their opinions in this respect. For instance, I am referring to a small towing company that handles ships upriver in the port of Miami, Florida. This is a tortuous waterway with many bridges and heavy traffic from pleasure as well as commercial craft. Both banks of the river are lined with docks, ship-yards, and vessels of all descriptions, all of them vulnerable to damage from passing vessels. The ships, small island freighters for the most part, are all towed upriver and down, just as often stern first as bow first, since in many parts of the river there is insufficient room to turn a vessel.

The small handy tugboats do a phenomenal job employing the only method available to them due to the restriction in width at the bridges. The tug on the head of the ship (or whichever end is foremost) makes fast with a fiber hawser bridle. The tug on the after end runs two head lines to opposite quarters of the vessel. The ships must be handled with great precision, especially when passing under the bridges, as the width of the draw is often barely wide enough to accommodate them. Many of the ships are so large that a vessel's superstructure would strike the raised portions of the bridge before the hull came into contact with the fender-works. Many of the bridges are located close together and at a consider-able angle to each other. It requires careful maneuvering to get the ship through without doing damage.

This is precision work. Almost anyone can get a ship halfway through a bridge. The hard part is getting the last half of the vessel through without hitting anything. The leading tug steers the forward part of the ship, but the tailboat must sheer the after part of the vessel, as is needed, for it to pass safely through these narrow openings. In practice, it resembles the maneuvers that a hook and ladder fire truck is required to make while transiting narrow city streets with one of the firemen steering the rear end of the truck.

For such close quarters work, the lead tug must be made up with a very short towline, and bridles are definitely needed. Gate lines might also prove useful for this type of work. These gate lines are separate lines led from either bow of the tow to the opposite quarter of the tug. The tailboat would, of course, put up two head lines that lead to the stern of the vessel on either side. It might better to lead these lines directly to the bitts on the bow of the tailboat rather than through the bullnose, since it helps if the bow extends a short distance forward of where the head lines are made fast. This permits the tug to sheer the stern of the vessel to one side or the other more readily, or perhaps lie on an angle to act as a brake. I have no doubt that there are many ports where similar situations exist, and shiphandlers might profit by watching some of these tugs in action (Fig. 19-1).

However, it is not only in small ports where this method of handling is appropriate, nor is it only ships that are handled this way. Immense offshore oil platforms are loaded on huge barges and handled similarly. Usually there are two or more tailboats, and perhaps two or more tugs towing the unit. Drill rigs and other large vessels and structures can also be handled this way, but they will all be under the command of those familiar with using tugs.

Somewhat similar methods are also in use in other ports. In one port, which can accommodate vessels as large as VLCCs, the ships proceed under their own power through the channel with tugs fast alongside forward to aid in steering, but use tailboats aft that are fast on the quarters. These tailboats have flanking rudders and help keep the vessels under control at slow speed as they can steer the stern effectively. They can also assist in slowing the ship's headway (Fig. 19-2).

In the Gulf Coast area, a practice known as *coon-assing* is common. (This slang term is used by the boatmen of southern Louisiana.) In this case, the tailboat makes fast to the center of the stern of the barge, floating derrick, or other piece of floating equipment. The tug assists in propelling the vessel by pushing and in steering the vessel as it can push the stern to one side or the other. This might not work on many ships because of the configuration of the stern, but the effect is similar to having a tug steer a vessel when it moves ahead or astern by pressing

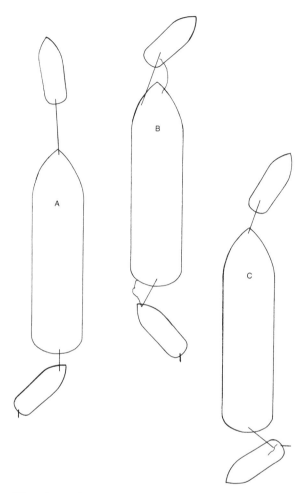

Fig. 19-1. Three examples of the use of tug and tailboat.

Vessel A is being towed in open waters by a tug with a fairly long towline. The after tug is made fast with a single head line led to the center chock. The after tug can back to check the ship's speed, and can sheer the vessel's stern to a limited extent.

Vessel B is being handled in confined waters. The forward tug is made fast with bridle or gate lines. The after tug is made fast with a short bridle led to the ship's quarters and secured directly to the tug's forward bitts. The forward tug will be able to maintain excellent control of the ship's bow and the after tug will be able to check the vessel's way and to sheer the vessel's stern for steerage.

Vessel C is being shifted to another berth. The forward tug is secured with a short towline. The after tug is used for braking and is towed—slowly—stern first. A gobline is used to keep the after tug from being tripped.

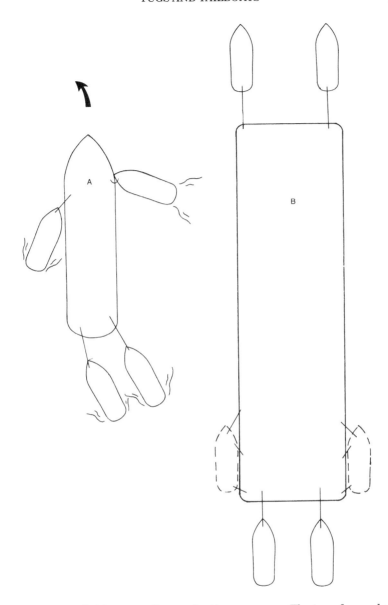

Fig. 19-2. Vessel A is proceeding under its own power. The tugs forward assist in steering; the tugs aft are fitted with Kort nozzles and flanking rudders which enable them to steer the stern as well as brake the vessel. Vessel B is a large barge of the type used to transport offshore drill rigs. The after tugs may hip up to the barge in protected waters for better control if the structural limitations permit it.

against the side of the bow or the stern to direct the vessel's movement. This maneuver has been more fully described in Chapter 11.

There are occasions when the after tug may work stern first. This is usually only for short distances, since the vessel must proceed very slowly to avoid endangering the tug. Handling this way can control the after end of the ship very well and the tug can often act as a brake simply by letting itself be towed along while it lies at an angle. This must, of course, be done with a great deal of care to avoid girding the tug. For safety's sake, it would be a good idea for a gobline to be used to avoid capsizing the tug. Offshore oil rigs are also moved in this fashion. Due to their size and configuration, they are unwieldy tows and are directionally unstable. Depending on the horsepower of the tugs, they may require two or more powerful tugs to tow, with tailboats on either side aft, made fast with head lines to provide the braking effect necessary for directional control. The riskiest part of this operation often occurs when the tugs are connecting up. The rigs are often located in areas exposed to rough seas and strong currents. It helps if the rig personnel are alert and familiar with the line-handling process since the tugs may have difficulty maintaining position if there are any delays in passing the towing pendants that connect to the tugs' towing cables (Fig. 19-3, Position 2).

There is another variation on the tug and tailboat theme that is seen in some waters where the channel is fairly long and narrow with ship berths close to the channel. The purpose here is to retard the speed of the vessel transiting these waterways so that the suction will not cause vessels docked in this area to surge in their berths and perhaps part mooring lines or cargo hoses. Large motorships in particular use this practice since even "dead slow" speed on their engines may be excessive for the circumstances. In practice the forward tug is made fast alongside to assist in steering and the after tug usually puts up two head lines—one to each quarter—and backs its engines to reduce the ship's headway in critical areas (Fig. 19-3, Position 1). The ship, of course, proceeds ahead at its slowest speed, depending on its own rudder and the forward tug for steerage and the after tug to reduce its forward way.

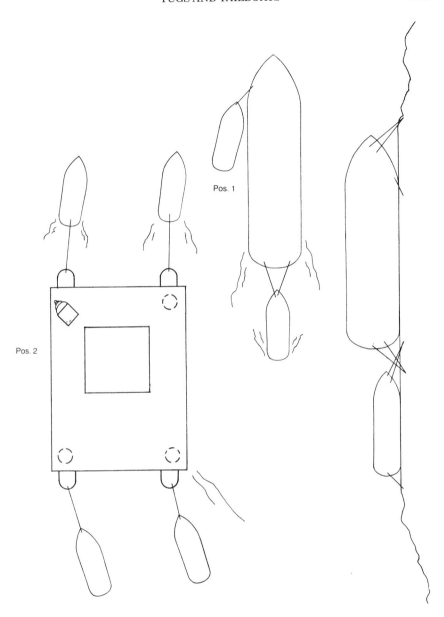

Fig. 19-3. Position 1: a large motorship is underway in a congested waterway. The forward tug's purpose is to assist in steering the vessel. The after tug's function is to act as a brake and reduce the ship's headway when passing near other vessels in their berth. This will keep the docked ships from surging and parting lines. Position 2: a typical arrangement for using tugs in shifting oil rigs.

STUDY QUESTIONS

1. What is a tailboat?
2. What is its purpose?
3. How does it accomplish this purpose?
4. Explain how braking works.
5. How does "sheering" the stern work?
6. How is steering the stern accomplished?
7. How is a tailboat "made up" to the ship?
8. What precautions should be taken when a towline is used?
9. What service is this method best suited for?
10. What kind of ships can be handled in this fashion?

CHAPTER TWENTY

HANDLING THE ITB

Before I begin my discussion on the handling of the ITB (integrated tug-barge), I want to explain what kind of an ITB I am referring to. The United States Coast Guard's Bureau of Marine Inspection has defined as follows two entirely different types of vessels as an ITB:

1. *Pushing-mode ITB* which consists of a propelling unit that is *rigidly* connected to a barge, and which is designed to remain so for the duration of the voyage. Some units with an articulated connecting system are also included in this category.

2. *Dual-mode ITB* which consists of a tug capable of operating either in the pushing or towing mode, and a barge fitted out to accommodate either mode of propulsion.

Since the pushing-mode ITB is for all practical purposes treated as a ship, my interest here is confined to the dual-mode ITB, which is also sometimes referred to as the deep-notch tug-barge unit.

For the sake of convenience these dual-mode ITBs are divided—perhaps arbitrarily—into three basic types: first, second, and third generation units, the principal distinction between these categories being their relationship to the depth of the notch.

The first generation ITB has a small notch at the stern of the barge, 4 to 7 feet. The tug pushes the barge (usually in protected waters) when weather permits, and when the draft of the barge permits the tug to make up safely in the notch. This usually requires that the barge be either fully or partially loaded, so that the tug is not likely to be damaged under the after rake as it might be if the barge were light.

The second generation ITB has a deeper notch, perhaps 7 to 20 feet, that permits the tug to push the barge offshore in fair weather. Furthermore, the range of the barge's draft may be less critical for the tug to make up safely.

The third generation ITB often has a notch more than half of the length of the tug and in some instances the walls of the notch are contiguous with the skegs. This usually permits the tug to make up safely even if the barge is light and to push the barge at sea in fairly boisterous weather.

In many instances the tug is "dedicated" to a particular barge, though there are some fleets in which a number of the tugs and barges are interchangeable. The tug is structurally reenforced and fendered for this work and usually has an elevated pilothouse in addition to the regular bridge to permit visibility over a light barge, or one loaded with a high deck load. Ordinarily the tug is secured in the notch by a head line or safety lines, and the cables or fiber lines that make up the pushing gear. These are referred to variously as slings, skeg wires, push wires, etc. They are secured and tightened in several different fashions, and sometimes utilize the tug's towing winch to heave the pushing cables tight.

When circumstances permit, the ITB is operated in the pushing mode, especially when the barge is loaded. The reason for this is that pushing the barge eliminates the drag caused by the towing hawser or cable and the loss of speed caused by the yawing of the barge. This loss of speed due to yaw, however, with a light barge may be relatively insignificant.

COMMON CHARACTERISTICS OF THE ITB

As you can see the ITB is much too diverse in its potential makeup for generalizations to be applied. Some are large, some are small. Some must be handled on the hip when light, others may be handled from the notch when they are in this condition. There are, however, some characteristics shared by all of them.

1. When the ITB is light, it is affected by wind conditions, and the tug handler must anticipate and compensate for the effect the wind will have upon the ITB when maneuvering in confined quarters, and when docking and undocking.

2. With the tug in the notch when the barge is loaded, the ITB will often have a tendency to skid or slide sideways when making a turn. This is usually the result of starting a turn too late or trying to power through a turn. If this tendency is not checked or is not anticipated, the whole rig might go aground or cause some damage (see Fig. 20-1).

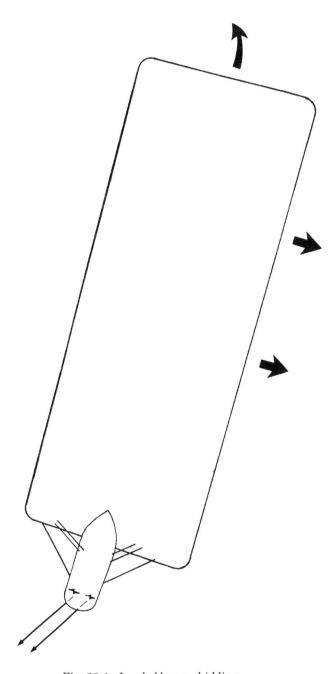

Fig. 20-1. Loaded barge skidding.

3. The tug should exercise care when backing its engines when the barge is deep loaded and barely afloat. In this case the tug is usually not as deep as the barge and some of the wheel wash will strike the notch and the rest will deflect downward by the after rake of the barge. In deep water the barge will respond normally, but in shallow water the barge may move erratically to the side or even move ahead as the confined wheel wash jets out to the side or astern (Fig. 20-2).

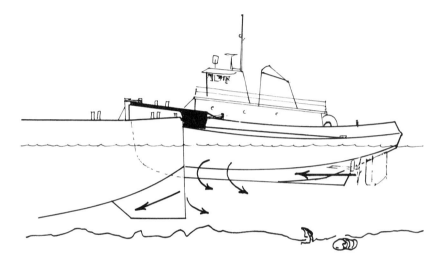

Fig. 20-2. Shallow water effect.

4. In the pushing mode the ITB must be handled fairly gingerly since the strain of maneuvering (backing, turning, etc.) falls mainly on the pushing gear—especially with first and second generation units. If the pushing gear parts, it could lead to an accident.

5. Almost all large, deep-loaded barges have a pronounced tendency to yaw or sheer when towed astern. At sea this characteristic may be more of a nuisance than a hazard. However, in confined waters with the barge being towed on a short hawser or cable, it can be extremely dangerous. With the ITB this situation normally occurs when the unit is crossing the bar, inbound or outbound, when sea conditions are too rough to permit the barge to be pushed by the tug in the notch.

It is this last situation that I particularly wish to address in this chapter. When the barge is entering from seaward, it should avoid shortening the tow cable more than is absolutely necessary since the shorter the tow cable is the greater the likelihood that the tug will become girt and might be tripped or capsized. It is essential that the barge's speed be kept slow especially when there are large turns to be made. The tug's captain should take particular care that the barge does not accelerate as the tug changes its heading, and thereby overpowers the tug (Fig. 20-3).

A speed in excess of 3 to 3½ knots might be excessive in this situation. If the barge must be towed faster than is prudent, in order to overcome current for example, then it is best to wait for sea conditions to abate and handle the barge with the tug in the notch. If the tug captain elects to tow the barge across the bar in adverse conditions, the towing winch should be tended so that the cable can be slacked in the event that the barge becomes unmanageable. It is better in this instance to have the barge go aground than for the tug to be rolled over and sunk.

Some tug captains will handle the barge with the tug in the notch even in fairly heavy seas when outbound by employing a practice often called coon-assing (described above). In this instance, the tug works free in the notch without the push wires (since they would most likely part) but with either a slack head line or safety lines. The tug controls the barge by steering its stern. In this case the tug becomes the rudder since it pushes the stern of the barge *away* from the desired direction of the turn (Fig. 20-4). Once the unit is outside, the tug will back clear of the notch, connect its tow cable to the barge's "shock line," and take the barge in tow astern. *Only a seasoned tug handler* familiar with this method of barge handling should attempt this maneuver, particularly when sea conditions are unfavorable.

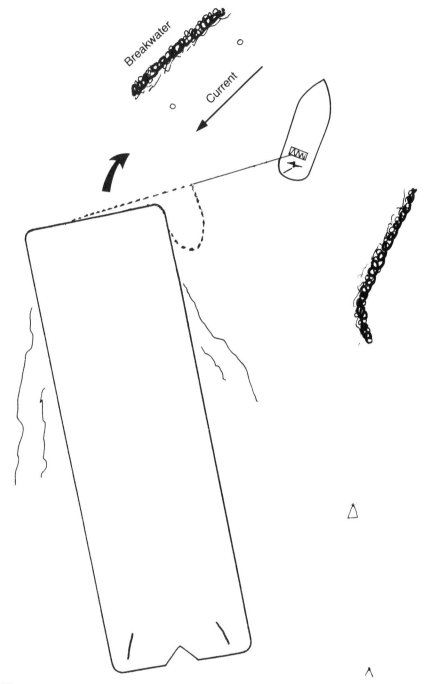

Fig. 20-3. Tug towing barge into an inlet with current ahead. Tug may become girt if barge fails to respond to the tug's change of direction.

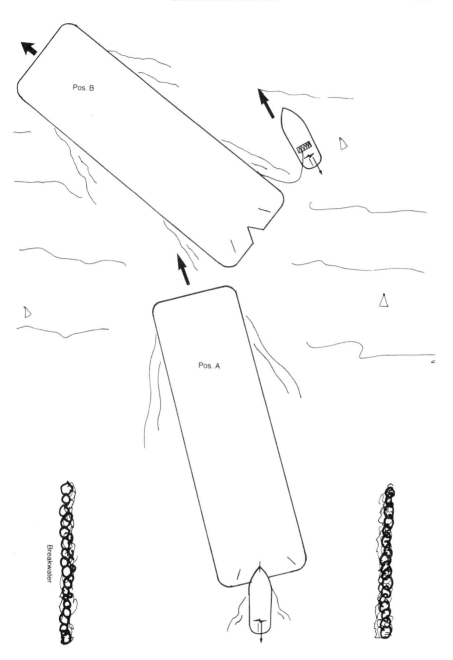

Fig. 20-4. Position A: tug is coon-assing barge (i.e., steering the stern) until it is clear of the inlet. Position B: barge is clear of inlet and tug is taking it in tow.

STUDY QUESTIONS

1. What is a dual-mode ITB?
2. When will the tug push the barge?
3. What factors determine when the tug can push the barge?
4. How do wind and sea conditions affect this?
5. When the tug is pushing, what precautions should the captain take?
6. What characteristics are shared by most large, deep-loaded barges on a towline?
7. When a deep-loaded barge is entering a channel from seaward, how must it be handled?
8. How may a tug control a barge by pushing without using pushing gear?

CHAPTER TWENTY-ONE

CONCLUSION

In concluding, it is necessary to emphasize some differences in technique employed in shiphandling with tugs as opposed to handling vessels without tug assistance. This relates particularly to the amount of engine power used when maneuvering a vessel and to the speed of the ship. For example, unassisted by a tug, a light ship with a lot of exposed freeboard might require a fair amount of power to kick it through a turn on a windy day. However, the same amount of power applied with a tug alongside would not be necessary and, in fact, may destroy the tug's effectiveness. A recent study undertaken by the United States Maritime Administration (see Appendix 2) confirmed this point; a tug's thrust begins to diminish rapidly at speeds over three knots and is severely diminished at excessive speed. In other words, a tug's effectiveness is almost inversely proportionate to the speed of the ship. The moral to this story is that if tugs are there to assist the vessel, let them work.

In reality the interaction between the tug and the ship is a collective effort—like that of an orchestra. The pilot or shiphandler, of course, is the conductor. The success or failure of the performance is contingent upon several factors: the knowledge of the shiphandler, the quality of the instruments (both ship and tug), and the skills of all of the performers—this includes the tug's captain and crew as well as the officers and crew of the ship.

A deficiency in any aspect of this operation (whether of equipment or personnel) can prejudice or mar the final outcome. One pilot's commentary in this respect was very interesting. He works in small ports where ships only call infrequently, and consequently the tug crews are not familiar with shipwork since they handle mostly barges. He said, "It's always a pleasure when the big city tugs are in port, because they

are a lot sharper at shipwork than the hometown tugs." He was referring to the tugs from nearby large ports like New York and Baltimore
which the pilots preferred to use, when they were available instead of
the local tugs, since they were more proficient at shipwork. The familiar
aphorism "If you don't use it, you lose it" applies to tug captains as well
as other shiphandlers.

The employment of tugs in shipwork is sometimes referred to as
harbor service. The use of this term is appropriate, for tugs do provide a
service for the pilot, for the ship, and for the community at large.

ANSWERS TO THE
STUDY QUESTIONS

3. THE TUGS

1. Efficiency, since on a horsepower for horsepower basis, a single-screw tug will develop about 20 percent more thrust.
2. Lack of maneuverability, inability to steer astern, and inability to maintain position (i.e., 90°) when backing. Power astern is less than power ahead.
3. Excellent maneuverability, ability to maintain position when backing (if ship is stopped), and ability to steer astern.
4. May require a stern line when backing, is less efficient than a single-screw tug, and backing power is less than power ahead.
5. Tugs fitted with flanking rudders, steerable Kort nozzles (Kort rudders), and PS (propeller-steered) tugs.
6. The ability to steer astern and maintain position when backing.
7. 1. PS tugs
   2. Tugs with flanking rudders
   3. Tugs with Kort rudders
8. There are two types of PS tugs: the "pusher" tugs which have the rudder propellers (RP) located aft as in a conventional tug, and "tractor" tugs which have their RPs located forward.
9. "Pusher" tugs are operated like conventional tugs except that they have superior maneuverability and can maintain position while backing. "Tractor" tugs are intended primarily for towline work and are less likely to become "girt" because of the forward location of the RP. When they push, they normally work stern first against the ship.

4. PROPULSION AND STEERING

1. Because the diesel engine is lighter (in weight to horsepower ratio), more compact, and more fuel efficient.
2. It has greatly extended the power and range of tugs.
3. Higher engine speeds which may require a reduction gear in order to utilize an efficient propeller, and limited speed range (dead slow is often about one-half of full speed).
4. There are several methods used, listed below:
   1. Direct reversing (DR)
   2. Diesel electric (DE)
   3. Controllable-pitch propellers (CPP)
   4. Reverse and (usually) reduction gears with hydraulic or pneumatic clutches.
   5. Magnetic couplings which are often used in conjunction with two engines driving a single-propeller shaft. The engines are direct reversing, and the maneuvering is accomplished by running one engine ahead and the other astern, and engaging them as is required.
5. The DR system is the simplest system of maneuvering. The engine is directly connected to the propeller shaft, and the direction of its rotation is the same as that of the engine. The engine must be stopped between maneuvers or when changing maneuvers from ahead to astern and vice versa. The engines are started by compressed air injected into a reservoir cylinder. These engines may be fitted with wheelhouse controls so that they need not be tended by an engineer.
6. Low cost.
7. Limited number of maneuvers, engine speed may not permit a propeller of the most efficient size, vulnerability to mishap (i.e., failure to start, or starting up in wrong direction).
8. The DE system consists of engine-driven generators that supply current to the electrical-drive motors connected to the propeller shaft. The direction and speed of the drive motors is determined by the control of the current developed by the generators.
9. A wide range of speeds available from stop to full speed ahead or astern. The fact that the main engine (or engines) runs at a constant speed.

10. High costs, vulnerability to salt, and dampness.

11. The SCR system employs an AC generator whose current is then converted by silicon control rectifiers (SCRs) to DC current for driving the propulsion motors.

12. The SCR system is a more modern development of the DE drive. It is less costly than DC installations, and the main engine generators can furnish current for ship supply.

13. The controllable pitch propeller is not only an energy converter (rotative force to thrust), but it is also a transmission since it changes the direction of thrust by reversing the pitch of the propeller blades. The amount of thrust is also regulated by reducing or increasing the pitch as required by the circumstances. Stopping is achieved by flattening the pitch so that it is in neutral and does not develop thrust ahead or astern even though the propeller continues to turn. The pitch is controlled by an inner shaft inside the drive shaft that engages cams on the propeller blades in the hub of the drive shaft.

14. Usually not, since only half the horsepower would be available because one engine is customarily run ahead and the other astern when maneuvering and only half of the tug's aggregate power would be used to assist the ship.

15. In PS tugs the rudder propellers direct the thrust ahead, astern, and to the side, and are, in effect, both a steering system and a transmission.

16. Heavy fuel is a residual oil called bunker C (No. 6 oil). This is sometimes mixed with light diesel oil (No. 2 oil) to make blends which are cheaper than light diesel oil, and can be burned in low- and medium-speed engines.

17. It must be heated and centrifuged before being used, and the engines require more maintenance since there are more residues after combustion than with light diesel oil.

18. Solid propellers (fixed pitch), CP propellers, and cycloidal propellers (Voith-Schneider).

19. Propellers used aboard tugs are usually of large diameter with fairly flat pitch to avoid overloading the engine in a high-slip situation. They usually have three or more blades. More blades are less efficient but may reduce vibration.

20. They are cheaper and less vulnerable to damage than CP or cycloidal propellers. However, they are most efficient at one speed,

and the direction of rotation must be able to be changed for maneuvering.

21. Fuel efficiency since the pitch can be adjusted to suit the load ("light" tug vs tug with a tow), maneuverability, and a practically infinite range of speeds.

22. High costs, susceptibility to damage. A vessel's steering qualities are affected when in neutral pitch. Since the propeller is always turning, it is liable to foul lines in shipwork.

23. One with reverse and reduction gears with hydraulic or pneumatic clutches is favored for service aboard tugs in this country. Hydraulic clutches are available for engines up to about 1,500 hp, and pneumatic clutches (with inflatable tires instead of clutch plates) are suitable for installations up to about 4,000 hp. Some of these transmissions have two-speed gear boxes for "light" and loaded conditions. Some may also be fitted with a "slip" mode that can be used for short periods of time when very slow speed is desired.

24. Relatively low costs, unlimited number of maneuvers, convenience for maneuvering.

25. The principal disadvantage is the limited range of speeds unless the "slip" mode is used for very low speeds.

26. The VSP consists of a number of airfoil-shaped vanes that rotate about a vertical axis. The angle of incidence of these vanes is governed in such a way as to determine the direction and amount of thrust generated. VSP functions as a propeller as well as a maneuvering and steering system.

27. Other PS systems, like Schottel drive, "Z" drive, and SRAD (steerable right-angle drive), employ conventional propellers driven by vertical shafts that can be rotated through 360° to provide steering and backing. The propellers are often used in conjunction with nozzles.

28. A Kort nozzle (and other type nozzles) are airfoil-shaped rings installed about the perimeter of the propeller. They enhance the propeller's thrust ahead by up to 40 percent. Propellers enclosed in such nozzles are often referred to as shrouded propellers.

29. Balanced or semi-balanced rudders are constructed so that the leading edge of the rudder extends forward of the rudder post. This is done to provide more effective steering and a mechanical advantage to the steering gear.

30. A "spade" rudder is one that is not supported at the bottom by an extension of the vessel's keel or skegs.
31. Flanking rudders are installed ahead of the propellers, and there are usually two of them for each propeller. They are operated by a separate steering system from the regular one installed aft of the props and provide steering control of the vessel when it is maneuvered astern.
32. A Kort rudder is a steerable nozzle installed around the perimeter of the propeller which is turned to direct the propeller wash and provides steering when maneuvering ahead or astern.
33. Bollard pull is the pull in pounds or kilos generated by a tug pulling against a fixed object. In conventional tugs it is estimated to be about one long ton (2,240 pounds) per 100 hp, depending upon the configuration of the tug and whether or not nozzles are installed. Bollard pull can range betwen 22.5 and 38 pounds per hp.
34. Not always since other factors, like "stiffness" and maneuverability, are important too.

5. STRUCTURAL CONSIDERATIONS

1. A tug for shipwork will have a heavily constructed hull with low freeboard. It should be "stiff" enough so that a strain on a line leading to the side will not capsize it. The bulwarks are "tumbled home" so that they will not be damaged when the tug goes alongside a ship even if they are both rolling a bit.
2. Yes, the bow of a conventional tug is heavily reenforced since this is the area that comes in contact with the ship when the tug is pushing full ahead against the vessel. The bow in powerful tugs should be of ample radius so that large fenders can be used to distribute the tug's force over a large area of the ship's side. Heavy rub rails are usually installed along the tug's sides, fore and aft, above the waterline to reenforce and protect the hull. In "tractor" tugs the stern is usually strengthened since tractor tugs normally push stern first against the ship.
3. The deckhouse and/or wheelhouse on a harbor tug is set inboard to prevent it from coming into contact with the ship's side when the tug is working under the flare of the ship's bow or overhang at the stern and when the two vessels are rolling.
4. A "bullnose" is a large closed chock installed near the bow of a tug to

provide a fairlead for the tug's head line and springline. It should be large enough for the large working lines and the splices to pass through freely.

5. There is usually a large H bitt installed fore and aft in the foredeck, another H bitt installed athwartships aft of the deckhouse (approximately one-third of the tug's length forward of the stern), and there are quarter bitts installed forward and aft along the rails on either side of the tug. If there is no "bullnose," another small cruciform bitt will usually be set up near the stem to provide a fairlead for the forward working lines.

6. The bitts and deck fittings must be large enough on which to belay the large size working lines, and strong enough to withstand the heavy strains imposed upon them. The "bullnose," forward cruciform bitt, and the quarter bitts must be set inboard enough so that they will not come in contact with the ship's hull and cause damage.

7. A "dipping" mast should be installed so that it can be lowered when working under overhanging obstructions on the ship.

8. The wheelhouse should be constructed in such a fashion that the tug captain's vision is as nearly unobstructed as possible. The controls for the helm and engines should also be located so that his view is unobstructed.

9. Because they are less likely to do damage if they come into contact with the submarine's hull than either twin-screw or chine- (V-bottom) hulled tugs.

10. Poorly located chocks and bitts installed too far forward or aft or beneath overhanging structures can damage or endanger the tug. External hull fittings on the ship's side (i.e., sponsons, pipes, and rub rails) can also be a nuisance or a hazard.

11. "Pocket chocks" are set into convenient locations in the ship's side in such a way that they have a bar or pin for the tug's lines to be secured to. They are particularly helpful in the case of some passenger vessels, container ships, and car carriers that have short forward and afterdecks.

6. GEAR AND RIGGING FOR SHIPWORK

1. The fender system, connecting gear, and auxiliary equipment are the basic components.

2. The fender system on a tug is designed to protect the tug and the ship from damage when they come into contact with each other. The conventional harbor tug has a heavy bow fender to absorb and distribute the thrust when the tug is pushing against the ship. A tractor tug has a heavy stern fender since it usually pushes against the ship stern first. A tug also has fenders along its sides to protect it when it lies alongside the ship.

3. The bow (and stern) fenders are, currently, usually made from heavy synthetic rubber extrusions. These are sometimes used for fendering on the sides although in many instances side fenders are made up from heavy-duty tire casings. Both bow and side fenders are sometimes covered with rope and yarn which make them bulkier and less likely to slip when working against the ship.

4. Yes, they are sometimes used to compensate for structural deficiencies on the tug, such as padding out the tug's width if the deckhouse is too close to the tug's side and alongside the wheelhouse if the tug's bridge is too wide.

5. Underwater fenders, and they can affect the handling qualities of the tug.

6. This term refers to the head lines, springlines, quarter lines, and towlines that are used to secure the tug to the ship.

7. Synthetic fiber lines. In some instances wire rope pendants are attached to the ends of the working lines and in some areas (Mississippi River, etc.) tugs make fast with all wire rope working lines.

8. Dacron, polypropylene, polyethylene, and various blends and mixtures of Dacron and polypropylene are favored for shipwork.

9. Never, they are much too elastic.

10. It is mostly used for head lines and springlines because Dacron is very strong, but it does sink.

11. They are mostly used for quarter lines and occasionally for towlines because of their light weight, and the fact that they float.

12. In all applications because they are stronger than polypropylene and polyethylene, but are lighter than Dacron, and they also float.

13. They protect the working lines from chafe where they pass through the chocks on the ship. They are usually between 15 and 25 feet in length.

14. They are usually regular-lay, three-strand or eight-strand plaited

lines since they are frequently respliced, and are cheaper than double-braided lines.

15. "Yacht" braid or double-braided lines (like Samson lines) are most often used in service aboard powerful tugs where their high strength and light weight offset their higher costs.

16. 6×19 or 6×37 construction made from improved plow steel or extra improved plow steel.

17. Heaving lines, tag lines, goblines, and quick-release straps.

18. They are usually about 15 fathoms in length and ⅜ inch to ½ inch in diameter to provide a handhold for the deck force on the assisted vessel. A "monkey's fist" or other form of weight is secured to the outboard end to facilitate throwing.

19. Tag line is a length of line 30 to 40 feet in length about 1 inch in diameter to provide a handhold for the deck force of the ship. It is attached to the outboard end of the working line or wire rope pendant and is intended to facilitate heaving it aboard.

20. Yes, manila is suitable for this purpose since it provides a good grip. Slippery lines like polypropylene should be avoided.

21. A gobline is a stout line used to tie down the towline of a tug when the tug is doing a towline job. Its purpose is to secure the towline nearer to the stern of the tug and restrict its arc of movement so that the tug will not be girt or tripped. It is especially useful when the tug is being towed stern first.

22. A quick-release strap is a relatively short length of line secured to the after H bits on a tug and that is rove through the eye of a hawser used as a towline. Its purpose is to provide a safe method of "slipping" the towline without endangering the crew of the tug.

7. COMMUNICATION BETWEEN SHIP AND TUG

1. Usually VHF radiotelephone, but whistle signals given on the ship's whistle and on handheld whistles are still occasionally used.

2. The tug may respond on the radiotelephone or use its whistle.

3. Most tugs are fitted with a "beeper" that gives a distinct signal, and when one of the tugs answers with this distinct signal the pilot can determine if his orders are properly understood.

4. They tend to echo off of high buildings which can cause misunderstandings.

5. "Go ahead" if the tug is stopped, or "stop" if the tug is maneuvering ahead or astern.
6. The tug is to "go astern" if it is stopped.
7. Operate engines at "full speed" ahead or astern.
8. Go at "slow speed."
9. "Cast off" or shift the tug.

8. HANDLING THE "LIGHT" TUG

1. Conventional single-screw tugs will respond to the rudder ahead but many of them will not steer when the tug goes astern since the torque effect of the propeller overcomes the effect of the rudder.
2. It is steered when moving astern by giving an occasional "touch" ahead on the engine to correct the heading. This is done briefly enough so that it does not destroy sternway.
3. It is turned by "backing and filling," i.e., alternately going ahead and astern on the engine with the helm turned toward the direction of the turn.
4. Usually it will since the stern will be cast to one side or the other when the tug backs its engine. This will be to port with the standard right-hand propeller. Tugs with nozzles may not react the same way.
5. They enable a single-screw tug to steer astern and maintain position when backing during shipwork.
6. No, because when the tug is backing and filling to make a tight turn, the rudder angle must be reversed between the engine maneuvers ahead and astern.
7. Yes.
8. Usually not. It will probably tend to back toward the opposite side from that of the propeller being backed.
9. That the tug is being maneuvered with one engine ahead and the other astern. The tug can be turned completely about without moving ahead or astern.
10. Flanking means moving a tug laterally by using its engines and rudders in opposition. For example, if the tug's port engine is maneuvered ahead with the rudder to port and the starboard engine is backed, the tug will move sideways to starboard.
11. Yes.
12. Yes.

13. The bow of the PS tractor tug is steered *toward* the direction of the turn. The PS pusher type tug is steered *away* from the direction of the turn as is the stern of the conventional tug.

14. By coming ahead on a springline until the stern is open and then backing clear of the dock. However, a twin-screw tug may "flank" off of the dock.

15. It will usually approach the dock at an angle of 15° to 20°, stop its engine, then bear off, and back its engine when close alongside. It can then be worked ahead on a springline until it is in position.

16. Yes.

17. It should make a "flatter" approach to the dock and put out a stern line first instead of a springline.

18. By practicing turning and stopping maneuvers in an unobstructed area and making touch and go landings at a dock.

9. BASIC TUG HANDLING FOR SHIPWORK

1. Coming alongside and moving at a good rate of speed because the handling qualities of the tug are affected by the hydraulic effect caused by the ship's passage through the water.

2. It draws the tug toward the ship by the suction aft and it pushes the tug away from the ship forward.

3. By pacing the ship long enough to see how the tug is affected and then gently easing the tug in alongside. You can best do this by letting the tug be drawn in slowly by the suction aft with the helm turned slightly away from the ship, but you will usually have to work the tug in against the hydraulic forces forward.

4. The tug may be "sucked" in too quickly aft. The danger forward is from "overcontrolling" and hitting the ship heavily. If the suction is heavy near the stern, it is often prudent to land the tug farther forward and allow it to slide back into position. Pacing the ship for a bit forward will usually resolve the problem of overcontrol.

5. No, since this might cause the tug to swing heavily towards the ship. The tug may, however, stop its engine in order to reduce its speed.

6. The tug will normally land alongside the ship slightly aft of its own midships. The helm should then be put over towards the ship to

keep it pressed against the ship's side. The engines should be kept running ahead to hold the tug in position until the lines are made fast to the ship.

7. Because the momentum of the tug moving astern could develop enough force to part the line.

8. Because if the ship is maneuvered with too much power, it could cause the tug to "girt," or the towline could trip the tug causing it to capsize or some other serious damage.

9. By watching the vessel's propeller wash, anticipating its movements, and running the tug parallel to the ship if necessary.

10. "Stemming" can occur when a tug takes a towline from the bow of a moving ship. If the tug comes in contact with the ship's side it may lose steerage, in which case the tug may be caught by the ship's bow and rolled over.

11. The propeller may cavitate.

12. If the tug is overtaking the ship and backs its engine, the tug may not respond and can cause damage to itself and to the ship.

13. *Negligence* which includes excess speed, careless handling (of ship or tug), poor line handling, mistakes made in shifting control stations on the tug, and misunderstood communications.

14. Excess speed, because if it is on the part of the ship, it can overpower a tug on a towline and trip or *gird* it. Excess speed can also capsize a tug using a quarter line and even endanger a tug fast alongside with only a head line out. It will also destroy the tug's ability to assist the ship. When the tug uses excess speed, it can part lines (injuring personnel) and lead to collisions with the ship it is assisting.

10. THE *HOWS* AND *WHYS* OF SHIPWORK

1. A tug can push, pull, or apply resistance passively.

2. They are applied independently in conjunction with, or against, the other forces affecting the ship. These include wind, current, and the effect of the vessel's own momentum.

3. To turn the vessel, to assist it to steer, to check its way, and to move it laterally.

4. At the geometric center of the submerged portion of the ship's side.

5. The pivot point moves toward the direction of movement and will be

near the bow when the vessel is going ahead and near the stern when the vessel has sternway.

6. At the greatest distance from the pivot point.
7. At a position nearest to the pivot point.
8. No, it will pivot about a point that is closer to the opposite end of the ship.
9. Approximtely two ship lengths unless the ship assists with its engine and rudder.
10. One tug can move a vessel laterally by pushing or pulling at the pivot point. Two tugs can accomplish this by pushing or pulling at opposite ends of the vessel.
11. One tug forward can push against the bow while the ship's rudder is turned towards the tug to "lift" the stern of the ship. A tug "hipped" to the bow of a ship can also move a vessel laterally if the ship operates ahead with the rudder turned opposite to that of the tug.
12. A tug on the inboard side of the ship making a bend can assist by backing which will slow the ship and cant the bow toward the tug—the ship's rudder will have a more pronounced effect. The tug on the outboard side can push effectively but only if the vessel is going slow enough to permit it to assume a satisfactory angle (45° to 90°).
13. Yes, but the ship must be going slowly.
14. The tug on the inboard side of the bend can assist by pushing. It can also be used backing which will have a twin-screw effect with the ship continuing to come ahead. A tug on the outboard side of the bend can do nothing unless it is hipped up so that it can come ahead on its engine with its helm turned toward the ship while the ship backs.
15. Yes, by pushing on the inboard side of the stern.
16. By backing. However if there is only one tug, the ship's bow will cant toward the tug. As the ship slows a single-screw tug's torque may swing the tug out to the side so that it has a turning effect.
17. Yes, it can help by backing and it can also act as a drogue by putting its helm over so that it is towed along on an angle.
18. Yes, the shiphandler should consider the sequence of maneuvers (i.e., steering, turning, checking, and moving laterally) and try to place the tug where it will be most effective. Generally speaking, it is customary to put the more powerful tug forward on a

large deep draft ship and perhaps place it aft when the ship is in ballast. However, a very maneuverable tug will usually be placed where it may be required to shift to another side of the vessel or another position.

11. WORKING A TUG ALONGSIDE

1. It takes less time for the ship to respond to the tug's efforts, and working the tug alongside is safer than towline work.
2. Ordinarily, the ship provides its own propulsion ahead and astern.
3. The conventional tug uses a quarter line to maintain a position at approximately a right angle to the ship when backing, otherwise the effect of the torque of the tug's own propeller, the vessel's motion, or wind and current might move the tug out of position.
4. This often depends upon local custom. In some ports a tug will work with a head line only, in other ports a tug may automatically put up three lines (head line, springline, and stern line) whether it needs them or not.
5. Spring lines are led through the bullnose on the tug so that the tug can pivot freely on the bow fender.
6. Yes, especially if the ship is high out of the water, or if the wind is blowing very hard.
7. The ship must steer a little wide of its course since the tug will have to come ahead against the ship to get in position, and this will push the ship a bit.
8. The tug can steer the bow of the ship as it moves astern by pushing on either side of the bow near the stem as its moves astern. A tug can also steer the stern of a ship as it moves ahead by pushing on either side of the stern or if it is a transom stern by working against a head line.
9. No, in some instances the flare of the bow or a bulbous bow will prohibit a tug assisting in this fashion. A tug will normally be used only to work the stern of a deep-laden ship with a cruiser or transom stern.
10. It may not require a line when working the stem, but it will require a head line when working the stern because of the effect of the ship's wheel wash.
11. Quite often, sometimes a tug is stationed on the inshore side of a ship landing at a tanker berth (it lies between the dolphins). A tug

may also assist a vessel to depart a berth by working its way inside when the ship has sprung its stern clear of the dock.

12. Gently! By that I mean the lines should be slacked down easily rather than let go on the run.

12. WORKING TUGS ON A TOWLINE

1. It is convenient when transiting narrow channels, locks, and bridges.

2. It is more time-consuming than working tugs alongside, and the tug is subjected to the risk of being capsized.

3. No, but it is often used for undocking and transiting narrow waterways.

4. The principal difference is that in towline work the tug actually propels the ship to a certain extent in addition to steering it, turning it, etc.

5. Usually about 100 to 150 feet between the tug and ship.

6. This occurs when a tug with a ship or barge in tow astern makes a hard turn and at the same time applies more power. Since the tug's rudder will set the stern of the tug in the opposite direction, the bow of the towed vessel will often also be set in the opposite direction of the turn at first.

7. If a ship or barge is setting down on a buoy or an obstruction, the tug may turn toward the obstruction while applying more power. This will cause the tow's bow to swing in the opposite direction.

8. Tripping or girding the tug which can be caused by the ship overtaking the tug, and stemming which is caused by the tug being caught "in irons" against the ship's side while picking up a head line.

9. By employing "tractor" tugs or requiring that the ships go at slow-to-moderate speeds.

13. USING TORQUE TO ADVANTAGE

1. It tends to "kick" the stern one way or the other when the engine is reversed. This will be to port in the case of a standard right-hand propeller.

2. The ship must move in the same direction at the same speed as the tug if it is to remain in position (approximately 90°).

3. Because it is often simpler to dispense with the stern line or quarter

line if the tug only has to back for a little while or is required to shift.

4. Sometimes, by using a longer towline and having the tug start backing at a smaller angle so that its stern must swing through a longer arc before it is out of position.

14. USING TUGS IN CURRENT

1. Sometimes.
2. Almost never.
3. The tug is affected by the same forces that affect the ship, so it must be made up in such a fashion that if it is required to maneuver it will not adversely affect the ship.
4. In several different fashions. It may be fast with only a head line; with a head line, stern line, and springline; on a towline; hipped-up; and working without a line at all—depending upon circumstances.
5. When it is only required to push. This often occurs when the tug is working "inside" at a tanker berth where it can lie between the dolphins to check a vessel's swing toward the dock or to breast the vessel clear when it is unberthing.
6. It may be hipped up forward or aft depending upon circumstances. It will usually be made fast forward with a fair current, and aft with a head current.

15. HANDLING DEAD SHIPS

1. With a "dead" ship the tug is the prime mover, with a powered vessel the tug is merely assisting.
2. Yes, just as tugs frequently handle fairly large barges unassisted.
3. The tug should be hipped up on the inboard side of the turn, since even if the tug backs the ship will continue to swing in the direction of the turn. If the tug (especially a single-screw tug) is on the outboard side of the turn, it may not be able to back as this would "kill" the swing.
4. Yes, this is caused by the offset location of the propelling and steering forces.
5. Yes, the number of tugs required (unless stipulated by port regulations) will depend upon the size of the ship and the horsepower of the tugs.

6. Yes, but extra care should be taken when docking to avoid damaging the rudder and propeller.

7. "Toe-in" is the inclination of the centerline of a tug on the hip toward the keel of a vessel. Its purpose is to compensate for the offset position of the tug's rudder and propeller, which otherwise might make the vessel difficult to handle.

8. With two tugs: a powerful tug aft on the hip to propel and a smaller tug forward for steering placed on either bow. With three tugs: a powerful tug aft on the hip with two smaller tugs forward on each side for steering, or two tugs aft with one tug forward for steering. With four tugs: two tugs forward and two aft on the hip for very large ships.

9. Because two moderately powered tugs can propel a sizeable vessel since both tugs are moving the ship. The forward tug can steer the vessel, and the after tug can back to check its way. This is an efficient use of power especially for longer shifts.

10. By using the tugs as if they were components of a twin-screw ship and by using their engines in opposition for steering effect.

16. SALVAGE AND EMERGENCY SITUATIONS

1. The resistance of ground effect (the weight of the vessel resting on the bottom) times the coefficient of friction of the bottom and the effect of wind, current, and heavy seas.

2. 1. Wait for a high tide to float vessel.
   2. Discharge ballast or fuel.
   3. Discharge cargo into lighters.
   4. Pull vessel off with tugs.
   5. Heave vessel off with beach gear.
   6. Jettison some of the cargo.

3. Jettisoning the cargo is considered to be the last resort since the vessel's cargo is sacrificed to save the ship.

4. The vessel's draft should be checked to see how much buoyancy it has lost; soundings should be taken around the perimeter of the ship's side to determine what portion of the hull is aground; and the bilges should be sounded to determine if the vessel is holed.

5. Only if there are enough pumps or compressors to keep it afloat.

6. The buildup of sand or mud around a grounded vessel that will make refloating it difficult.

7. They can force a vessel farther aground and hamper salvage opera-

tions. Conversely, they can also help refloat a vessel by breaking the bottom suction or grinding down soft coral and limestone bottoms.

8. Lead out its anchors to restrain it, or ballast it down until the seas subside or assistance arrives.

9. The vessel may require assistance steering to avoid broaching when it is refloated.

10. A small tug can take a strain on the ship that will prevent it from broaching or "climbing the beach" until more assistance arrives.

11. "Beach gear" consists of heavy wire rope falls that are set up by a winch. They are attached to a heavy cable that is in turn attached to a shot or two of heavy chain and an anchor (usually an Eell anchor) which is spotted offshore of the stranded vessel. This gear was often set up on the ship's deck or on a barge attached to the ship, but modern salvage tugs sometimes are equipped to place the anchors and are attached to the ship by their own tow cable.

12. Yes, since they can apply their force from several different directions and "swing" the ship back and forth while beach gear can only pull in one static direction.

13. To assist in beaching a vessel that has been holed, remove a burning tanker from an oil dock, breast a listing ship to the dock, and assist a vessel that has lost power or steering.

14. First, the tug should have its own crew in fire-fighting gear or oilskins and have hoses led out and ready to provide some protection to the tug's crew. Then, the tug should back down and connect its towing gear to the vessel's fire warps and take the vessel easily in tow after streaming about 250 feet of towline or cable.

15. *Usually,* but the vessel will have a tendency to sheer away from the tug. It will be more easily controlled if there is another tug on a towline or pushing at the other end of the ship.

16. By taking the vessel in tow astern or on the hip.

17. By handling the ship with a towline to the vessel's bow; making fast alongside of the vessel forward; and by steering the stern of the ship.

18. Stay well to weather of it, or clear out!

19. The safety of his crew, the safety of his vessel, and the safety of the

vessel being assisted. His crew's safety should not be risked unless lives are at stake.

17. USING TUGS IN EXPOSED WATERS

1. The tug should be very heavily fendered and its working lines should be stronger than those required for normal harbor service.
2. Large pneumatic fenders (like tires) that are set on axles in a well in the bow of the tug. They are useful for shipwork in exposed areas since they will roll if the tug is pitching heavily as the tug pushes against the ship.
3. Work the tugs on the lee side when possible and give the lines a longer lead to prevent parting them in the rise and fall of the swells.
4. No, it takes the tug longer to respond to helm and engine in a seaway than it does inside a bay or harbor.
5. It usually puts up a line on the lee bow clear of the chocks where the mooring lines are passed and assists the vessel to hold its position while the gear is being run. The tug can also assist the steering while the vessel is making its final approach and backing to stop.

18. TUGS AND ANCHORS

1. Because when a vessel uses its anchors, it can dispense with the services of a tug. There are also occasions when the use of the anchors is preferred.
2. The anchor is essentially a "passive" device that cannot push nor pull like a tug unless it has been "spotted" beforehand and is used as a "deadman" to heave against, or is used as a "brake" to check a vessel's way.
3. The anchor is essentially used as a "restraint." The anchor can stabilize the bow of a ship in ballast on a windy day if enough chain is slacked out so that it drags along the bottom. When the anchor is slacked out to the right amount (usually a shot to a shot and a half of chain at the water's edge—depending upon the type of bottom and depth of the water), the ship will be able to steer at very slow speeds which is handy for docking.
4. The anchor may be used to "fix" the bow of a ship so that the ship can pivot about it. The anchor can also be used to heave the vessel

out of its berth if the anchor has been dropped in the right position beforehand.

5. The anchor continues to function passively except when used as a "deadman." The anchor is also used to provide directional stability when the vessel is towed by the tug, and it can "fix" the position of the bow while the ship is turned.

6. Stern anchors may be used to keep ships from swinging with the tide, and are often used on passenger ships to hold up the stern of a vessel to provide a lee for the launches. When used with tugs they are often used in docking in fair tide situations.

7. The possibility of the ship overriding the anchor and as a result doing damage to the rudder or propeller.

19. TUGS AND TAILBOATS

1. It is a tug made up to the stern of a vessel that is being towed by another tug.

2. The tailboat's principal function is to assist the lead tug to steer the vessel.

3. It may "brake" the vessel, "sheer" its stern, or steer the stern of the ship.

4. The tailboat simply backs whenever it is necessary. This slows the ship and allows the tug ahead to control the bow of the ship without concern for becoming girt.

5. A tailboat with a head line up steers to one side or the other of the vessel's stern. This acts like a paravane to set the stern to the side to which the tug is sheered.

6. A tailboat with flanking rudders can steer the stern by backing in the appropriate direction; a conventional tug can steer the stern by pushing on one side or the other; and a tug on a towline can pull the stern to one side or the other.

7. Usually with a head line or bridles from its bow to either quarter of the ship. However, it is occasionally made up with a towline.

8. The tailboat should rig a gobline, and the ship should be maneuvered slowly.

9. Moving a vessel in narrow waterways and offshore where it is not practical for the tug to go alongside the vessel.

10. Everything from interisland freighters to VLCCs and drill rigs.

20. HANDLING THE ITBs

1. A dual-mode ITB is an integrated tug-barge unit that can be operated in either the pushing mode or the towing mode.
2. Whenever conditions permit since pushing is a more efficient way to propel the barge and provides good control over it in confined waters.
3. Wind and sea conditions, the size of the notch on the barge, and the barge's draft.
4. A dual-mode tug cannot usually push a barge in rough seas, and it may find it dangerous to handle a "light" barge from the notch in high winds.
5. He should avoid making full-powered turns and backing heavily because the strain might part the pushing gear and cause an accident. He should guard against the ITB's tendency to skid when making a turn with too much power. He must also be aware that backing hard with a deep-loaded barge in shallow water can cause the tug-barge unit to react erratically.
6. Most of them tend to yaw or sheer to a certain extent. This can be dangerous in confined waters, and the barge may overpower a tug on a short towline if the barge is traveling too fast.
7. *Very carefully.* Its speed should be held to a minimum and the towing winch tended.
8. By "coon-assing," i.e., steering the stern of the barge. This is sometimes used to depart inlets in rough seas with the intention of taking the barge in tow outside.

APPENDICES

The three appendices that follow are drawn from technical papers and studies of tug performance, and are based on trials or ongoing practices. This material is included because it is relevant to the shiphandling process and is not readily available to professional mariners. The subject matter is selectively confined to those portions of the text that are likely to be of interest to the shiphandler.

Readers interested in referring to the complete texts for technical reasons should contact those who have generously made portions available for publication in this volume.

APPENDIX ONE

SHIP HANDLING AT RAS TANURA SEA ISLAND

Whereas this paper is officially entitled "Ship Handling at Ras Tanura Sea Island," during its preparation, I decided to broaden its scope in order to reflect our experience dealing with other large ports. The title should be changed to "Rationalized Design Parameters for Ship-Assisting Tug Boats" or "Study of Tugboats for Port Hypothetical".

If one were to attempt on a worldwide basis to cover the entire spectrum of techniques used by ship-assisting tugboats, describing in detail their methods, the diversity of procedures would produce a huge volume on the subject.

Virtually every seaport has its own features, peculiarities and problems. The methods used at each port have evolved through experience and generally in an empirical manner. Tugboat sizes and characteristics have kept pace with the increase in size of the vessels calling at that port.

This paper is an attempt to provide a broad background of information concerning ship-assisting tugboats and then to provide a rational approach toward recommending the type, size, and thrust requirements as well as the number of tugs required for Port Hypothetical. This method has been used and tested in determining the requirements for a major Alaskan oil port as well as a major Arabian Gulf oil port.

In this computer age, naval architects turn to the computer to generate the characteristics of their vessel designs in conjunction with their own personal training, experience and skill. This new design tool has furnished a refinement in the design process which was out of reach heretofore.

SHIP ASSISTING METHODS

Broadly, there are two distinct methods of assisting ships by the use of tugboats. First is the "towing on the hook" method as generally practiced in Europe and known as the "European" method. The other is the "towing alongside" method which is generally practiced in the United States and known as the "American" method.

The "European" method requires at least a head tug and a stern tug connected to the ship's bow and stern, each with a tow line attached to the tugboat's towing hook. This method provides very good control over the ship, particularly in a fore and aft direction. In many European ports with high tidal ranges, a vessel preparing to berth must first enter and pass through a narrow pair of locks before entering the enclosed harbor basin. It is seen that tug assistance under these circumstances is only possible by means of a head tug towing on a towline attached to the bow of the ship. A stern tug is similarly connected astern to control the ship's stern. Even before entering the lock system, in many cases, the ship is subjected to strong tidal forces and must be controlled by the assisting tugboats.

The head tug, in order to take the ship's headline while underway, must maneuver close under the ship's bow. In this hazardous position, a conventional single screw tugboat must maneuver with greatest care in order to prevent "stemming." After the head tug has taken its position ahead of the ship on the towline, the tug is subjected to the hazard of "girting" (fig. 1). These hazards were thoroughly discussed at the First North American Tug Convention held in Vancouver, B.C., Canada in 1974 (ref. A).

In the United States, tidal action is generally much less, and there are no harbor basins enclosed by a lock system. However, river currents and tidal currents must be accommodated in many United States ports. Traditionally, as in New York City, older finger piers project outwardly at right angles from the shoreline. Lately, terminal construction in the United States has been influenced by the "container revolution," and are now of the "quay" type, with great shoreside container marshalling areas. Oil ports and bulk cargo ports are usually constructed of the "tee" type with the ships laying off the face of the "tee." A system of pile dolphins and catwalks is provided for securing the ship's mooring lines.

FUNDAMENTAL HAZARDS ASSOCIATED WITH CONVENTIONAL SHIP-HANDLING TUGS

Wind

Stemming

Girting

SHIP HANDLING METHOD: PORTLAND, OREGON, U.S.A.

Step 1
Positioning

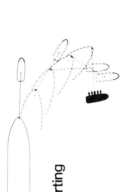

Figure 1

Excerpts from "Ship Handling at Ras Tanura Sea Island" by Philip F. Spaulding (M.Sc.; Life Fellow, S.N.A.M.E.; David Taylor Medal, M.A.S.N.E.; President, Nickum & Spaulding Associates, Inc.) presented at the Seventh International Tug Convention and Exhibition, London, England, 15-18 June 1982. Courtesy: Nickum & Spaulding Associates, Inc., Seattle, Washington.

tugs are used to turn the ship, then breast her up to the pier. The ship's athwartship momentum is then checked by the tugs backing down on their headline.

When moving a "dead" ship by the "American" method (fig. 3), a third tug is placed at the stern of the ship opposite the "alongside" tugs. This tug is made up to the ship by the use of three lines. A headline leading through the bow towing eye or around the bow bitt, is lead forward on the ship. A second line is also lead through the same chock tending aft as a spring line. The third line is a stern line leading athwartship directly to the ship's stern.

Properly designed American tugboats have a pronounced shoulder at the forward quarter of the hull, so when making up to handle a "dead" ship, the two forward lines are set up by the use of winches or gypsies. Then, by horsing in the stern line with a stern towing winch or capstan, the tug pivots on its shoulder setting all lines up violin string tight. This stern tug then provides the power and steering control to move and maneuver the "dead" ship in much the same manner as if the ship had her own power.

"DEAD" SHIP

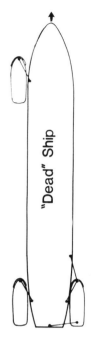

"Dead" Ship

Figure 3

Step 2
Breasting

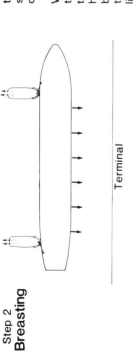

Terminal

Step 3
**Checking
or Departing**

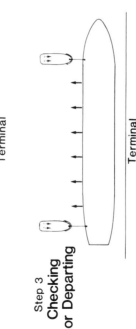

Terminal

Figure 2

The "American" method, illustrated as that used in Portland, Oregon fig. 2), evolved as the most effective way for assisting ships while they are being maneuvered into finger piers. This is accomplished by using at least two tugboats secured alongside the ship, opposite the side to which the ship would lay to the pier. While in the river or channel with the tugs alongside, the ship's power and steering is used to move the ship, with the tugs giving little control or assistance. The tugs are secured to the ship by the use of their headline leading through a towing eye or around a cruciform bitt located on top of the stem head. While turning into the berth, the

It is noted that positioning tugs alongside, using the "American" method, they are comparatively safe, and the danger of "stemming" and "girting" is minimized. It is not necessary for the forward tug to maneuver under the ship's bow in order to pass its headline to the ship, nor seldom is the tug positioned ahead on a towline, eliminating the danger of "girting."

SHIP-ASSIST TUGBOAT FEATURES AND CHARACTERISTICS

American tugs are usually equipped with a winch or anchor windlass fitted with two gypsies on the fore deck and a towing winch with gypsies or a towing bitt and capstan aft. American tugs are not fitted with towing hooks similar to European tugs, as a quick release of their tow line is not considered paramount. Ship assistance is just one of a multitude of the harbor and coastwise towing duties that American tugs are called upon to perform; therefore, they must be designed for great versatility in their operation. Their deck gear and its location must also reflect these varied requirements.

Europeans have been most active in promoting the tractor tug concept amongst American tugboat operators, and have been very critical of their reluctance to adopt this "modern" design concept. Tractor tugs were developed in Europe to prevent the danger of "stemming" and "girting" which is attendant to the "European" method of ship-assisting, but not so to the "American" method. Whereas it is admitted that tractor tugs have outstanding maneuverability, the issues that have provided the greatest resistance to tractor tug adoption include: first cost and maintenance; being dedicated to ship assistance; as well as their deeper draft and modest towline pull.

At this point, it is interesting to note that the first vertical axis propeller, similar to the Voith-Schneider propeller, was developed by an American. Professor Kirsten, Professor of Aeronautical Engineering at the University of Washington in Seattle, developed this propeller in the early 1920s.

First, cost is always foremost on the minds of American tugboat operators. For this reason, most new tugs are twin screw because of their better maneuverability and off-the-shelf American diesel engine selection. They are fitted with the largest, slowest speed open-water propellers that can be accommodated within the dimensional constraints of the hull and available reverse reduction gear ratios. Some tugs are equipped with triple steering rudders and when fitted to a high, displacement/length ratio hull form, they possess unusual maneuverability.

The next advance in design sophistication is to add four flanking rudders in a fashion similar to that used on the Mississippi River towboats. This feature enhances the tug's maneuverability while it is backing down.

With acknowledging that Dip. Ing. W. Baer of J. M. Voith GmBH, was the father of Thrust Vector Diagrams in a paper he presented at the First Tug Conference, (ref. B), with apologies, I will borrow his thunder. The thrust diagram shown (fig. 4), is used as a basis of comparison with all other tugboat types illustrated and discussed in this paper. The performance of an open-water, propeller-driven twin screw tug in forward thrust, is taken as 100% and all other diagrams are factored therefrom. The dotted lined envelope in figure 4 illustrates the improvement in maneuvering range astern by the addition of flanking rudders.

In cases where American companies have elected to dedicate their vessels to ship assistance, the ultimate designs of American tugboats are known as flanking rudder tugs (FR) of 6000 HP. They are twin screw and fitted with the largest diameter specially-developed fixed propeller nozzles possible, within the di-

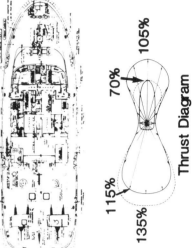

CONVENTIONAL STERN DRIVE TWIN SCREW WITH NOZZLES & FLANKING RUDDER

Thrust Diagram

105%

70%

115%

135%

Figure 5

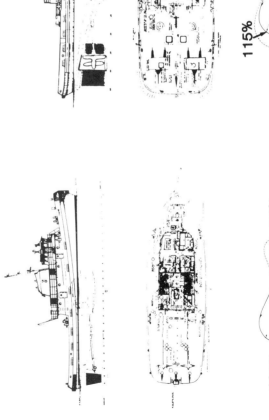

CONVENTIONAL STERN DRIVE: TWIN SCREW

Thrust Diagram

74%

100%

Figure 4

to push against the bow fender then back away hard on the two headlines. Note the virtual equality between the forward and astern thrust, a most important feature for tugs using the "American" method.

The dotted lined envelope in figure 5 illustrates the thrust derived from a conventional nozzle as compared to the specially developed nozzle and propeller combination used on the lastest flanking rudder tugs.

It is possible, by the proper placement of the steering rudders and flanking rudders, together with rotating the propellers in opposite direction, to physically move the tug athwartship smartly without advancing. Also, the tug can be easily rotated about its axis without forward movement.

Figure 7

mensional constraints of the hull. They are fitted with three steering rudders and four flanking rudders and have a cutaway afterbody to enhance their astern thrust. These flanking rudder tugs (fig. 5), by using the "American" method, perform most of their ship assisting by the bow. They are, however, equipped with a towing hook and capstans on the after deck for an occasional towing assignment.

Two very large headline spooling winches, (fig. 6), are located on the large foredeck of the tug. The winches are equipped with powerful brakes and the two headlines lead forward under a large double cruciform bitt (fig. 7), then to the ship. The tug has an unusually large bow radius and the bow is heavily fendered (fig. 8). The flanking rudder tug's principal ship-assisting maneuver is

Figure 6

CONVENTIONAL STERN DRIVE:
TWIN "Z" DRIVE

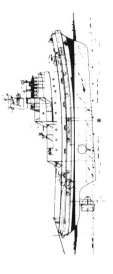

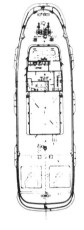

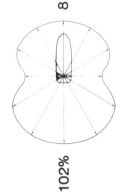

102%   87%

Thrust Diagram

Figure 9

Figure 8

In order to complete the spectrum of ship-assisting tugboats, the following illustrations are included with their trust diagrams. Each of the following tug types incorporates some propeller manufacturer's product, hence, our assessment may be open to argument. However, the illustrations do reflect our experience and unbiased opinion.

The twin propeller "Z" drive with the units located at the stern is typical of Japanese and Korean tugs (fig. 9). Actually, for ship-assisting work, this type of tug configuration acts as a reverse water tractor, in that the vessel works by pushing with the bow or backing down on the headlines in reverse mode.

The astern thrust diagram (fig. 10) was prepared to compare the stern drive propeller "Z" drive with water tractor types. The illustration clearly shows that the aft drive permits designing a vessel of minimum draft, however, astern bollard pull is reduced by propeller wash impingement on the hull itself (thrust deduction).

Two basic types of water tractor tugs are shown. The water tractor with twin propeller "Z" drive (ref. C), with its thrust diagram, (fig. 11), can be compared with a water tractor tug with twin Voith-Schneider (VSP) drive (ref. B), and its thrust diagram (fig. 12). The features of tractor tugs have been broadly discussed at previous tug conferences, however, salient features and advantages are repeated here in order to relate to the assistance of large tankers while berthing at Port Hypothetical:

1. Steering propulsion units are located forward of the "hook" eliminating the risk of "girting", (fig. 1).

2. With the steering propulsion units located forward, after taking the ship's bowline, the tug can pull away from the vessel's bow, eliminating the danger of "stemming." (fig. 13).

3. The forward position of the steering propulsion units minimizes the risk of fouling the towline.

4. Tractor tugs push with their sterns when the propulsion units are in the astern mode. If they want to take a strain on their towline, the propulsion units are quickly placed in a head mode without a change in direction of the tug.

5. The Voith-Schneider (VSP) tractor tug can change its direction and thrust by simply adjusting the angle of attack of their rotating blades with no change in engine speed, hence, they have the quickest response time. They steer with equal ease in any direction — backward, forward or sideways.

ASTERN THRUST DIAGRAM
ASTERN DRIVE TUG VS. WATER TRACTOR TUG

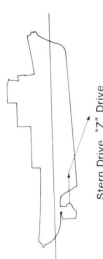

Stern Drive, "Z" Drive

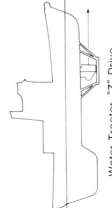

Water Tractor, "Z" Drive

Water Tractor, Voith Schneider

Figure 10

WATER TRACTOR:
TWIN VOITH-SCHNEIDER DRIVE

92%

96%

Thrust Diagram

Figure 12

WATER TRACTOR:
TWIN "Z" DRIVE

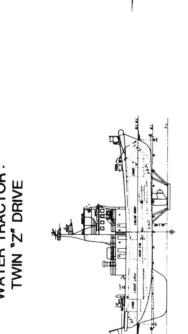

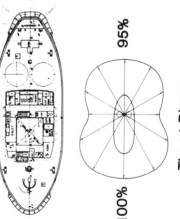

95%

100%

Thrust Diagram

Figure 11

TUGBOAT THRUST

PROPULSION TYPE	BOLLARD PULL #/ SHP	
	AHEAD	ASTERN
TWIN SCREW W/ OPEN PROPELLERS	25.9	19.4
TWIN SCREW W/ OPEN PROPS. & FLANK. RUD.	25.8	19.1
TWIN SCREW W/ CONVENTIONAL NOZZLES	34.9	18.1
TWIN SCREW/SPEC. NOZZLES & FLANK. RUD.	29.7	27.2
STERN PROPELLER "Z" DRIVE	26.4	22.5
WATER TRACT, TWIN PROP. "Z" DRIVE	25.9	24.8
WATER TRACT,TWIN VSP DRIVE	24.9	23.7

Service Factor 10%

Figure 14

SHIP-ASSIST TUGBOAT OPERATING PHILOSOPHY

Dispatch and safe operation in berthing large ships must be foremost when rationalizing the parameters for a ship-assisting tugboat system. Dispatch is essential when one considers the hourly cost of operating large tankers or container ships with their valuable cargoes. Safe operation is paramount, as damage to the vessel or pier can be astronomical in cost, to say nothing about the casualty's affect on the environment.

When observing the berthing operations at the oil port of Valdez, Alaska (two million barrels of oil per day); Ras Tanura, Saudi Arabia (ten million barrels of oil per day); and the container port of Seattle (second largest in the United States) one thing must be borne in mind. Procedures for the berthing operation are discretionary with the pilot and ship's master, and not all pilots

TAKING THE BOWLINE

(NO DANGER OF STEMMING)

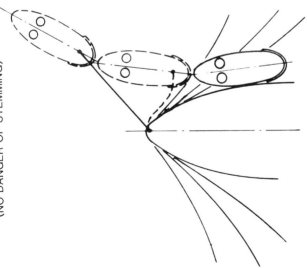

Figure 13

Figure 14 summarizes the bollard pull of the various types of ship-assisting tugs in pounds of bollard/SHP.

approach a problem in exactly the same manner. For this reason, any plan for developing a tugboat ship-assisting system must be reviewed and approved by the harbor pilots.

Because different ports vary greatly in the number of terminals, together with vastly different number of ship arrivals and departures requiring tug assistance, this paper's analysis is confined to those tugs required for each ship assist. As Port Hypothetical is to be an oil port, ship-assisting procedures are to follow the general practice already established through successful operating experience.

OIL PORT SHIP ASSISTING PROCEDURE

In this procedure, usually two, three or more tugs are positioned and secured on the offshore side of the ship in such a way as to produce the thrust control, primarily for the breasting movement of the vessel. Fore and aft thrust as well as minor steering control is produced, or at least augmented, by the ship's propeller and rudder. The ship normally will be brought "dead" in the water, parallel to the berth a short distance out. The ship will then be breasted up to the face of the berth with the tugs supplying the lateral thrust necessary. At the proper time, at the pilot's discretion, the tugs will back down applying the necessary thrust to check the vessel's athwartship motion (fig. 2).

It will be shown herein that a certain aggregate thrust is required in the tug flotilla being used to berth a ship of a given mass under the most unfavorable conditions anticipated at a given location. Obviously, this aggregate thrust can be obtained with a small number of very powerful tugs or a greater number of less powerful tugs. The upper limit of tugboat power is directly related to the design of the fendering system so as to prevent damage to the ship's hull structure. All things being proportional, the fewer the tugs, the less the cost; and because of communication, it is easier with fewer tugs for the pilot to manage the berthing operation.

As a typical example, when making a study for a specific port's ship-assisting tugboat system, we dealt with the Marine Department and Terminal Pilots in Ras Tanura, Saudi Arabia. They considered that the largest suitable tug was a twin screw flanking rudder tug producing 6000 HP with an overall length limitation of 136 feet, (fig. 5).

At Ras Tanura, where they handle the largest vessels in the world on a regular basis, they have developed an advanced phase of the "European" method for ship assistance. The head tug and stern tug are both water tractor Voith-Schneider-propelled (VSP) tugs of 4000 HP each and are used for positioning the tug abreast the berth (fig. 12). Amidship, depending on the weather, one or two flanking rudder (FR) tugs of 6000 HP each are used for the breasting operation, and they then check the athwartship movement as the vessel approaches the pier, (fig. 15). When departing, a fully loaded tanker requires less critical tug assistance, as the operation does not involve bringing a large mass to rest against a stationary object. However, the mass of the departing loaded tanker will be more than twice that of the ballasted tanker coming in.

SHIP HANDLING METHOD: RAS TANURA, SAUDI ARABIA

Step 1
Positioning

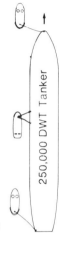

250,000 DWT Tanker

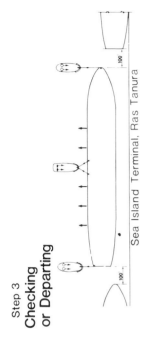

Step 3
Checking
or Departing

Sea Island Terminal, Ras Tanura

Figure 15

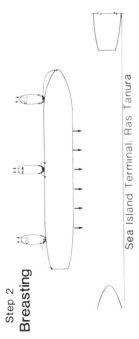

Step 2
Breasting

Sea Island Terminal, Ras Tanura

FULL-SCALE TRIALS . . .DURING BERTHING OF TANKERS

The *EXXON Garden State* is a 105-foot-long twin screw tugboat of 29-foot beam and 11-foot draft. Propellers are mounted in Kort nozzles. Engine power is provided by two supercharged Caterpillar diesels, driving through two-speed reduction gear boxes. All trials were conducted in the low-speed gear range (6.44 ratio); a nominal 850 horsepower per shaft at 170 propeller rpm is available in this configuration. The combination of Kort nozzles and two-speed reduction gearing allows the *Garden State* to produce much higher low-speed thrust than typical for tugboats of this installed power. Hull design is intended for harbor maneuvering, and is quite fine aft with minimal skeg. This type of tug usually would not be employed in offshore towing or escort. Steering and flanking rudders are ganged, so port and starboard rudders move in unison; this characteristic is not typical of many flanking rudder tugboats (although it is the conventional steering arrangement for river tow boats). A final feature of importance is the shape and construction of the bow fenders. These are molded of hard rubber, horizontally applied, and almost square in contour. As a consequence, the tug had little contact area when pushing at an angle to the ship hull, and tended to "slip" along the hull at higher power levels.

The tanker USNS *American Explorer* is 600 feet long, 80 feet in beam, and was ballasted to 20.75 feet (20.5 fwd; 21.0 aft). The 22-foot diameter single screw propulsion system is driven by a steam plant capable of 22, 875 SHP at 113.4 rpm. During standardization trials the

Excerpts from U. S. Department of Transportation, Maritime Administration. *Full-Scale Trials to Examine Tugboat Performance During Berthing of Tankers.* Technical Report 8011-5. Report prepared by J. Zseleczky and R. Altmann of Hydronautics, Incorporated, Laurel, Maryland. Washington, D. C., 1982.

ship made 21.3 knots when ballasted to 32 feet under these conditions. The ship is formally classified as a T5-S-RM2a tanker. Features are shown in the photographs of Figure 2 and the drawings of Figure 10 [not shown]. Data from the original ship characterization trials (all performed at a laden draft of 32 feet) are included in Appendix A for reference [not included].

*Conclusions.** This report is primarily a data presentation, and the bulk of the text is a compendium of measurement tables and graphs. The data do permit some nondimensional relationships to be constructed on the basis of the maximum bollard thrust capability of the tugboat, and these may be of some use in scaling the present results to other tugboat sizes. However, the majority of measurements in this report have not been analyzed at the present time. In particular, ship response to tug forces will require considerable computer simulation work before these data are correlated and completely understood. Successful correlation will greatly enhance the confidence with which a given computer simulation of tug maneuvering can be used.

Although most of the analysis work associated with these data remains to be done in the future, a number of important conclusions can be drawn from the performance characteristics without further detailed study.

From the operational viewpoint, the envelope curve of Figure 36 is most important. The tugboat cannot exert significant control forces on a ship, either pushing or pulling, unless it can maintain a large angle to the hull. This clearly is not possible at speeds through the water in excess of three knots. However, Figure 36 also shows that tug operation is possible alongside a tanker at speeds in excess of six knots, given a heading that provides some leeward shelter for the tug. Similar observations were made in the Reference 5 test program. These velocities are considerably higher than the *nominal* speeds at which most tug cap-

*The principal purpose of these trials was understood to be for the development of mathematical models for incorporation into computer-simulator systems. Of particular interest to the mariner will be the conclusions indicating the degradation of the tug's effectiveness at speeds exceeding three knots. This is graphically illustrated in figures in Figures 35 and 36.

The last paragraph of this study may be of further interest to the shiphandler since it refers to lateral forces generated by the rudder. This effect is demonstrated in practical applications when a tug is 'flanked' (Chapter 8), when a tug is hipped-up to the vessel forward or aft (Chapter 10), and when snapping a vessel on a towline (Chapter 12).

tains consider safe for work alongside a moving vessel, but apparently can be achieved without jeopardy if weather conditions are not extreme.

The performance limits shown in Figure 36 only apply to a tugboat not restrained by auxiliary lines. A three-point make-up (such as used in Reference 5 [not shown]) would allow significantly higher angles to be achieved at the lower operating speeds, and would permit the full thrust-producing capability of the tug to be used for tanker control (rather than maintaining tug position). However, Figure 70 clearly shows that even this thrust capability falls off rapidly with forward speed, and clearly illustrates the desirability of assisting from a head line, with tug propellers reversed, whenever this mode of operation is practical.

A most interesting conclusion from the test measurements is the large percentage of ahead or astern thrust that can be converted to lateral force simply by rudder action. The *Garden State* generated side forces which approached one-third the bollard thrust value, (Figures 68 and 69 [not shown]).

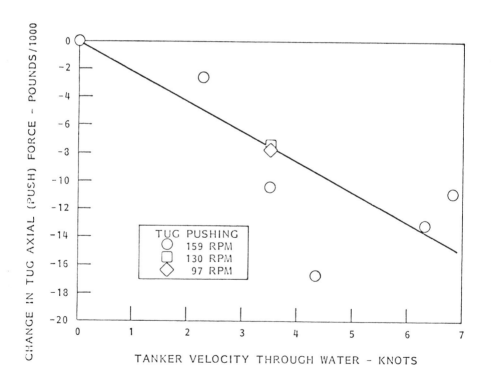

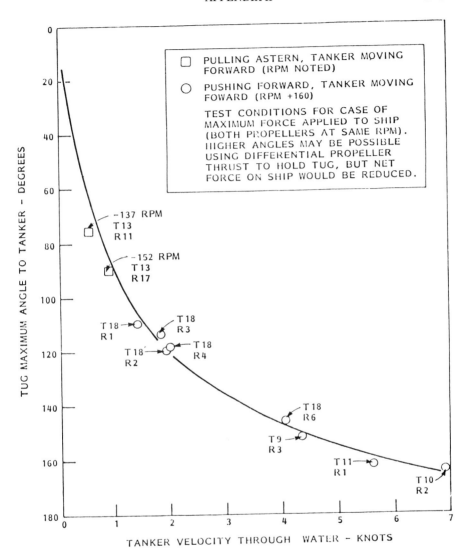

PULLING ASTERN, TANKER MOVING FORWARD (RPM NOTED)

PUSHING FORWARD, TANKER MOVING FOWARD (RPM +160)

TEST CONDITIONS FOR CASE OF MAXIMUM FORCE APPLIED TO SHIP (BOTH PROPELLERS AT SAME RPM). HIGHER ANGLES MAY BE POSSIBLE USING DIFFERENTIAL PROPELLER THRUST TO HOLD TUG, BUT NET FORCE ON SHIP WOULD BE REDUCED.

TUG MAXIMUM ANGLE TO TANKER – DEGREES

TANKER VELOCITY THROUGH WATER – KNOTS

APPENDIX THREE

SAFETY IN TOWING

SAFETY in towing concerns the following three fundamentals:

(1) Safety for the tow;

(2) Safety for the harbour installations, the waterways and everything within the area of operation;

(3) Safety for the tug performing the towing work.

Despite the subdivision into these three classifications, it should immediately be stated that the requirement of safety in towing is only fulfilled it it applies to all three, i.e. when the ship or any other tow is moved safely to its destination, when the surroundings have not been damaged during this operation and when the tug itself and the crew have not sustained any damage. This statement may seem to be a matter of course, but this is far from the truth, for there are devices—particularly on tugs—which, while safeguarding the tug itself, may, when applied, seriously endanger the tow. I am thinking of slipping the hook when the tug is in danger of capsizing.

Safety in towing is assuming increasing importance. This is due to various reasons and the following is an attempt to assess these in detail.

(A) 1. Traffic density in river estuaries, ports and harbours and on inland waterways is steadily increasing.

2. The speed of manoeuvring is increasing.

3. The size of the tows is getting larger all the time, resulting in longer times for acceleration and retardation manoeuvres and, evidently, in substantially larger space requirements for turning manoeuvres.

4. The ratio of power to displacement is progressively declining in the big ships so that with falling speed they lose their manoeuvrability before the smaller ships.

5. The ratio of ship channel depth to draught deteriorates rapidly with increasing ships' dimensions, and controllability is no longer adequate in the roadstead. This applies in particular to changing water depths and in the neighbourhood of sloping banks.

6. Cargo and fuel are becoming more dangerous both in respect of quantity and quality. I am thinking of oil, liquified gas and acids or other chemicals. Ships driven by atomic power should also be mentioned.

7. In many districts it becomes increasingly difficult to find crews who can satisfy the more exacting requirements of today's towing.

An assessment and improvement of safety during towing requires, first of all, knowledge of where the risks lie. To get this we must consider the various towing tasks.

(B) 1. Giving assistance to sea-going ships from the roadstead to the berth in the harbour and vice versa.

other countries, with a total of 62 men being killed. Seventeen of these tugs capsized and 15 were run down. These statistics, however, do not take into account the many tug sinkings where, fortunately, no lives were lost. (Source: SAFETY AT SEA, Sept. 1972). In Germany, between 1951 and 1964 a total of 15 tugs were turned over and 10 men lost their lives, but the statistics do not show which manoeuvres were responsible for these accidents. (Source: ANNUAL OF SCHIFFBAUTECHNISCHE GESELL-SCHAFT, 1965, page 540). The statistics show that accidents occur not only when working forward as head tug, but also when the tug is being used for braking and steering. Whereas tugs are prone to being turned over both during pushing and towing, tugs using the towrope mainly sustain damage during braking and steering manoeuvres. Using the towrope, however, offers too many decisive advantages, particularly for the safety of the tow, for this method to be waived. The risks associated with using the towrope can be eliminated, as will be shown later. The following analyses a towing manoeuvre which has proved to be particularly dangerous.

(C) 1. Manoeuvring in the forebody range of a ship under way.

A typical example is the tug *Fairplay I* which was run down by the passenger ship *Italia* in Cuxhaven roadstead.

Photographs taken of the accident show the tug was first moving parallel to the *Italia* (see **Fig 1**) and then moved forward on the starboard side to get into the range below the bow. The tug performed this manoeuvre with great care, since, as you know, tugs sometimes drop back on to the approaching ship. This last manoeuvre is, I believe, substantially more dangerous since it is difficult to estimate

2. Moving sea-going ships in the harbour area, with their main engines not operating.

3. Long-distance towing of sea-going ships which are not in running order or of floating equipment with inadequate self-propulsion or none at all.

4. Towing lighters over long inland waterways.

5. Moving lighters in river roadsteads and inland harbours including LASH and SEABEE.

6. Salvage work at sea:
   (a) Rescue of human beings;
   (b) Keeping damage under control and preventing further damage;
   (c) Salvaging the damaged ship.

7. Giving assistance to stationary equipment (platforms or similar off-shore equipment).

When examining the assigned tasks, we find certain towing duties and operations which are repeated and can be regarded as typical such as taking over the towrope, braking, steering, turning manoeuvres, towing or pushing and, in salvage work, taking off the crew of the damaged ship, fire-fighting and salvaging the ship itself.

Accident statistics show the following:

In Great Britain 16 tugs have been turned over during towing manoeuvres from 1952 to 1972 in which 47 men lost their lives. Of these 16 tugs, six were capsized and 10 run down. According to the same statistics, between 1962 and 1972, 32 tugs were turned over in

Excerpts from "Safety in Towing" from International Tug Conference Papers by Dipl.-Ing. Wolfgang Baer (Director, Maschinenfabrik·J. M. Voith GmbH). Courtesy: Voith Schneider America Inc., Great Neck, New York. Dipl.-Ing. W. Baer is credited with the development of the tractor-tug configuration for shipwork.

American mariners will note that longer towlines are used in shipwork in Europe (space permitting) than is customary in this country.

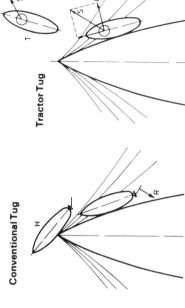

Fig. 2 *(above)* **tug under the bow of the 'Italia'**

Fig. 2a *(below)* **taking the bowline of an incoming vessel**

Conventional Tug

Tractor Tug

Fig. 1 'Fairplay I' running alongside the 'Italia'

the relative speed between two ships. In this case, however, the accident happened despite the captain making the safer approach. Before the forward shoulder of the ship underway is reached, the tug is subjected to a deflecting tendency, but then in the range of the forward shoulder there is a tendency for the tug to move in the opposite direction and the tug turns towards the ship (see HANSA, 1964, No. 12). At this phase rudder movement no longer had any effect on the stern-controlled tug *Fairplay I* since her stern touched the side of the ship and could no longer turn away. **Figs 2** and **2a** show the following critical phase. The captain of the tug then apparently tried to get more pressure on the rudder by going 'full speed ahead' hoping to free the tug in the forward direction but this manoeuvre, regrettably, did not succeed.

from the forward direction but the forward tug captain cannot be absolutely sure for how long the ship will still carry headway.

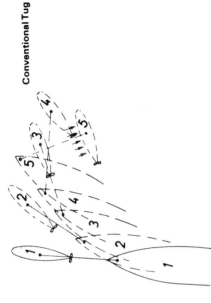

Conventional Tug

Fig. 3 Showing the increased risk of capsizing to the tug

It is at this point that complications can arise. If the tug captain starts a turning circle which is too tight and the ship continues to move forward, the tug runs the risk of being overtaken by the tow so that eventually the towrope lies at an angle of 90 degrees to the tug's fore and aft line. At this juncture there is an increasing risk of the tug capsizing (**Fig. 3**) and it is difficult for the tug to get out of this situation unless there is sufficient time to turn back and follow the tow's course. Should the ship continue to steam ahead and not turn then the tug is in serious difficulties and must take drastic action. The normal course is to slip the hook, but even if this is successful and saves the tug, it robs the ship of vital assistance. Safety can be improved by using radial-arm towing gear or by the use of a guest rope to haul the towrope tight to the after bitts. But

The stern-driven tug, apparently, could have got clear of the dangerous forward range of the *Italia* only by a braking manoeuvre.

This and similar accidents occurring when working in the forebody range of a sea-going ship under way, prompted the German Ministry of Transport and Traffic to ask the Hamburgische Schiffbau-versuchsanstalt (Hamburg Tank) to conduct investigations as to how accidents can occur during these manoeuvres and to find out in particular how to avoid such accidents. Models of tugs of different types were tested in conjunction with ships to be handled. It would be beyond the scope of this paper to mention all the details of this investigation but reference is made to the Hansa publication SCHIFF UND HAFEN, 1964, No. 12. In condensed form the conclusions were as follows. A conventional tug without bow control cannot turn away from the forebody of the incoming ship, once the tug has come alongside in contact with the tow. Tugs with a very powerful bow thruster can get clear under certain favourable conditions, but the only tug which could get clear virtually under any conditions was the *Voith Water Tractor*, a tug equipped with Voith-Schneider propulsion in the forebody. Even if the Voith Water Tractor were in contact with the bow at frame 5—she could still turn away.

But such critical situations should never arise since the tractor is fully controllable even when her aft-body is in contact with the tow, and can sheer away before getting into the dangerous bow range. The explanation is that the full installed engine power of the Voith Water Tractor is available for turning the forebody away from the danger zone, since this power can be converted into a steering force irrespective of the tug's speed.

2. Turning manoeuvres.

In discussing turning manoeuvres it is assumed that the incoming ship is under headway and, on reaching the turning area, brakes using her own screw to stop the forward movement. At this moment the tug initiates the turning manoeuvre by moving away

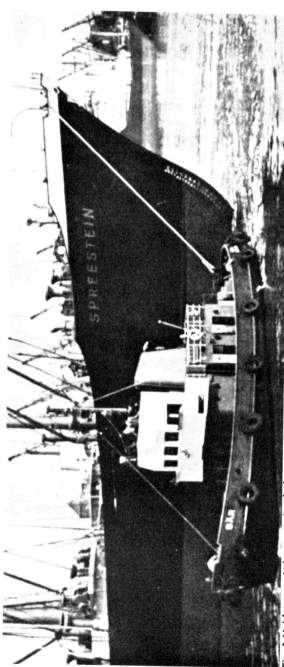

Fig. 4 Voith tractor being overtaken by her tow

this is a difficult manoeuvre and sufficient time may not be available. It is also a hazardous operation for the tug's crew to carry out.

If the forces effective during these manoeuvres are analysed it will be found that the risks are basically attributable to the fact that with the stern-driven and stern-controlled tug the main forces—towrope pull and screw propeller thrust— are in unstable equilibrium, since the towrope pull acts ahead of the total forces formed by rudder force and thrust. The *Voith Water Tractor* was conceived to eliminate these risks by ensuring that the propeller thrust and the steering force act ahead of the point of attack of the towrope pull. **Fig. 4** shows a tractor performing the above mentioned manoeuvre. While the ship continued steaming ahead the tractor—because of the favourable position of the towhook aft—was not pulled by a force of a towrope athwartships but in the direction of the towrope, so that the tractor continuing ahead could maintain the turning circle and automatically swing into position to stop the still moving ship.

BRAKING AND STEERING TUG

Reverting to the screw-propelled tug and after the ship is turned she becomes a braking and steering tug. For this work it is general practice to make the towrope fast farther aft. This is usually done with the help of a guest rope also called a bridle or gob rope. The guest rope must be firmly bowsed down since it must always be expected that the change from the turning manoeuvre to running astern is instantaneous. If the guest rope cannot be hauled tight during this period, there is the risk of capsizing as described in connection with the turning manoeuvres. With the help of the guest rope, it is possible for the tug to follow the ship at a safe angle. However, a precondition is that the ship runs at a steady speed. If, however, this speed for some reason or other increases, even with the use of the guest rope there is a real risk of the tug capsizing. This

danger may be due both to the higher speed of the ship and also, with a tug at the stern of the ship, to the wake from the ship's screw. In river road-steads, the current is another potential danger; in particular when a train, consisting of head tug, sea-going ship and braking/steering tug, coming from the river enters a dead-water harbour area. **Fig. 5** shows the situation when passing from a river to a harbour basin such as in the area of the port of Bremen where a tug was lost.

The stern tug entrained via the towrope and the guest rope is virtually braking only with the lateral resistance of her hull; thus, her braking resistance is the higher the faster the towing manoeuvre is performed. Generally, such braking is undesirable but, as there is no alternative, it must be accepted. The drawback for the safety of the whole manoeuvre is that, with decreasing speed, the braking effect of the tug diminishes and becomes virtually 'zero'. Thus, the tug in this position cannot assist in the final braking phase and must get stern on. This requires a difficult manoeuvre in a critical phase with the risk that the manoeuvre is too late, and braking is not initiated as desired.

With the *Voith Water Tractor*, however, braking and steering manoeuvres are entirely different.

It is of major importance for the safety of the tow that the tug, working at the stern, can change from one side to the other. This, within limits, is possible with screw-propelled tugs which, made fast via towrope and guest rope, follow the ship. However, the sector in which the tug can work is only about 120 degrees. To this—as mentioned above—must be added the undesirable braking effect. Therefore, when operating over long distances as stern tug, the tugs are often used without guest rope on one side (see **Fig. 6**). The centre of this photo shows a screw-propelled tug, while in the foreground the stern of a *Voith Water Tractor* entrained by her sternpost is visible. The screw-propelled tug, while running—as shown in this example—cannot leave the starboard side of the ship and, should she want to change sides, her towrope would have to pass over her superstructure with the possibility of fouling and cap-

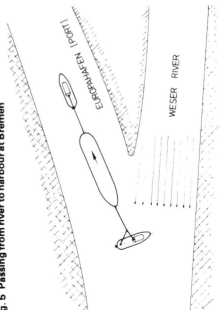

Fig. 5 Passing from river to harbour at Bremen

Fig. 6 Tow wires used without 'guest' ropes

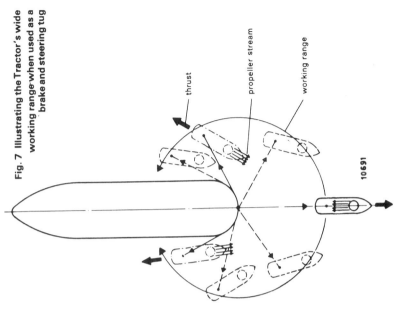

Fig. 7 Illustrating the Tractor's wide working range when used as a brake and steering tug

thrust

propeller stream

working range

10691

sizing the tug. The *Voith Water Tractor* on the other hand can, without any risk, change from the starboard side to the port side of the ship. The angle range in which the *Voith Water Tractor* can operate is thus approximately 360 degrees. The tractor, as shown here, can sheer away to starboard, can drop back and apply a braking effect and can then sheer to port until running parallel to the ship. (**Figs. 7** and **8**) and at no time during these operations is the tractor running any risk (see also 'Location of the Towing

Hook'—Proceedings of the 2nd International Tug Conference). Thus the tractor substantially increases the safety of the sea-going ship and of the entire towing operation, since there is no risk that stern and steering tugs may fail during manoeuvres as a result of delayed towrope changes or inability to move from side to side. The tractor is always in the correct position to carry out the pilot's orders.

PUSHING AND PULLING

Many manoeuvres require instantaneous changeover from braking to acceleration and vice versa in order to ensure the safety of the assisted ship or equipment. These quick reversals are dependent not only on the changeover time of the engine equipment but also on the ability of the tug to change from pulling to pushing without major loss in time. The larger the time loss the greater is the risk for the tow. Since time losses during reversals generally cannot be avoided, the practice is to put more tugs on the job some of which are used for pushing and the others for braking. Thus, the one group of tugs, so to speak, works against the other group. While, in this way, safety is ensured, considerable effort must be expended.

By using *Voith Water Tractors* these difficulties can be overcome since the tractor performs with the same efficiency in either direction and can push equally by her stern as pull in the forward direction. The changeover from pushing to pulling with the tractor is very quick and depends on the towrope length. With directly attached tractors it is a maximum of a few seconds and, since the tractor does not have to move, the ever increasing powers and dimensions play a role of growing importance. In restricted harbour basins it is often impossible to operate the tug groups mentioned above. From the safety aspect, therefore, it is preferable to use the tractor with a short towrope or connect her directly to the ship. When moving ships in docks or narrow passages these constrictions play a vital role in the last phase of the berthing manoeuvres and although in all these operations the safety of the tug itself is not endangered, there is a danger to the safety of the tow and the dock structures and facilities.

forward). Therefore, the head tugs can transmit only a small turning moment to change the course. In contrast, the Voith Water Tractor operating at the stern is much more effective. This tractor, shown shearing at the bottom of the photo, is being towed with her stern turned foremost. The Voith-Schneider Propeller allows to choose the setting angle with the direction of running so as to achieve the required athwartship towrope pull. Most of the towrope pull is provided by the flow pressure which develops at the large stern fin and the lateral surface of the ship's hull. The athwartship towrope pull provided by this method exceeds the static towrope pull when the tug is towed at a speed of 6 knots, and far exceeds this value when the towing speed is increased. The power requirements of the driving engine of the Voith Water Tractor are at such time low only, as the Voith-Schneider Propellers are only required to control the shearing angle.

Fig 8 This photo shows the handling of the tanker "Pacific Glory" which has been destroyed by fire. The course of the tanker is to be changed towards port so as to provide against shearing off towards starboard. The tugs at the head of the tanker have already moved far athwartships in the starboard direction. Their oblique towrope pull towards starboard has little effect on the change in course, as the pivoting point of a ship under way is located far forward (in this case at about 20% of the ship's length from

REFERENCES

Hooyer, Henry H. *Behavior and Handling of Ships*. Centreville, Md.: Cornell Maritime Press, 1983.

MacElrevey, Daniel H. *Shiphandling for the Mariner*. Centreville, Md.: Cornell Maritime Press, 1983.

Noel, John V., Jr., and Bassett, Frank E. *Knight's Modern Seamanship*. 17th ed. New York: Van Nostrand Reinhold, 1983.

Plummer, Carlyle J. *Ship Handling in Narrow Channels*. 3d. ed. Centreville, Md.: Cornell Maritime Press, 1966.

Reid, George H. *Boatmen's Guide to Light Salvage*. Centreville, Md.: Cornell Maritime Press, 1979.

———. *Primer of Towing*. Centreville, Md.: Cornell Maritime Press, 1975.

———. *Simulator Training Manual*. Centerport, N. Y.: Ship Analytics, Inc., 1983.

INDEX

A

After control station, 50, 92, 99
Aircraft carriers, 50, 117, 124
Alongside towing, 112, 121-36, 138, 149, 150, 161, 162, 164-69
Atlantic Marine, 185

B

Backing, 5, 13, 15, 17, 18, 20, 21, 22, 30, 31, 33, 36, 38, 42, 72, 73, 74, 76, 77, 79, 86, 87, 92, 95, 96, 107, 108, 119, 122, 125, 131, 133, 134, 135, 136, 143, 144, 146, 147, 168, 169, 206
Backing and filling, 12, 112, 115, 121, 164, 165
Beach gear, 171, 172
Bird-Johnson, 27
Bitts, 50, 52, 60, 117, 119, 146, 197
    bullnose, 46, 48
    cruciform, 46-47, 48
    H, 47, 49
    quarter, 45, 47, 48, 87, 124
    tow, 49, 67, 138
Bollard pull, 19, 36, 173
Brake horsepower, 36
Braking, 117, 197
Breasting, 8, 117, 127, 129, 136, 148, 158, 192
Bridles, 197
Bullnose, 46, 124, 197
Bulwarks, 42, 44

C

CAORF, 6
Capsizing, 18, 42, 49, 66, 91, 93, 94, 98, 117, 124, 138, 207
Capstan, 47, 60
Cavitation, 30, 92, 96, 99
Center of lateral resistance, 102, 105
Checking, 107-8, 131
Chocks, 13, 50, 51, 52, 115, 117, 119, 124, 125, 126, 146
    pocket (recessed), 51
    rolling, 46, 51
Cleats, 49
Clutches
    hydraulic, 27-28, 37
    mechanical, 27-28, 37
    magnetic, 28-29, 37
    pneumatic, 28, 37
Coming alongside, 90-92, 94, 96, 99, 122
Current, 81, 86, 87, 88, 102, 121, 127, 128, 149-63, 171, 184, 186, 187, 200, 208

D

"Deadman," 190
Dead ship, 164-69, 181
Deckhouse, 42, 47, 51, 57
Docking, 86-88, 102, 107, 117, 127, 128, 135, 138, 149, 150, 154, 161, 166, 168, 184, 189, 192, 194, 195

Dock lines, 59, 148
Drogue, 108, 112

E

Engines, 4, 15, 24-25
   diesel, 24-25, 29
   diesel-electric, 26, 36-37; AC system,
      26; DC system, 26; SCR system,
      26, 37
   direct-reversing, 25-26, 29, 36-37,
      122
   horsepower of, 8-9, 11, 13-15, 27, 28,
      29, 37, 62, 172, 173, 185

F

Fairleads, 49
Fenders, 43, 45, 50, 52, 56, 177, 184,
      185, 186, 204
   bow, 55, 56-57, 58
   roller-type, 57
   stern, 57
   systems, 54-57
Fire, 178
Fire wires, 178
Flanking, 79-81, 82, 86, 87
Flare (of bow), 11, 42, 50, 99, 125, 126
Free agent, 149, 150
Freeboard, 42, 43, 122, 171, 211
Fuel, 29

G

Gate lines, 197
Girding, 92, 93, 145, 200, 207
Goblines, 66, 139, 167, 198
Ground effect, 171
Grounding, 170-77

H

Harbormaster, xi, 18, 38-39
Head lines, 42, 46, 57-58, 92, 95, 96,
      97, 98, 99, 108, 112, 115, 122, 123,
      125, 127, 129, 136, 146, 147, 148,
      149, 150, 166, 197, 200, 207
Heaving lines, 62-63, 122-23, 124
Heavy seas, 171, 184, 200, 207

Hipped up. *See* Alongside towing
Holing, 173, 178-81
Hull, 42
   chine (V bottom), 43, 46
   configuration, underwater, 18, 34, 36
   double-chine, 35
   model (round-bottom), 43
   multichine, 32, 45
   of submarine, 13

I

Immersion scale, 171
International Organization of Masters,
      Mates and Pilots, 6

J

Jettison, 171, 172

K

Ka-Me Wa, 27
Kedging, 3, 190
Keel, 34
   bilge, 46
   fin, 18
Kort nozzle, 11, 12, 15, 16, 17, 21, 22,
      30, 33, 36, 38-39, 74, 146, 173,
      185, 199
Kort rudder, 30, 33, 36, 38-39, 74-76,
      86, 119, 213

L

Lightering, 7
Lines. *See* particular types
   length of, 138-39
Loss of power, 181
Loss of steering, 181

M

Making up, 90-91, 117, 122, 149, 181,
      203
Marine Safety International, 6
Maritime Institute of Technology and
      Graduate Studies, 6
Mast, 11, 42

Masters
 docking, 6, 7, 122
 mooring, 6, 7
Mediterranean moor, 190
Metacentric height, 172
Mooring lines, 60
Moving (a ship) laterally, 104, 112, 117
Murray & Tregurtha, xi, 18

N

Nickum & Spaulding, xi, 28, 31, 32, 45, 50

O

Oil rigs, 197, 199, 200, 201
On the hip. *See* Alongside towing
Overhang, 11, 42, 50, 99, 117, 119, 127, 173

P

Paddle wheel effect, 80-81, 146, 147, 148
Panama Canal, 7, 8
Pendants, 61
Pilothouse, 11
Pilots, 4, 6-10, 122, 138, 148, 149, 164-65, 173, 177, 190, 211
 bar, 7
 license of, 7
 Panama Canal, 8
 river, 7
Pivot point, 102-4, 105, 106, 107, 116
Propellers
 controllable pitch, 26-27, 28, 29, 30, 32, 33, 34, 38-39, 50, 74, 99
 conventional (solid), 18, 24-26, 29, 30
 cycloidal, 18, 34
 single-blade, 30
 steerable, 12, 13, 15, 16, 17-18, 21, 22, 33, 35
 tip speed of, 30
 two-blade, 30

Propelling (pushing), 104, 105, 107, 112, 129, 134, 135, 168, 169, 181, 197

Q

Quarter lines, 9, 13, 59, 98, 99, 122, 123, 124, 128, 134, 135, 146, 147, 150, 159. *Also see* Stern lines
Quick-release straps, 54, 67-68

R

Reduction gears, 27, 28
Refloating, 170-77
Reverse gears, 27
Rub rail, 52
Rudders, 30-31, 107
 angles, 72, 75, 77, 78, 79, 81
 double, 33
 flanking, 11, 12, 15-17, 21, 33, 34, 74, 75, 86, 119, 121, 146, 166, 185, 197, 199
 leading edge of, 30-31
 single, 33
 spade, 31, 35-36, 38-39

S

Salvage, 170, 172, 173
Salvors, 170, 171, 172
Schottel, xi, 18, 19, 21, 30, 33, 35, 83, 84, 119
Sea buoy, 7
Searchlight, 49-50
Sheering, 117, 181, 197, 198, 206
Shiphandling Training Center, 6
Shock lines, 60
SHP, 38-39
Silicon-controlled rectifier, 26, 37
Single-point mooring, 6, 186-87
Sinking, 178-81
Skeg, 18, 31, 34, 35, 204
Slip, 29-30
Springlines, 42, 46, 59, 86, 87, 107, 112, 122, 123, 124, 129, 130, 149, 150
Stack, 11

Steering, 102, 104, 107, 116, 117, 125, 126, 129, 130, 168, 177, 197, 209
Steering gear, 17, 31, 33
    Towmaster, 31
Stemming, 92, 94, 98
Stern lines, 13, 15, 20, 21, 22, 31, 49, 59, 60, 87, 112, 122, 123, 124, 134, 149. *Also see* Quarter lines
Stern post, 34
Submarines, 13, 43-44, 50, 56, 57
Suction, 91-92, 125, 171, 173, 174, 200
Suez Canal, 7
Superstructures, 12, 42, 43, 44, 50, 196

T

Tabernacle, 42
Tag lines, 63-64
Tailboat, 115-17, 164, 167, 196-201
Tides, 171, 172, 173, 177
Tie downs. *See* Goblines
Torque, effect of, 12, 13, 15, 31, 72, 74, 87, 121, 124, 146-48
Towing, 3, 4, 33, 54
    gear, 54-68
    hooks, 47, 49, 50, 67
Towlines, 9, 13, 18, 22, 27, 42, 47, 59, 60, 61, 66, 95, 98, 99, 107, 112, 117, 121, 138, 139, 142, 143, 144, 145, 149, 150, 166, 167, 174, 177, 178, 181, 186, 187, 197, 198
    work, 92-95
Transmissions, 27-28, 33
Trim, 81, 86, 102
Tripping, 66, 92, 93, 144, 207
Tugs
    canal, 11
    harbor, 11, 20, 29, 42, 45, 46, 49, 50, 54, 56, 87, 90
    history of, 3-4
    light, 82-83
    limitations of, 8-10, 11-22
    oceangoing, 29
    pusher, 18, 21, 22, 82, 86
    railroad, 11

single-screw, 8, 12-13, 14, 15, 16, 17, 20-21, 28, 31, 32, 33, 43, 46, 50, 72-76, 86, 87, 88, 121, 122, 127, 129, 146, 164
tractor, 18, 19, 20, 22, 42, 43, 57, 82, 86, 92, 117
twin-screw, 12, 13-15, 16, 17, 18, 21-22, 31, 33, 36, 43, 46, 77-84, 86, 87, 88, 121, 122, 129, 185
Turning, 13, 104, 106, 107-12, 125, 130, 144, 148, 166, 206

U

U. S. Merchant Marine Academy, 6
ULCCs, 4, 13, 185
Undocking, 86, 102, 127, 129, 138, 142, 143, 147, 150, 162, 184, 190, 195

V

VHF radiotelephone, 69, 70, 100
VLCCs, 4, 13, 185, 197
Voith-Schneider, xi, 18, 19, 20, 33, 34, 38-39, 43, 44, 85, 119

W

Walkie-talkie, 69
Walking (sideways), 17
"Weathervane," 187
Wheelhouse, 11, 42, 43, 49, 50, 57, 96, 99
Wheel (propeller) wash, 17, 87, 92, 99, 108, 112, 125, 126, 130, 131, 139, 174, 177, 206
Whistles, 69-70, 96, 100
Winches, 172, 176, 207
Wind, 81, 86, 102, 115, 121, 124, 127, 130, 146, 164, 170, 171, 186, 187, 189, 192, 204
Windlass, anchor, 47
Working lines: fiber, 59-62, 184
    blends, 60-61
    dacron, 60, 61
    hockle, 61
    manila, 59-60, 61
    nylon, 60, 95

polyethylene, 60, 61
polypropylene, 60, 61
samson, 62
strengths of, 64-65
Working lines: wire, 61-62, 63, 112,
    172

fishhooks in, 61
sizes of, 62
strengths of, 63

Z

Z drive, 18

ABOUT THE AUTHOR

Captain George H. Reid was born in Birmingham, Alabama, and raised in Florida, where he now resides. He started to sea in the early 1940s, and received his original license as third mate in 1944. He has since served as mate and master aboard tankers, freighters, windjammers, fishing vessels, and tugs. In addition he has had experience as pilot, docking master, and salvage master. About half of his time at sea, however, has been spent aboard tugs, which he regards as more interesting and challenging than service aboard conventional vessels.

For a number of years he worked primarily in the Caribbean and Latin America; he speaks fluent Spanish. (He speaks of this period as his TTT [Typical Tropical Tramp] days.)

He still goes to sea on occasion, but his principal activity is presiding over the activities of his firm, Harrison Reid & Associates of Cape Canaveral, Florida, which provides consulting, surveying, and marine engineering services to the maritime industry.